# WOODSMITH CUSTOM WOODWORKING

# Kitchen & Dining Room

WOODSMITH CUSTOM WOODWORKING

# Kitchen & Dining Room

By the editors of Woodsmith magazine

# Kitchen &
# Dining Room

## KITCHEN ACCESSORIES 6

Glass-Front Breadbox

**Country Harvest Table**

**Country Pie Safe**

# KITCHEN ACCESSORIES

**H**ow your kitchen is organized determines whether your time spent there will be a pleasurable experience or a chore.

With the knife rack, a set of hardwood dividers keeps your knives protected from nicks and dings that other utensils could cause. Laid flat in a drawer or hung on a wall, your counters stay clear. And no more digging through cupboards for a hidden spice container. Now they're right at your fingertips, stored in a spice cabinet that features a second set of shelves built into the attractive arch-paneled doors.

And you'll like the recipe card box with two drawers sized to hold hundreds of recipe cards. Its tilting top keeps your cookbook propped up and out of the reach of wayward ingredients.

Lastly, the glass-front breadbox not only stores bread but has an optional cutting board that can be built and conveniently stored in the space below the breadbox.

# Knife Rack

*This versatile rack can be displayed on a wall or tucked in a drawer. Either way it ends kitchen clutter without using up any counter space — protecting your knives, while keeping them close at hand.*

Good kitchen knives are like a fine set of woodworking chisels — quality doesn't come cheap. So you want to take good care of them. And in a busy kitchen, they get used a lot, so they should be within easy reach. You also want them to stay sharp, and that means the blades should be protected.

**STORAGE OPTIONS.** When it came time to design this Knife Rack, I used a couple of methods used for storing chisels as inspiration. I've seen some shops with the woodworking chisels hung on the wall behind a workbench, just within arm's reach. And I've also seen them stored in a separate drawer in a cabinet or workbench, where they're protected from other tools.

Both of these woodworking solutions inspired the design for this rack used for storing kitchen knives. It's designed so you can hang it on the wall or set it in a drawer. In either place, your knives can be kept close at hand without taking up any valuable counter space. And I used thick hardwood dividers to protect them from other utensils if you decide to store them in a drawer.

**OPEN SLOTS.** This rack works in out-of-the-way places because it's designed with open slots. Rather than burying the knives in slots cut in a heavy block of wood where you have to pull them straight out, this rack allows you to pull (or lift) the knife away from the rack in one safe and easy movement.

**MATERIALS.** Choosing the wood for my Knife Rack was easy. It has to stand up to the nicks and dings it will get from everyday use. But it also has to look nice. So I chose hard maple for all the rack parts. It's not only durable, but it has a neutral color that allows it to blend in with almost any decor.

**CONSTRUCTION.** A simple jig makes cutting the tapered dividers a snap. You'll find a description of how I built it in the Shop Jig box on page 10.

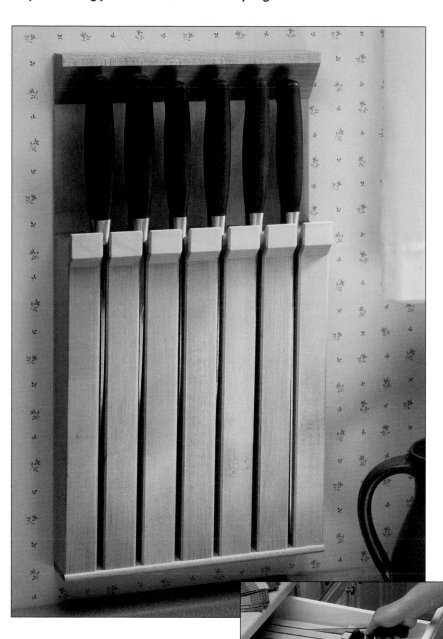

**COUNTRY KNIFE RACK.** If your kitchen decor leans more toward country than contemporary, you'll be pleased with the simple changes you can make to the rack. To learn more about these changes, see the Designer's Notebook on page 13.

# EXPLODED VIEW

OVERALL DIMENSIONS:
$8\frac{9}{16}$W x $2\frac{7}{8}$D x $16\frac{1}{2}$H

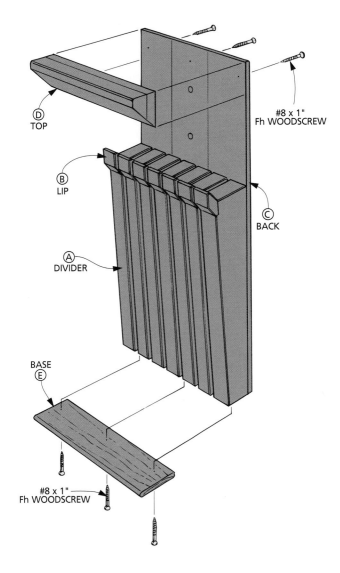

D TOP

B LIP

C BACK

A DIVIDER

#8 x 1"
Fh WOODSCREW

BASE
E

#8 x 1"
Fh WOODSCREW

## MATERIALS LIST

**WOOD**

| | | |
|---|---|---|
| A | Dividers (7) | $1\frac{1}{16}$ x $2\frac{1}{8}$ - $10\frac{1}{2}$ |
| B | Lips (7) | $\frac{1}{2}$ x $1\frac{1}{8}$ - $1\frac{1}{16}$ |
| C | Back (1) | $\frac{1}{4}$ x 9 rough - $16\frac{3}{4}$ rough |
| D | Top (1) | $1\frac{1}{4}$ x $1\frac{5}{8}$ - $8\frac{9}{16}$ |
| E | Base (1) | $\frac{1}{4}$ x $1\frac{7}{8}$ - $8\frac{9}{16}$ |

**HARDWARE SUPPLIES**

(6) No. 8 x 1" Fh woodscrews

## CUTTING DIAGRAM

$1\frac{1}{16}$ x $5\frac{1}{2}$ - 48 (3.7 Bd. Ft.)

| A | A | A | A |
|---|---|---|---|
| A | A | A | B |

$\frac{3}{4}$ x $3\frac{1}{2}$ - 24 (.6 Bd. Ft.)

| D | D |
|---|---|

$\frac{1}{4}$ x $3\frac{1}{2}$ - 72 (1.8 Sq. Ft.)

| C | C | C | E |
|---|---|---|---|

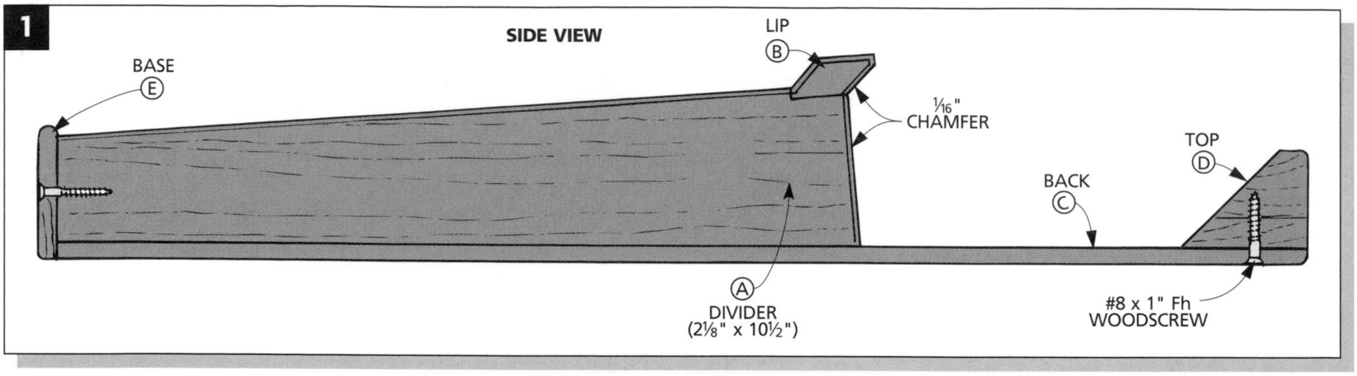
1
SIDE VIEW
BASE
E
LIP
B
1⁄16" CHAMFER
TOP
D
BACK
C
A
DIVIDER
(2⅛" x 10½")
#8 x 1" Fh WOODSCREW

## DIVIDERS

To begin work on the rack you need to first decide how many knives you'll be storing in it. Mine holds six knives, but customizing it is easy — all you need is one more divider than the number of knives you plan to hold in it.

Start with the dividers (A), cutting 1$^1/_{16}$"-thick maple into oversize blanks (refer to *Fig. 1a* in Shop Jig below). (Mine ended up being 2$^3/_8$" x 11".)

**Note:** This knife rack is designed to hold knives with blades up to 2" wide and 10" long, so adjust the length and width

## SHOP JIG ........ *Taper Jig*

The tapers on the front edge of the divider serve two purposes: they reduce the weight of the rack and they make the dividers look more graceful.

To add the tapers, I decided to use a taper jig on the table saw *(Fig. 1)*. The jig is easy to use. It acts as an angled spacer between the rip fence and the divider. To use it, you push the workpiece past the blade, and the cleat causes the jig to simply ride along, while holding the workpiece at the correct angle.

**MAKING THE JIG.** This can be done with a jig that can be made quickly from a piece of scrap hardwood stock.

To make the jig, cut a piece of $^3/_4$"-thick stock to the same length as the dividers (11") *(Fig. 2)*. Then rip the stock to width and lay out the taper.

I used the band saw to cut the taper and then I sanded the cut edge smooth. Finally, to hold the workpiece in the jig, I screwed the hardwood cleat to the narrow end *(Fig. 2)*.

**CUTTING THE TAPERS.** To cut the tapers, the thing to keep in mind is that you want the top of each divider to end up wide enough to hold your widest knife. (It should be at least $^1/_8$" wider.) I wanted the rack to be able to hold a 2"-wide knife, so when setting the rip fence on the table saw, I made sure the dividers tapered to 2$^1/_8$" at the top *(Fig. 1a)*.

Now each divider can be tapered by sliding both the jig and the workpiece along the fence *(Fig. 1)*.

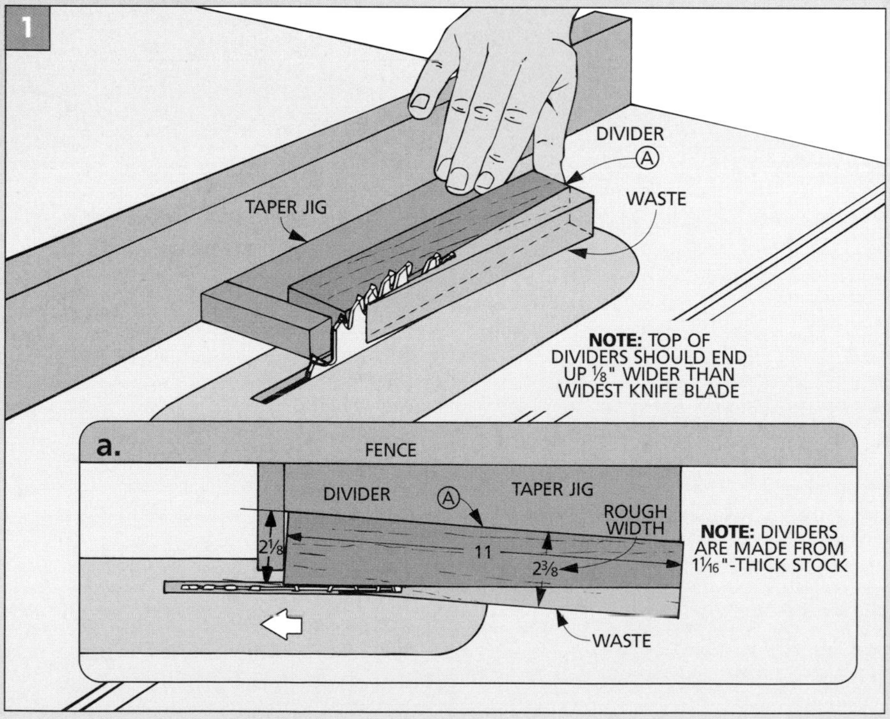
1
DIVIDER
A
TAPER JIG
WASTE
NOTE: TOP OF DIVIDERS SHOULD END UP ⅛" WIDER THAN WIDEST KNIFE BLADE
a.
FENCE
DIVIDER
A
TAPER JIG
ROUGH WIDTH
2⅛
11
2⅜
WASTE
NOTE: DIVIDERS ARE MADE FROM 1 1⁄16"-THICK STOCK

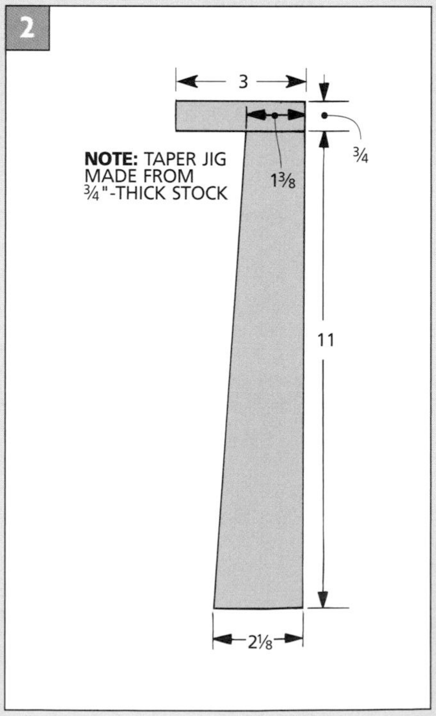
2
3
NOTE: TAPER JIG MADE FROM ¾"-THICK STOCK
1⅜
¾
11
2⅛

of your dividers to fit your knives. Later, when you glue them to the back piece, you'll use spacers between the dividers to ensure even spacing for your knives.

With the dividers roughed out, the next thing I did was to taper them slightly along the front edge *(Fig. 1)*.

To taper the dividers, I used the table saw and a shop-made jig (see the Shop Jig box on the previous page).

With the tapers cut on the dividers, the next step is to cut a 1/8"-deep rabbet in each divider *(Fig. 2)*. This creates a recess to hold the lip pieces that are added later *(Fig. 1)*.

To cut the rabbets, I used a dado blade on the table saw with an auxiliary fence to back up the cut. (Just make sure it's long enough to extend past the blade to reduce the chance of chipout.) Because this cut doesn't go all the way through the divider, I was able to use the rip fence as a stop. This way, all the rabbets are exactly the same length (3/4") *(Fig. 2a)*.

**LIP PIECES.** Once the rabbets are cut, I worked on the lip (B) pieces *(Fig. 1)*. They help the knives slide in place. They also help prevent the knives from tipping out if the rack is wall mounted.

But these lip pieces are pretty small to work with safely. So I decided to do most of the work on a single 1/2"-thick blank

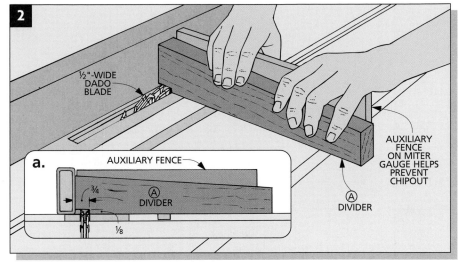

oversized in both width and length (my blank was 2" x 12") *(Fig. 3)*. Then later, I cut the individual pieces from the blank like slicing bread from a loaf.

First, rout a 45° chamfer along one edge of the blank with the bit set to leave a 1/8" shoulder *(Figs. 3 and 3a)*.

Next, the blank can be ripped to final width *(Figs. 4 and 4a)*. The important thing here is that the inside face of the lip blank matches the width of the rabbets cut earlier in the dividers (3/4") *(Fig. 4a)*.

To complete the lip blank, I routed a second chamfer on the corner opposite

the first *(Fig. 5)*. Here, I wanted the shoulder left by the chamfer to match the depth of the rabbet I cut in the dividers (1/8") *(Fig. 5a)*.

At this point, the lip pieces can be sliced from the blank to match the thickness of the dividers (1 1/16") and glued in place *(Fig. 6)*. These pieces are small enough that instead of using clamps, I just held each piece until the glue set.

Finally, to make it as easy as possible to slide the knives in place, I routed a 1/16" chamfer around the front and top edges of each divider *(Figs. 1 and 6)*.

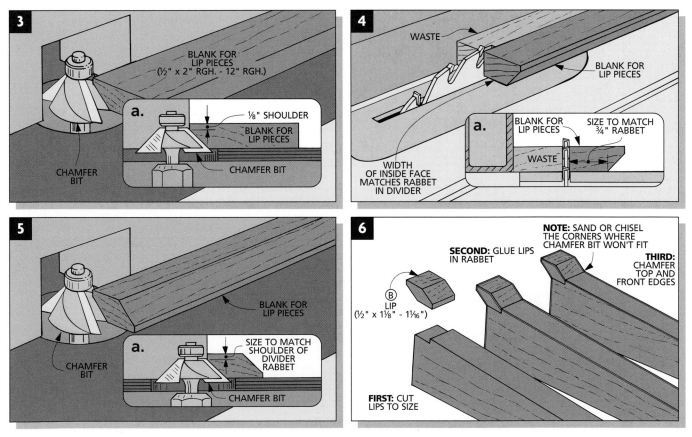

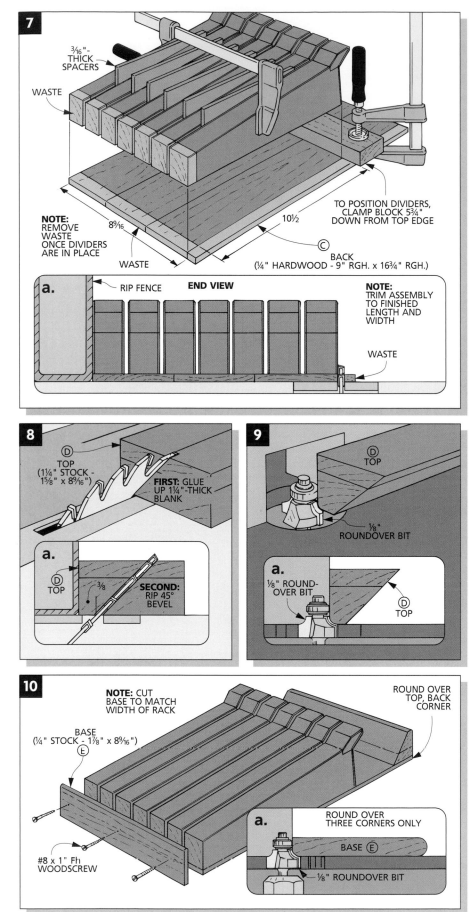

**7**

3/16"-THICK SPACERS

WASTE

NOTE: REMOVE WASTE ONCE DIVIDERS ARE IN PLACE

8 9/16"

WASTE

10 1/2"

TO POSITION DIVIDERS, CLAMP BLOCK 5 3/4" DOWN FROM TOP EDGE

C

BACK
(1/4" HARDWOOD - 9" RGH. x 16 3/4" RGH.)

**a.**  RIP FENCE    **END VIEW**

NOTE: TRIM ASSEMBLY TO FINISHED LENGTH AND WIDTH

WASTE

**8**

D

TOP
(1 1/4" STOCK - 1 5/8" x 8 9/16")

**FIRST:** GLUE UP 1 1/4"-THICK BLANK

**a.**  D TOP    3/8"    **SECOND:** RIP 45° BEVEL

**9**

D TOP

1/8" ROUNDOVER BIT

**a.**  1/8" ROUND-OVER BIT    D TOP

**10**

NOTE: CUT BASE TO MATCH WIDTH OF RACK

BASE
(1/4" STOCK - 1 7/8" x 8 9/16")
E

ROUND OVER TOP, BACK CORNER

#8 x 1" Fh WOODSCREW

**a.**  ROUND OVER THREE CORNERS ONLY

BASE E

1/8" ROUNDOVER BIT

The dividers are easily the most difficult part of this project to build. Now that they're complete, it's time to glue them to a back panel, and add a top and base.

**BACK.** The back (C) is just a 1/4"-thick glued-up panel *(Fig. 7)*. I started by making the panel a little wide and long (9" x 16 3/4"). This way it can be trimmed after the dividers have been added.

Which brings up a slight problem. How do you glue seven dividers to a panel so they all end up parallel — with even spaces between them to hold the knife blades? My solution was to clamp the dividers together with 3/16" spacers between them. This way, I was able to glue the dividers to the back panel as a single unit *(Fig. 7)*.

Also, I clamped a temporary block to the back 5 3/4" down from the top. Then with something to butt the assembly against, I glued each of the dividers flush with one edge of the back panel.

**Note:** Remove the temporary block after a few minutes (enough time to let the glue just start to set up) to make sure it doesn't get glued in place.

With the dividers glued to the back panel, I trimmed the assembly to final length (16 1/4") and width *(Fig. 7a)*. (My rack ended up 8 9/16" wide.)

**TOP.** Now a beveled top (D) can be added. Like the lips on the dividers, it helps hold the knives in place when the rack is lying flat in a drawer.

To make the top, I glued two 3/4"-thick pieces together and ripped them 1 1/4" thick. Then I cut them to length to match the width of the rack (8 9/16") and beveled one edge *(Fig. 8)*.

Next, I rounded over the top front edge *(Fig. 9)*. And after screwing the top (D) to the back, I rounded the top edge of the back *(Fig. 10)*.

**BASE.** To cover the ends of the dividers, I added a 1/4"-thick base (E) *(Fig. 10)*. It stands 1/8" proud of the dividers. (Mine was 1 7/8" wide.) Then after rounding over three edges, the base is glued and screwed to the rack.

Finally, I wiped on a couple of coats of an oil finish and screwed the rack to the wall (see the Exploded View on page 9).

**COUNTRY KNIFE RACK.** If you'd like to achieve a country look for your Knife Rack, all that is needed are a few simple changes to the design. For more on this country-style rack see the Designer's Notebook on the next page. ∎

# DESIGNER'S NOTEBOOK

*A gently curved profile added to the back and new side panels really change the look of this project. The Country Knife Rack has a down-home style that's perfectly suited for a more traditional kitchen.*

## CONSTRUCTION NOTES:

■ To change the look of the wall-hung rack to give it a "country" look, I added a gentle curve at the top and added side pieces for a more traditional appearance.

■ Start by making the lipped dividers as before, but with one minor change. Instead of routing a chamfer all the way around the front edges on all seven dividers, leave an outside edge of two of the dividers square so they'll butt up flush against the side pieces (see drawing).

■ With the dividers complete, begin making the oversize panel. You'll trim it to size *after* the dividers are added.

**Note:** Because of the difficulty in gluing the dividers to the base so they end up parallel, the curved detail at the top also has to be cut to shape after the dividers are glued to the base and the back has been trimmed to size.

Start by gluing up a 9" x 18¼" panel for the back (C) from ¼"-thick stock.

■ Now you can glue the dividers to the back panel. Use the same spacer technique to glue them to the base as before, but this time clamp the temporary block 7¼" down from the top edge of the back.

■ Trim this assembly to width and length (8⁹⁄₁₆" x 17½"), cutting the excess from the edges at the bottom and one side.

■ Next, lay out the gentle curve on the back blank (I laid mine out freehand).

Then I cut it to shape using a band saw, but you could also use a jig saw to cut it (see drawing). I made sure to cut on the waste side of the layout line and then I used a drum sander to clean up the rough edges.

■ Now the beveled top piece can be added. Once again, you'll want to roundover the top front edge of the top piece (see drawing).

■ With the dividers and top glued in place and the back cut to size, the next thing to do is to cover up the ends of the dividers with the base. Round over the three edges, then glue and screw it in place.

■ To complete the rack, add a pair of side panels (F). They're just pieces of ¼"-thick stock with a curved edge cut to shape on the band saw. To make it easier to cut them, first lay out the curves using the side pattern (see drawing). Then to get a perfectly matched pair, use carpet tape to attach them to each other with their back edges flush. Make your cuts on the waste side of the layout line and sand the edges using a drum sander.

■ Finally, glue the sides in place, positioning the back edges flush to the back of the rack and the bottom edge ¾" below the base (see drawing).

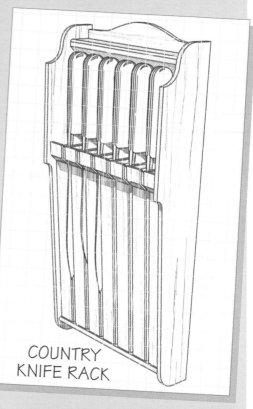

COUNTRY
KNIFE RACK

## MATERIALS LIST

**CHANGED PART**

| | |
|---|---|
| **C** Back (1) | ¼ x 9 rough - 18¼ rough |

**NEW PART**

| | |
|---|---|
| **F** Side Panels (2) | ¼ x 3 - 18 |

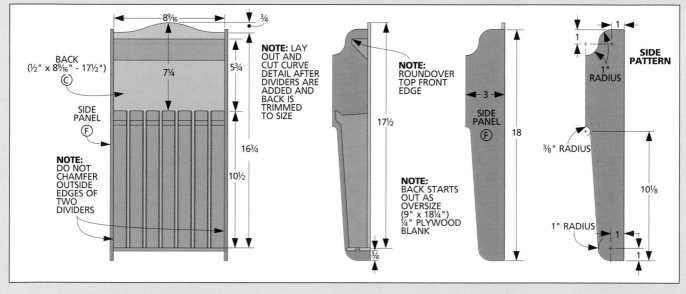

BACK
(½" x 8⁹⁄₁₆" - 17½")
C

SIDE PANEL
F

NOTE: DO NOT CHAMFER OUTSIDE EDGES OF TWO DIVIDERS

8⁹⁄₁₆    ¾
7¼    5¾
16¾
10½

NOTE: LAY OUT AND CUT CURVE DETAIL AFTER DIVIDERS ARE ADDED AND BACK IS TRIMMED TO SIZE

NOTE: ROUNDOVER TOP FRONT EDGE

17½

NOTE: BACK STARTS OUT AS OVERSIZE (9" x 18¼") ¼" PLYWOOD BLANK

¾

3
SIDE PANEL
F
18

SIDE PATTERN

1    1
1" RADIUS

⅜" RADIUS

10⅛

1" RADIUS    1    1

# Recipe Card Box

*With two drawers to hold all your favorite recipes, this card box is much more than just a food file. It also has a tilt-up cookbook holder that makes it an even more useful project for the kitchen.*

Isn't it interesting how a useful project can develop from a simple idea? For instance, this Recipe Card Box was originally designed as a simple one-drawer box to hold 3x5 note cards.

But then some of the more experienced "cooks" I know took a look at the original sketches and told me there wasn't nearly enough room for all their recipe cards. So I decided to add another drawer in a side-by-side arrangement.

**JOINERY.** After even more discussion, instead of making just a plain box for these drawers, I was encouraged to dress up the corners with miter and dovetail key joints. (Making this special joinery is explained in detail on pages 18-19.)

Since the box was joined with miters and dovetail key joints, I decided to make the drawers with this joint as well.

**TILT-UP FRAME.** By this time, the cooks approved of the box. But they also mentioned that their cookbooks often get in their way or get covered with flour when laid out on a countertop. So I added a simple tilt-up frame to hold a cookbook. It works great for clearing space and I even found it useful when I wanted to copy a few recipes to notecards.

But this caused a bit of a problem. The box now looked a little top heavy. So I added a second frame around the bottom of the box to balance the appearance of the top frame.

**MATERIALS.** This recipe box only takes a few short pieces of hardwood to build. I like the look of the red oak I used for my box, but you could use almost any hardwood. I ended up resawing and planing some 3/4"-thick stock to get the thin pieces needed for the box and drawers.

**OPTIONS.** As I said, project designs tend to develop as you get into them. One of the nicest features of this project is that you can leave off part of the design (the tilt-up cookbook frame) and still have a great project. The Designer's Notebook on page 23 takes this idea a little further and turns the project into a Mission Recipe Card Box. Don't worry, there's still plenty of room for your recipes.

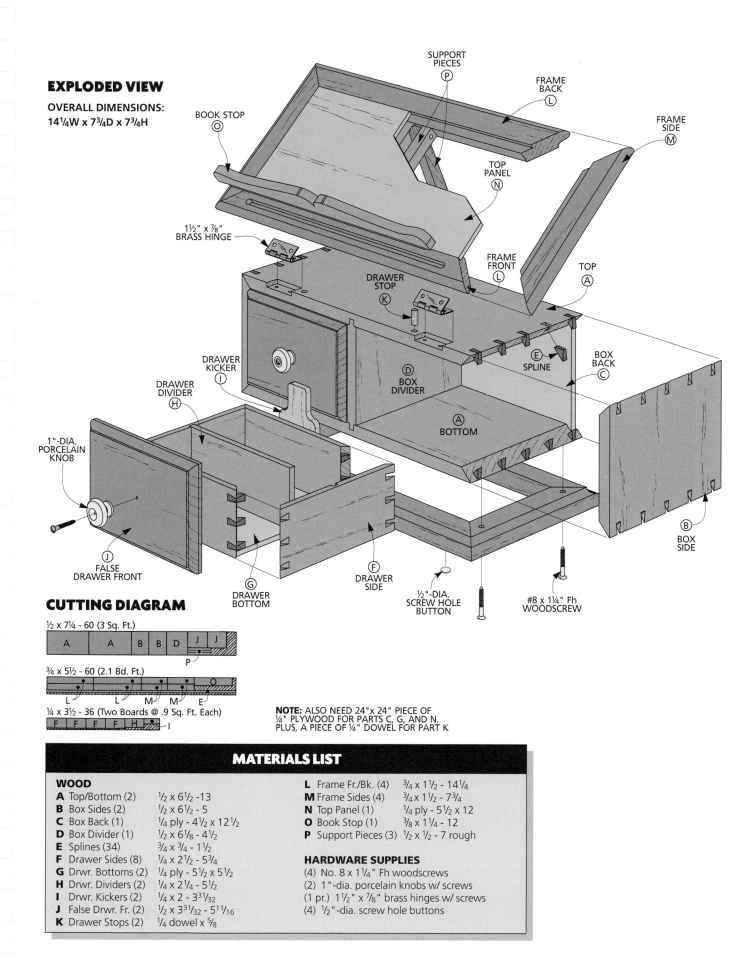

## EXPLODED VIEW

**OVERALL DIMENSIONS:**
**14¼W x 7¾D x 7¾H**

SUPPORT PIECES (P)

FRAME BACK (L)

FRAME SIDE (M)

BOOK STOP (O)

TOP PANEL (N)

1½" x ⅞" BRASS HINGE

FRAME FRONT (L)

TOP (A)

DRAWER STOP (K)

SPLINE (E)

BOX BACK (C)

DRAWER KICKER (I)

BOX DIVIDER (D)

DRAWER DIVIDER (H)

BOTTOM (A)

1"-DIA. PORCELAIN KNOB

DRAWER SIDE (F)

½"-DIA. SCREW HOLE BUTTON

#8 x 1¼" Fh WOODSCREW

BOX SIDE (B)

FALSE DRAWER FRONT (J)

DRAWER BOTTOM (G)

## CUTTING DIAGRAM

½ x 7¼ - 60 (3 Sq. Ft.)

| A | A | B | B | D | J | J |

P

¾ x 5½ - 60 (2.1 Bd. Ft.)

L   L   M   M   E   O

¼ x 3½ - 36 (Two Boards @ .9 Sq. Ft. Each)

F F F F F H   I

**NOTE:** ALSO NEED 24"x 24" PIECE OF ¼" PLYWOOD FOR PARTS C, G, AND N. PLUS, A PIECE OF ¼" DOWEL FOR PART K

## MATERIALS LIST

**WOOD**

| | | |
|---|---|---|
| **A** | Top/Bottom (2) | ½ x 6½ -13 |
| **B** | Box Sides (2) | ½ x 6½ - 5 |
| **C** | Box Back (1) | ¼ ply - 4½ x 12½ |
| **D** | Box Divider (1) | ½ x 6⅛ - 4½ |
| **E** | Splines (34) | ¾ x ¾ - 1½ |
| **F** | Drawer Sides (8) | ¼ x 2½ - 5¾ |
| **G** | Drwr. Bottoms (2) | ¼ ply - 5½ x 5½ |
| **H** | Drwr. Dividers (2) | ¼ x 2¼ - 5½ |
| **I** | Drwr. Kickers (2) | ¼ x 2 - 3³¹/₃₂ |
| **J** | False Drwr. Fr. (2) | ½ x 3³¹/₃₂ - 5¹¹/₁₆ |
| **K** | Drawer Stops (2) | ¼ dowel x ⅝ |
| **L** | Frame Fr./Bk. (4) | ¾ x 1½ - 14¼ |
| **M** | Frame Sides (4) | ¾ x 1½ - 7¾ |
| **N** | Top Panel (1) | ¼ ply - 5½ x 12 |
| **O** | Book Stop (1) | ⅜ x 1¼ - 12 |
| **P** | Support Pieces (3) | ½ x ½ - 7 rough |

**HARDWARE SUPPLIES**

(4) No. 8 x 1¼" Fh woodscrews
(2) 1"-dia. porcelain knobs w/ screws
(1 pr.) 1½" x ⅞" brass hinges w/ screws
(4) ½"-dia. screw hole buttons

To build the box, I started by resawing enough stock to about $^9/_{16}$" thick to make the top and bottom (A), the two sides (B), and the divider (D).

**Note:** You can eliminate resawing if you have access to $^1/_2$"-thick stock.

With the stock resawn, you can edge-glue one long blank (about 28") for the top and bottom pieces. Then edge-glue a second blank for both side pieces and the divider. These pieces are oversized to make it easier to mill them to width.

**Note:** You may be able to find $7^1/_4$"-wide stock. But since wide boards tend to warp, I prefer ripping them down or using narrower boards, then edge-gluing them.

Once the glue has set up, plane the blanks flat and down to $^1/_2$" thick.

**CUT TO ROUGH SIZE.** Next, rip both blanks to width ($6^1/_2$") and cut the top and bottom pieces (A) from the long blank to a rough length of 14". Now cut the two sides (B) from the short blank to a rough length of $5^1/_2$". (Save the cutoff piece for the divider.) I've cut all these pieces to rough length at this point, since I'll be mitering the ends later.

**RABBET FOR THE BACK.** Once all the pieces are cut to rough length, go ahead and rout a rabbet for the plywood back on the inside back edge of the top, bottom, and side pieces (*Fig. 1a*). The $^3/_8$"-wide rabbet allows a decorative set-back for the $^1/_4$"-thick plywood back.

**MITERS.** Next, miter the ends of each side piece (B) to length (5") (*Fig. 1*). (See the Technique article on page 18 for more on cutting these miters.)

**Note:** Be sure to cut the miters so they're on the same face as the rabbets.

Then miter the ends of the top and bottom pieces (A) to length (13"). This will allow plenty of room for the two drawers which hold the 3x5 recipe cards.

**DADO FOR DIVIDER.** Now that all the miters have been cut, you can rout a $^1/_4$"-deep dado centered across the inside face of the top and bottom pieces (*Fig. 2*). This dado will accept the tongues you'll be routing later on the divider.

Centering the dado in the top and bottom pieces is easy. To do this, simply set the fence near the middle of the workpiece. Then to rout the dado to width, make one pass, then rotate the workpiece 180° and make a second pass.

**BACK.** With the the top and bottom pieces complete, cut the back (C) to fit the rabbets you routed earlier (*Fig. 1*).

**DIVIDER.** To determine the length of the divider (D), first dry-assemble the box with the back in place. Then measure the distance from the inside edges of the top and bottom pieces and add $^1/_2$" for the dadoes (*Fig. 4a*). (Mine was $4^1/_2$".)

The width of the divider should match the distance from the front of a side piece to the shoulder of the rabbet in the back edge (*Fig. 4*). (Mine was $6^1/_8$".)

**TONGUES.** After cutting the divider to final size, rout tongues on each end using the router table (*Figs. 4a and 4b*). Depending on the width of your dadoes, you might have to sneak up on the final thickness of the tongues.

**ASSEMBLY.** Once the tongues fit snugly into the dadoes, glue up the assembly, making sure the divider is flush with the front edges. Then clamp the assembly with a couple of band clamps.

## DOVETAIL SLOTS & KEYS

When the glue was dry I added the dovetail slots and keys. These keys (or splines) are used to strengthen the miters on these small pieces. They also add a decorative touch to the box.

Routing these slots isn't difficult. But doing it safely will take a little thought and some extra attention to details.

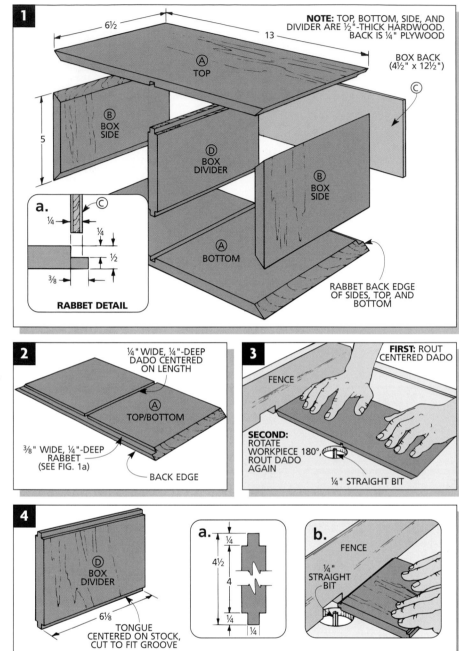

**1** | 6½ | 13 | **NOTE:** TOP, BOTTOM, SIDE, AND DIVIDER ARE ½"-THICK HARDWOOD. BACK IS ¼" PLYWOOD | Ⓐ TOP | BOX BACK (4½" x 12½") | Ⓒ | Ⓑ BOX SIDE | 5 | Ⓓ BOX DIVIDER | Ⓑ BOX SIDE | Ⓐ BOTTOM | RABBET BACK EDGE OF SIDES, TOP, AND BOTTOM

**a.** Ⓒ ¼ ¼ ½ ³/₈ **RABBET DETAIL**

**2** ¼" WIDE, ¼"-DEEP DADO CENTERED ON LENGTH | Ⓐ TOP/BOTTOM | ³/₈" WIDE, ¼"-DEEP RABBET (SEE FIG. 1a) | BACK EDGE

**3** **FIRST:** ROUT CENTERED DADO | FENCE | **SECOND:** ROTATE WORKPIECE 180°, ROUT DADO AGAIN | ¼" STRAIGHT BIT

**4** Ⓓ BOX DIVIDER | 6⅛ | TONGUE CENTERED ON STOCK, CUT TO FIT GROOVE | **a.** ¼ 4½ 4 ¼ ¼ | **b.** FENCE ¼" STRAIGHT BIT

The slots are routed with the help of a holding jig *(Figs. 5 and 6).* (See the Shop Jig box below and the Technique article starting on page 18.)

After all the slots are routed, make the dovetail keys using the router table once again. (This procedure is outlined on page 19 of the Technique article.) Then glue the keys into the slots.

After the glue for the keys has set up, saw the keys off with a fine-toothed back saw, staying close to the surface, and trim each one flush with a sharp chisel.

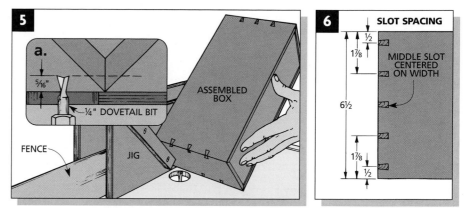

**5**

**a.**

5/16"

1/4" DOVETAIL BIT

FENCE

JIG

ASSEMBLED BOX

**6** **SLOT SPACING**

1/2

1 7/8

MIDDLE SLOT CENTERED ON WIDTH

6 1/2

1 7/8

1/2

---

# SHOP JIG . . . . . . . . . . . . . . . . . . . . . . . . . . . . . *Adjustable Holding Jig*

**W**hen it came time to make the dovetail key joints for the Recipe Card Box, I decided I would make an adjustable jig that could be used on both the router table and my table saw. This way I could use it for making splined miters as well as the dovetail keys I'm using on my box.

The jig has two plywood plates that ride over the fence. I can adjust it so the distance between the two plates matches the thickness of the fence, plus just a smidgeon extra for a smooth ride.

**Note:** Instead of using my regular router table fence (which has several knobs sticking out), I used a piece of scrap hardwood as a temporary fence.

To build the jig, begin by cutting two 3/4"-thick plywood plates to size *(Fig. 2).* Stick the plates together temporarily with carpet tape and trim the bottom edges so they're exactly flush.

**ROD HOLES.** With the two plates still stuck together, drill two counterbores in the front plate *(Fig. 2a).* Then drill shank holes the rest of the way through both plates for threaded adjustment rods.

**SUPPORT ARMS.** To locate the support arms, first determine the centerpoint on the bottom of the front plate. Then use a combination square to draw two 45° lines up from this point *(Fig. 2).*

Now cut two 1"-wide support arms and mount one to the front plate, positioning it 1/2" up from the bottom edge and flush with an angled reference line *(Fig. 3a).*

Use a framing square to line up the second support at 90° to the first arm *(Fig. 3).* Now screw the arm to the plate.

**ASSEMBLY.** Next, cut two lengths of threaded rod *(Fig. 1a).* Place a double nut and washer arrangement on the front plate. Add the remaining plate, wing nuts, and washers. Then straddle the two plates over the fence. Slide them against the sides and adjust the wing nuts so the jig rides smoothly along the fence and square to the table.

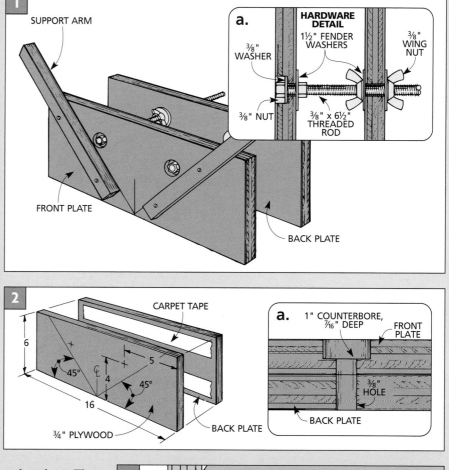

**1**

SUPPORT ARM

FRONT PLATE

BACK PLATE

**a.** **HARDWARE DETAIL**

1 1/2" FENDER WASHERS

3/8" WASHER

3/8" WING NUT

3/8" NUT

3/8" x 6 1/2" THREADED ROD

**2**

6

45°

4

45°

5

16

CARPET TAPE

3/4" PLYWOOD

BACK PLATE

**a.** 1" COUNTERBORE, 7/16" DEEP

FRONT PLATE

3/8" HOLE

BACK PLATE

**3**

DRILL

**a.** SUPPORT ARM

SUPPORT ARMS (3/4" x 1" - 12")

1/2

2

# TECHNIQUE ....... *Dovetail Key Joint*

The dovetail key joint may look like a through dovetail joint. But it's actually a miter joint with dovetail keys running across the miter.

These keys (sometimes called splines) transform what could be a weak miter joint into one that will hold up to a lot of use.

## GETTING STARTED

Start by cutting the workpieces to final width, but to rough length. (The pieces are cut to final length when they are mitered.)

**SET UP THE SAW.** Next, set up your table saw to cut the miters. First, you'll need to attach an auxiliary wooden fence to the miter gauge, making sure it's square to the blade. Then, to keep the workpiece from shifting along the fence, stick a strip of adhesive-backed sandpaper to the auxiliary fence (or attach some sandpaper with carpet tape) (*Step 1*).

**TEST CUT.** Now, tilt the blade to 45° and make a test cut on two pieces of scrap. Hold the two test pieces together and check them to ensure they are square.

## DOUBLE-CUT MITERS

Once the saw blade is set up at exactly 45°, you can begin working on the miters. Start by mitering one end of each workpiece (*Step 1 below*).

**Note:** I sneak up on miters by "double-cutting." It seems to give a cleaner, straighter cut that doesn't burn. Start by making an initial miter cut. Then make a

second cut so only half the thickness of the blade (about $1/16$") is cutting (*detail 'a' in Step 1*).

**DOUBLE CUT.** After the first end of each piece is mitered, clamp a stop block to the auxiliary fence so that the opposite end is cut about $1/16$" longer than the final length (*Step 2*). Cut the second end, and then move the stop block to double-cut the pieces to final length (skimming the last $1/16$" off the miter).

**BOTTOM.** Once all the pieces are mitered to final length, you're ready to glue the pieces together.

**Note:** To glue up a frame (or any assembly without a bottom), cut a piece of scrap plywood to fit inside. This scrap helps keep the frame square during assembly.

**ASSEMBLY.** Before assembly, test the bottom for final fit by dry-clamping the box together. Once it fits, go ahead and glue up the box.

On smaller mitered boxes, I find it easier to glue up the sides in pairs using a squaring jig to keep them aligned (*detail 'a' in Step 3*). And then I glue the pairs together. On larger mitered boxes

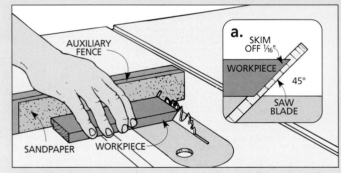

1 *Tip blade to 45° and cut one end. Then make a second cut to skim off another $1/16$" (half the blade's thickness). Sandpaper on auxiliary fence prevents the piece from slipping.*

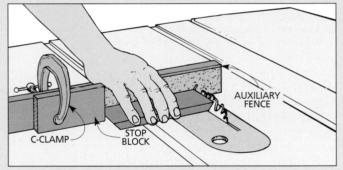

2 *Next, clamp a stop block to the auxiliary fence and cut the other end of the workpiece slightly long ($1/16$"). Then readjust the stop block to trim the workpiece to finished length.*

3 *Glue two sides together (a squaring jig helps while holding pieces tight). Slip the bottom into place to square up the box and glue the two pairs together. Clamp with two band clamps.*

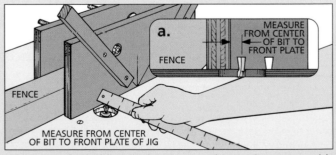

4 *Mount the holding jig (see page 17) over the router table fence. Determine the location of the slots by measuring from the front face of the jig to the center of the bit.*

though, I find it's a lot easier to glue up all four sides at once.

Either way, slip the bottom in place to hold the box square. Then wrap a couple of band clamps around the whole assembly and tighten *(Step 3)*.

## DOVETAIL SLOTS

After the glue is dry on the miters, the dovetail key slots can be cut across each corner. Begin by mounting a dovetail bit in the router table.

**Note:** I used a ¼" dovetail bit here, but you could use a ½" dovetail bit, or even a straight router bit for flat keys.

**JIG.** To hold the box at an angle to the router table, I built a jig that straddles an auxiliary router table fence (see the Shop Jig box on page 17). With the jig straddling the fence, determine the location of the slots by measuring from the center of the bit to the side of the jig *(Step 4)*. Now hold the box tight against the jig and push it through the bit *(Step 5)*.

**Note:** If the box you're building has an odd number of dovetail keys, locate the first slot so it's centered on the width of the box *(detail 'a' in Step 5)*.

**ROUT OTHER SLOTS.** Next, move the fence until the next slot location is centered over the bit and rout that slot. Then flip the box (don't move the fence) so the opposite edge is against the jig and rout the opposite slot. Continue with this procedure to rout all remaining slots.

## DOVETAIL KEYS

Once the slots are cut, remove the jig but keep the router bit at the same height to make the dovetail keys. The keys are made by first routing dovetail tongues on the edges of a piece of scrap.

Hold the workpiece against the fence with a piece of scrap *(Step 6)* and rout one edge. Then flip the workpiece so the opposite edge is facing the fence and rout the other edge *(detail 'a' in Step 6)*. Now test the tongue for fit — it should be snug *(Step 7)*. If it's still too tight, readjust the fence to take off a little more.

Rout the tongues on your workpiece and rip the keys off the strip *(Step 8)*.

**FINISH THE JOINT.** Now cut the dovetail keys into 1½" lengths, apply a little glue to each key, and slide it into the slot. After the glue dries, trim off the excess with a fine-toothed saw *(Step 9)*.

To make the keys perfectly flush with the side of the box, shave them off with a sharp chisel *(Step 10)*.

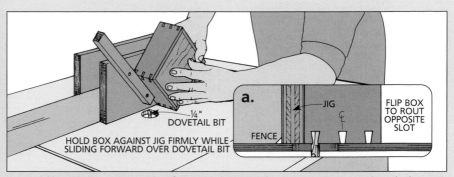

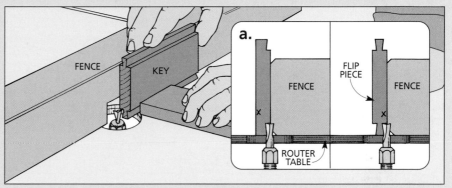

**5** Hold box tight against side of jig and down in the support arms and push through the bit. Corner of box should ride along surface of router table. (If needed, rout center slot first.) Then move fence for the next slot. Without moving fence, flip the box around and rout the slot on the other side (detail 'a'). Repeat for remaining slots.

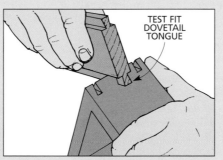
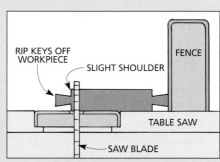

**6** With bit at same height, rout dovetail tongues on both edges of a piece of scrap. Use another piece of scrap to hold workpiece tight against the fence. Make the first pass on both edges of one face of the workpiece (detail 'a'). Then flip piece over and rout opposite face. If tongue is too thick, move fence and rout again.

**7** Test the dovetail tongue to see if it fits in the slots routed in the box. If it's just a little too thick, lightly sand the tongues to produce a good, snug fit.

**8** Rip the long dovetail keys off the workpiece so they fall away from the blade. Leave a slight shoulder to be sure the keys are wide enough.

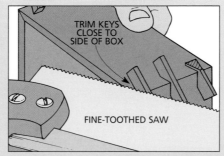

**9** Cut keys about 1½" long and glue them into the slots. Once the glue is dry, cut the keys off close to the side of the box with a fine-toothed saw.

**10** Shave excess off flush with a sharp chisel. Work from each corner toward the center of the box side to prevent the dovetail keys from chipping out.

After the box is complete, the drawers can be built to fit in the openings. I began work on the drawers by cutting eight drawer sides (F) to width (2½") from ¼"-thick stock (*Fig. 7*). Then crosscut the sides to rough length (6½").

**BOTTOM RABBET.** Before cutting the sides to final length though, you need to cut ⅛"-deep (wide) rabbets on the bottom edge of all eight pieces to hold the ¼"-thick plywood drawer bottoms (*Fig. 7a*).

**LENGTH OF SIDES.** After the rabbets are cut, the drawer sides can be cut to final length. To find the exact length, measure the width of the drawer opening in the box. (In my case, the opening measured 5¾".) Now cut the miters on the ends of all eight pieces so the length from point to point of the miters equals the width of the opening.

**Note:** The drawer openings are square so all eight sides are the same length. Once again, see the Technique article on page 18 to learn more on how I like to cut these miters.

**DIVIDER DADOES.** Once all eight drawer sides have been mitered to length, rout centered dadoes across four of the pieces (the sides of the two drawers) to accept the drawer dividers (H) to be added later (*Fig. 7b*).

**BOTTOMS.** Next, cut the ¼" plywood bottoms (G) to fit in the rabbets. Then glue up the drawers with the bottoms in place. Since the drawers fit tightly into the opening, check that they're square before clamping them together.

**DOVETAIL KEYS.** After the drawers have had plenty of time to completely set up, add the dovetail keys using the same technique as on the box (*Fig. 7c*).

After the dovetail keys are glued in place and cut off flush, you can sand or plane the sides slightly so the drawer

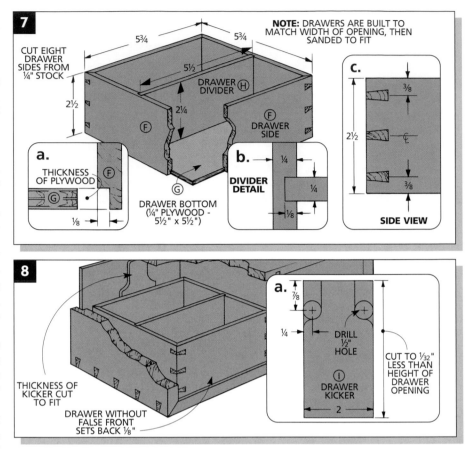

slides into the opening with about ¹⁄₃₂" clearance on each side.

**DIVIDERS.** Now cut the drawer dividers (H) to size so they'll slide into the dadoes in each drawer (*Fig. 7*).

**KICKERS.** To keep the drawer from tipping down as it's pulled out, I added a kicker (I) to the back of each drawer (*Fig. 8*). The kicker also acts as a spacer to keep the drawer from being pushed too far back into the box.

To determine the thickness of the kicker I pushed the drawer all the way into the box and measured the set-back. In my case this was ⅜". I wanted to add a ½"-thick false drawer front and have it

stick out ⅜" from the front edge of the box (*Fig. 9b*). This meant the kicker would have to be ¼" thick.

Once you've sized your kickers, cut them to thickness and to shape (*Fig. 8a*). Then, glue the kicker to the center of the drawer back, making sure it's flush with the drawer bottom.

**FALSE DRAWER FRONTS.** To complete the drawers, cut two false drawer fronts (J) from ½"-thick stock. The width is equal to the height of the drawer opening minus ¹⁄₃₂" and the length matches the front of the drawer (*Fig. 9*).

Now rout a ¼" roundover with a ³⁄₃₂" shoulder around the front face of the

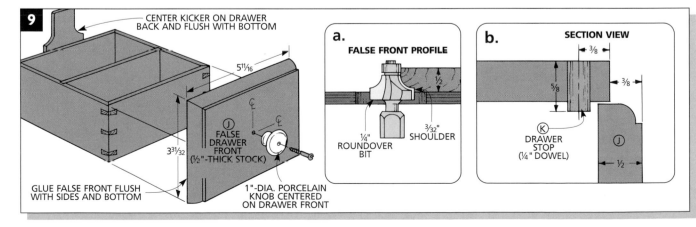

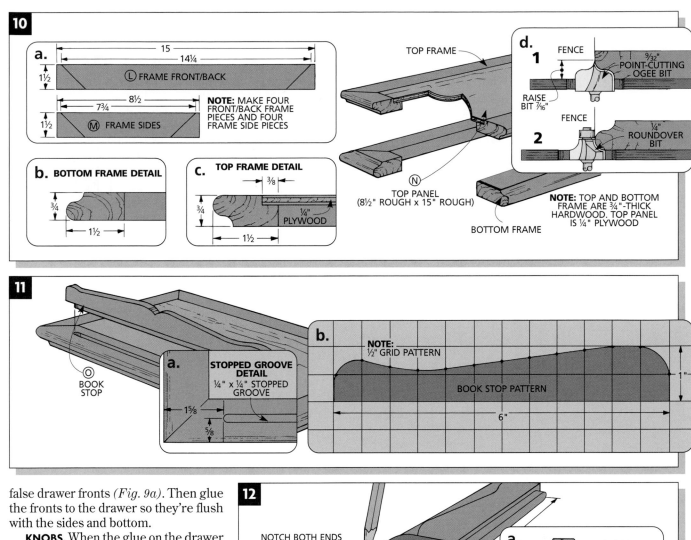

**10**

**a.**
15
14¼
1½ Ⓛ FRAME FRONT/BACK

**NOTE:** MAKE FOUR FRONT/BACK FRAME PIECES AND FOUR FRAME SIDE PIECES

8½
7¾
1½ Ⓜ FRAME SIDES

**b. BOTTOM FRAME DETAIL**
¾
1½

**c. TOP FRAME DETAIL**
⅜
¾
¼ PLYWOOD
1½

TOP FRAME

**d.**
**1** FENCE
9/32"
POINT-CUTTING OGEE BIT
RAISE BIT 7/16"

**2** FENCE
¼" ROUNDOVER BIT

TOP PANEL
(8½" ROUGH x 15" ROUGH) Ⓝ

BOTTOM FRAME

**NOTE:** TOP AND BOTTOM FRAME ARE ¾"-THICK HARDWOOD. TOP PANEL IS ¼" PLYWOOD

**11**

**a. STOPPED GROOVE DETAIL**
¼" x ¼" STOPPED GROOVE
Ⓞ BOOK STOP
1⅝
⅝

**b.**
**NOTE:** ½" GRID PATTERN
BOOK STOP PATTERN
1"
6"

false drawer fronts *(Fig. 9a)*. Then glue the fronts to the drawer so they're flush with the sides and bottom.

**KNOBS.** When the glue on the drawer fronts is dry, screw a porcelain knob to the center of each front *(Fig. 9)*.

**DOWEL STOPS.** To keep the drawer from pulling out too far, drill ¼" holes through the top of the box to accept ⅝"-long dowel stops *(Fig. 10a)*. (These stops catch the kickers.) Center the holes above each drawer opening.

## FRAMES

Once the drawers were complete, I added a tilt-up cookbook holder to the top and a matching frame to the bottom.

**CUT FRAME.** Start by ripping all eight frame pieces to width (1½"). Then cut the fronts (L), backs (L), and sides (M) to rough length *(Fig. 10a)*.

**TOP FRAME RABBET.** Next, cut a rabbet in the top frame pieces sized to accept the plywood top panel *(Fig. 10c)*.

**MITER TO LENGTH.** Now the frame pieces can be cut to final length. Measure the length and depth of the box and cut miters on the ends of the frame pieces so

**12**

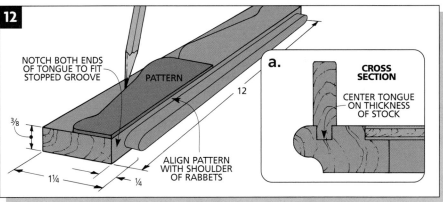

NOTCH BOTH ENDS OF TONGUE TO FIT STOPPED GROOVE
PATTERN
⅜
1¼
¼
12
ALIGN PATTERN WITH SHOULDER OF RABBETS

**a. CROSS SECTION**
CENTER TONGUE ON THICKNESS OF STOCK

thc finished length is 1¼" longer than the box *(Fig. 10a)*. This allows for a ⅝" overhang on each side. (In my case, the fronts and backs are 14¼" and the sides 7¾".)

**TOP PANELS.** Once the pieces are cut to length, glue up the frames. Then cut the ¼" top panel (N) to fit in the rabbets of the top frame and glue it in place.

**PROFILES.** After the frames are assembled, use the router table with a fence to rout profiles on the top and bottom edges of each frame. First, rout the point-cutting ogee profile *(Step 1 in Fig. 10d)*. Then flip the frame over and rout a ¼" roundover on the other side *(Step 2 in Fig. 10d)*.

**BOOK STOP.** The next step is to add a book stop (O) to the top frame. Begin by routing a stopped ¼" groove near the top front edge of the top frame *(Fig. 11a)*.

Then cut a blank for the book stop. Cut a centered tongue on the bottom edge to fit the groove *(Figs. 12 and 12a)*, notching both ends of the tongues to match the length of the groove.

Finally, lay out the profile on the blank, making sure the book stop pattern is lined up with the shoulder of the rabbet *(Figs. 11b and 12)*. Then cut the book stop to final shape. (But don't glue it in place yet; it's easier to continue with it off.)

## ATTACHING THE FRAMES

Once the top and bottom frames are complete, they can be attached to the box. I began by attaching the bottom frame.

**BOTTOM FRAME.** To do this, start by drilling six oversize ($^7/_{32}$") countersunk holes for the screws (*Figs. 13 and 14*).

**Note:** The bottom frame is not glued on, so oversized shank holes allow for expansion and contraction of the box during changes in humidity.

The Recipe Card Box sits on four $^1/_2$" screw hole buttons that act as "feet," and help keep the box from scratching your countertops. Drill $^3/_{16}$"-deep stopped holes for these buttons in the bottom frame and glue them in place (*Fig. 14*).

After the buttons are glued in, turn the box over on its top and position the bottom frame so it's centered on the box and mark and drill $^3/_{32}$" pilot holes. Then screw the bottom to the box.

**SUPPORT SYSTEM.** Before the top frame can be attached to the box, a support system (P) is added to the back side of the top frame. This system holds the frame at about 45° and acts as a support for an open cookbook (*Figs. 16 and 16b*).

Start building the support system by cutting a piece of $^1/_2$" stock $1^3/_4$" wide and long enough to fit snugly between the front and back of the frame (*Step 1 in Fig. 15*). Then drill a hole through one end of the blank to accept a 16d common nail that serves as a pivot pin.

Next, make two rip cuts to slice the workpiece into thirds with each piece measuring $^1/_2$" wide (*Step 1 in Fig. 15*). Then crosscut the middle workpiece down to a length of $4^1/_2$" and round over both ends (*Step 2 in Fig. 15*).

After rounding over the middle support piece, put all three back together, line up the holes, and epoxy a $1^1/_2$" piece of a 16d nail into the hole so the middle arm pivots (*Steps 2 and 3 in Fig. 15*).

Finally, glue the two outside pieces to the center (underside) of the top frame

(*Step 4 in Fig. 15*). I clamped the outside pieces with just enough gap between them so the middle piece pivots.

**MORTISES.** Once the support system is glued in place on top of the box, you can locate the mortises for the $1^1/_2$"-long hinges (*Fig. 16a*). To do this, I like to position the hinge so the knuckle is centered on the front edge of the box and mark the location of the hinge.

Now mortise deep enough so the knuckle is flush with the top of the box. Then drill holes for the hinge screws, and screw the hinges to the box.

**Note:** I had to file off the points of the $^1/_2$"-long brass screws since they came out into the box openings.

To mount the other hinge leaf to the frame, turn the box upside down so it's centered on the frame. Mark the position of the hinge, then drill for the screws.

**SUPPORT HOLE.** When the frame is tilted up, the support arm fits into a shallow $^3/_4$"-dia. hole centered on the length of the box (*Figs. 16 and 16b*).

**FINISH.** Finally I glued the book stop in place and finished the project with three coats of oil varnish. ∎

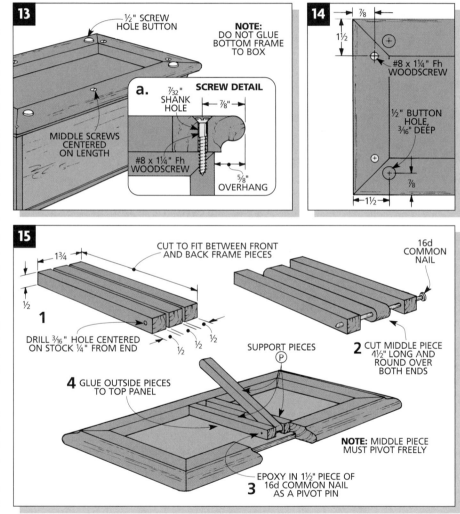

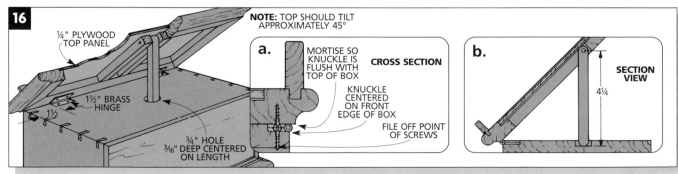

# DESIGNER'S NOTEBOOK

*Beveled edges, raised drawer fronts, and card pulls give this mission-style box an air of authenticity. It features dovetail key joinery for the box and drawers, with plenty of space for all your recipe cards.*

## CONSTRUCTION NOTES:

- The Mission Recipe Card Box has a solid wood top and bottom that will be glued to the box itself.
- Start by building the box with the divider and drawers as before. Once they're completed, you can work on the top and bottom (Q) pieces. To make them, start by ripping two pieces of $1/2$"-thick hardwood to width ($7^1/8$") and cutting them to length ($14^1/4$") *(Fig. 1)*.
- Once the workpieces are cut to size you'll need to cut the bevel along the front and sides of the top and bottom pieces. I used a table saw to do this, first tilting the blade to 27°. Then you can cut the bevels with the workpiece set on edge and the bottom face against the rip fence.

   **Note:** I left the back edge of the top and bottom pieces square since they'll be lined up with the back edge of the box when it gets assembled.
- Once the top and bottom are complete, you can glue them to the box *(Fig. 1a)*.
- The last pieces to make are the false drawer fronts (J). They also have a beveled profile, but this time I left a small shoulder at the top of the bevel and cut it all the way around the piece *(Fig. 2)*.

   Once again, I used the table saw to cut the profile. To do this, set the rip fence $5/16$" away from the outside edge of the blade and raise the saw blade $1/16$"

above the table top. Now, with the front face down, run all four edges of the workpiece over the blade. This will give you a square shoulder. Now raise the blade and tilt it to 45° to complete the profile.
- Finally, use a sanding block to remove any saw blade marks and glue the false fronts to the drawers.
- When the glue has completely set up, screw a brass index card frame pull to the center of each false front *(Fig. 2)*.

MISSION RECIPE CARD BOX

## MATERIALS LIST

**CHANGED PARTS**
**J** False Drawer Fr. (2)   $1/2$ x $3^{31}/_{32}$ - $5^{11}/_{16}$
**NEW PARTS**
**Q** Top/Bottom (2)   $1/2$ x $7^1/8$ -$14^1/4$
**Note:** Do not need parts L, M, N, O, and P.

**HARDWARE SUPPLIES**
(2) $2^3/8$ " x $1^5/8$" brass index card frame pulls w/ screws

---

**1**

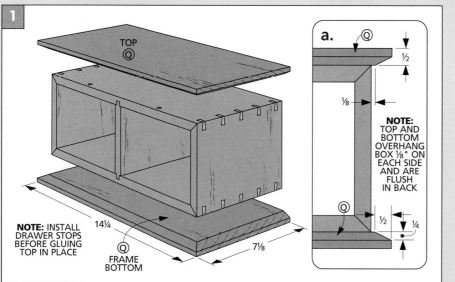

TOP
Q

NOTE: INSTALL DRAWER STOPS BEFORE GLUING TOP IN PLACE

$14^1/4$

Q
FRAME BOTTOM

$7^1/8$

**a.**

Q

$1/2$

$1/8$

**NOTE:** TOP AND BOTTOM OVERHANG BOX $1/8$" ON EACH SIDE AND ARE FLUSH IN BACK

Q

$1/2$

$1/4$

---

**2**

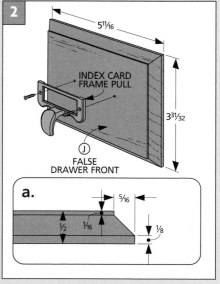

$5^{11}/_{16}$

INDEX CARD FRAME PULL

$3^{31}/_{32}$

J

FALSE DRAWER FRONT

**a.**

$5/16$

$1/2$   $1/16$

$1/8$

# Spice Cabinet

*Whether you are a beginner or a seasoned woodworker, building this small project will give you experience with woodworking techniques normally found only on larger pieces.*

**N**early everyone's reaction to this project has been the same — "It looks like a miniature armoire." And while I couldn't quite bring myself to call this a "spice armoire," it wouldn't have been too much of a stretch. After all, even though this project is small enough to sit on top of a kitchen counter, it's full of some of the same design details (and woodworking techniques) that you might find on a much larger project.

**ARCHED DOOR RAILS.** A good example of this is the arched rail on each door. This feature would look right at home on an armoire. Only with a project this size, your job is a lot easier. You won't have to cut curved panels to match the rails. The pieces are small enough so everything (except the rail) can be left square. With the pattern on page 29 and a little carpet tape, tracing the full size pattern of the arch for the upper rail is light work.

**STORAGE DOORS.** My favorite detail is a practical one. The doors on this case aren't your typical frame and panel doors. The front half of the case is attached to the doors so they can hold small spice containers (see inset photo). This means no more hunting for a spice you need. All the containers are out front in plain view.

**WOOD.** I used cherry hardwood for this project, but mahogany or maple would also look nice, depending on your home and kitchen decor.

**VENEER DOOR PANELS.** For a more dramatic look, you might want to build the door panels in a contrasting veneer.

For an example of how the doors can be "dressed up" with figured veneer, see the Designer's Notebook on page 29.

## EXPLODED VIEW

**OVERALL DIMENSIONS:**
13¾W x 6D x 14⅞H

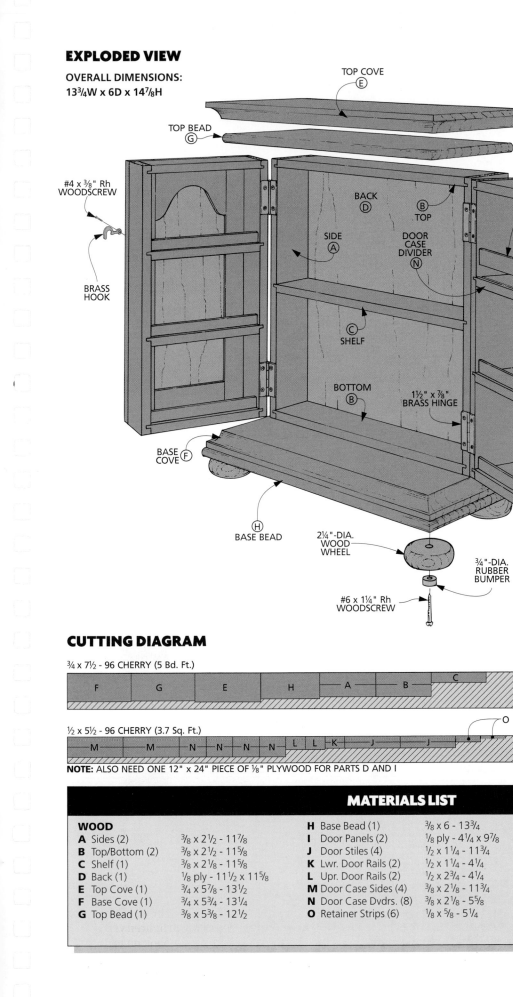

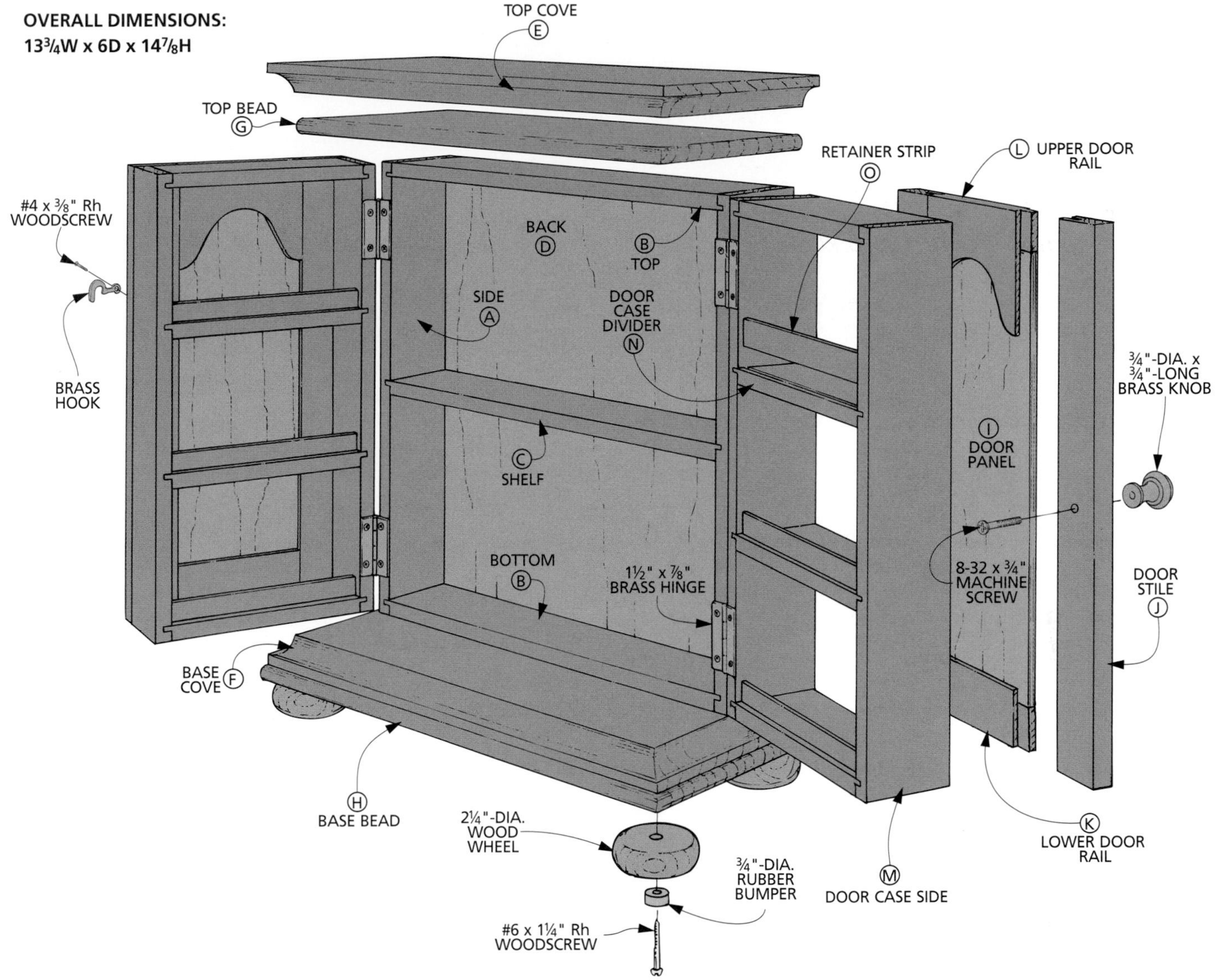

## CUTTING DIAGRAM

¾ x 7½ - 96 CHERRY (5 Bd. Ft.)

F  G  E  H  A  B  C

½ x 5½ - 96 CHERRY (3.7 Sq. Ft.)

M  M  N  N  N  N  L  L  K  J  J  O

**NOTE:** ALSO NEED ONE 12" x 24" PIECE OF ⅛" PLYWOOD FOR PARTS D AND I

## MATERIALS LIST

| WOOD | | | | HARDWARE SUPPLIES |
|---|---|---|---|---|
| **A** | Sides (2) | ⅜ x 2½ - 11⅞ | **H** Base Bead (1) | ⅜ x 6 - 13¾ |
| **B** | Top/Bottom (2) | ⅜ x 2½ - 11⅝ | **I** Door Panels (2) | ⅛ ply - 4¼ x 9⅞ |
| **C** | Shelf (1) | ⅜ x 2⅛ - 11⅝ | **J** Door Stiles (4) | ½ x 1¼ - 11¾ |
| **D** | Back (1) | ⅛ ply - 11½ x 11⅝ | **K** Lwr. Door Rails (2) | ½ x 1¼ - 4¼ |
| **E** | Top Cove (1) | ¾ x 5⅞ - 13½ | **L** Upr. Door Rails (2) | ½ x 2¾ - 4¼ |
| **F** | Base Cove (1) | ¾ x 5¾ - 13¼ | **M** Door Case Sides (4) | ⅜ x 2⅛ - 11¾ |
| **G** | Top Bead (1) | ⅜ x 5⅜ - 12½ | **N** Door Case Dvdrs. (8) | ⅜ x 2⅛ - 5⅝ |
| | | | **O** Retainer Strips (6) | ⅛ x ⅝ - 5¼ |

**HARDWARE SUPPLIES**
(2) No. 4 x ⅜" Rh woodscrews
(4) No. 6 x 1¼" Rh woodscrews
(2) 8-32 x ¾" machine screws
(4) ¾" x 2¼" wood wheels
(4) ¾"-dia. rubber bumpers
(2 pr.) 1½" x ⅞" brass hinges
(2) ¾" x ¾" brass knobs
(1) Brass hook

## CASE

The odd thing about this case is that it gets built in two halves. You're going to work on the back half for now *(Fig. 1)*. The front half will be assembled and attached to the doors later.

This case is simple enough. All the pieces are cut from ⅜"-thick stock (with a ⅛" plywood back) and are joined by tongues and dadoes.

**CUT TO SIZE.** After planing some stock ⅜" thick, you can cut the pieces to size *(Fig. 1)*. The sides (A) are identical, but I also cut the top and bottom (B), and shelf (C) the same. The shelf will end up a little narrower later on, but this way you can sneak up on its final fit.

**DADOES.** When joining pieces with tongues and dadoes, I generally cut the

dadoes first. It's a lot easier to sneak up on the final size of a tongue than it is to sneak up on the size of a dado.

To keep the dadoes in the sides as simple as possible, they're only ⅛" wide *(Figs. 1c and 2a)*. By doing this, they can be cut in a single pass with a regular blade *(Fig. 2)*. To back up these pieces, I added an auxiliary fence to my miter gauge and used the rip fence as a stop.

**Note:** Since you're not cutting all the way through the pieces, you don't have to worry about a waste piece kicking back.

**TONGUES.** With the dadoes cut in the case sides, the next step is to cut a rabbet that will leave a ⅛" tongue *(Fig. 3)*. This means getting out your dado blade and burying it in an auxiliary fence. Sneak up on the final depth of the rabbet until the tongue that's left fits the dado perfectly.

**BACK.** The other piece to take care of is the ⅛" plywood back. To do this, cut ³⁄₁₆"-deep grooves to hold the back panel *(Fig. 1a)*. Keep in mind that these grooves are cut on the case sides, top, and bottom — but not the shelf.

To determine the size of the back (D), dry-assemble the case and measure the opening. (Remember to allow for the grooves.) But I should mention something about the plywood you'll need for this project. Later, the door panels will need ⅛" plywood with two good faces. You can use this for the back as well.

But don't sweat it if you can't find plywood with two good faces — these small panels are very simple to veneer. Even with quality plywood on hand, veneered panels can give added distinction to this cabinet. For more on adding figured

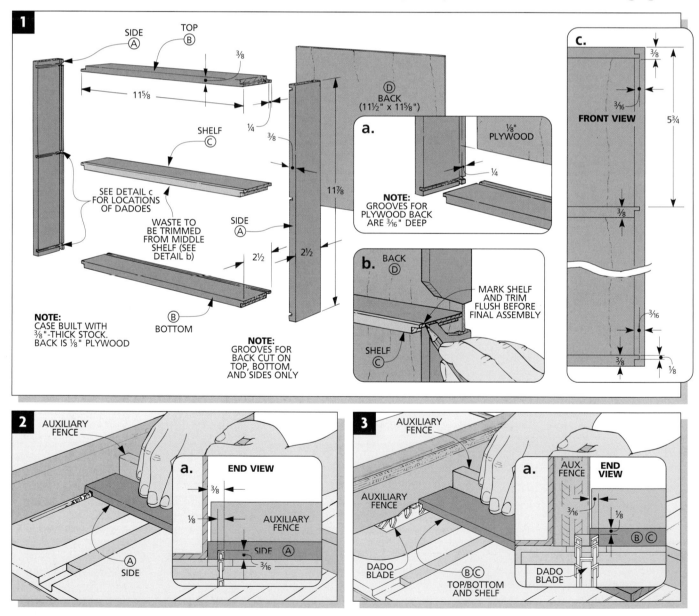

veneer to the door panels, see the Designer's Notebook on page 29.

**TRIM SHELF.** After the back has been cut to fit into the grooves, the last thing to do is trim the shelf to width *(Fig. 1b)*. All you need to do is rip one edge ensuring the piece will fit into the case flush with the front edges.

**ASSEMBLE CASE.** Now the case can be glued up. This assembly is pretty straight-forward. There are only six pieces to work with, and the plywood back helps keep the assembly square.

**MOLDING.** While the glue is drying, you can work on the molding for the top and bottom of the case *(Figs. 4 and 5)*. There are two kinds of molding: ¾"-thick cove molding and ⅜"-thick bead molding.

I started with the top cove (E) and base cove (F). These pieces can be cut to finished size right away. (The top cove is slightly larger.) Then a ½"-radius cove profile can be routed on the ends and front edges of these pieces *(Fig. 4a)*.

The top bead (G) and base bead (H) are thinner than the cove molding pieces, but the procedure is the same. After cutting them to finished size, the profile is routed with a roundover bit *(Fig. 5a)*.

**ATTACH MOLDING.** Gluing the two layers of molding together and then to the case is the same for the top and base. First I added small brads and snipped off their heads *(Fig. 5)*. With their back edges flush and the pieces centered side-to-side, I pressed them together so the

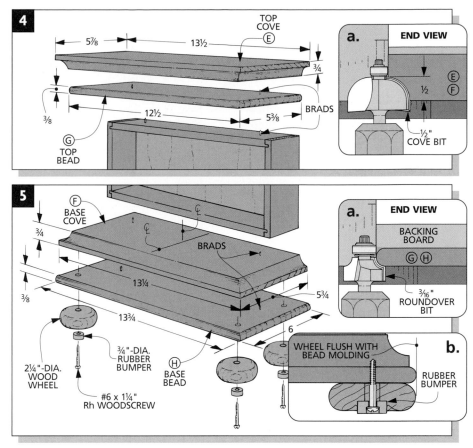

brads would "bite" into the wood. This way, when glued, the workpieces won't shift under the pressure of the clamps.

**FEET.** Once the top and base moldings are glued to the case, the last thing to do is add the feet *(Figs. 5 and 5b)*.

These bun-style feet are just wooden wheels. To give them more traction, add a rubber bumper to the bottom of each. This takes an extra counterbore, and working with round parts required some thought (see the Technique box below).

## TECHNIQUE . . . . . . . . . . . . . . . . . . . . . . . . . . . *Adding Rubber Feet*

The bun feet on the Spice Cabinet are just wood wheels used for toys. They look good, but they're slick. To keep the cabinet from sliding around every time a door is opened, I added a rubber bumper to the bottom face of each wheel.

**ENLARGE HUB.** To do this, a shallow counterbore is drilled, centered on the wheel's axle hole. But centering a counterbore on an existing hole is hard to do without some help.

Luckily, there's a simple solution that secures the wheel on the drill press so the axle hole is centered directly under the center of the drill bit.

This is done using a short length of dowel that fits in both the axle hole of the wheel and a piece of scrap secured to the drill press table *(Fig. 1)*.

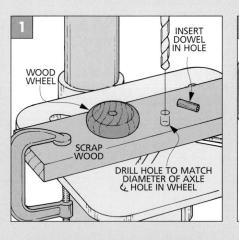

**Note:** The drill bit for the dowel must match the diameter of the axle hole, and the bit for the counterbore must match the diameter of the bumper *(Fig. 2a)*.

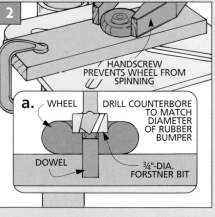

**ATTACH WHEEL.** Now the rubber bumpers can be pressed into place and the feet can be screwed to the bottom (refer to *Figs. 5 and 5a* above).

With the case done (or at least half done), I began work on the doors. These are frame and panel doors joined with grooves and stub tenons. But there are a couple of unusual things about them. For one thing, the upper rail on each door is arched (which helps the small cabinet to look much less "boxy"). Plus, after the front half of the case has been built, it will be glued to the back of these doors.

**DOOR PANELS.** To get started, the first thing I did was to get the door panels cut to rough size. (Note that all the dimensions in *Fig. 6* are finished sizes.) You need to have a rough panel on hand now because the joinery for the door frames is based on the thickness of this panel.

As I mentioned earlier, the panel here needs to have two good faces since you'll see the inside face when the doors are opened. I was able to find $1/8$" plywood with two good faces. But you can also apply veneer to one face of a regular plywood panel (or both faces of a piece of $1/8$" hardboard). You can even "dress up" the doors with a figured veneer panel, as described in the Designer's Notebook on the opposite page.

**DOOR FRAMES.** With the panels on hand, work can begin on the door frames. The first thing to do is figure out just how big to cut these pieces. Since I wanted $1/16$" gaps at the top and bottom of the doors, I simply measured the case opening and subtracted $1/8$". But the $1/16$" gap between the doors is a little trickier. To keep the numbers easy, I sized the doors to fit without a gap. Then later, the edges of the doors (and cases) will be sanded (or planed) to match the gap at the top and bottom.

The door frames require $1/2$"-thick stock *(Fig. 6)*. The door stiles (J) and lower door rails (K) are ripped $1^{1}/4$" wide, but the upper door rails (L) are wider ($2^{3}/4$") because of the arch at the top.

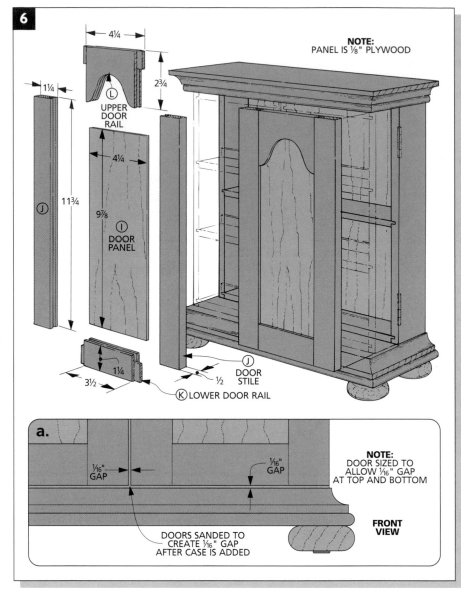

**GROOVES.** With the pieces cut to size, it's time to work on the grooves and stub tenons. I started with the grooves, sizing them to hold the door panels. They should also be centered perfectly — it'll make the tenons that much easier to cut.

So if your panel is exactly $1/8$" thick, you'll have to cut the grooves in one pass.

On the other hand, if the panel ends up slightly thicker than $1/8$", then you can center the groove automatically by cutting it in two passes, flipping the piece end for end between passes.

I cut the groove in each upper rail first *(Figs. 7 and 7a)*. Because of the arches that will be cut later, these grooves are

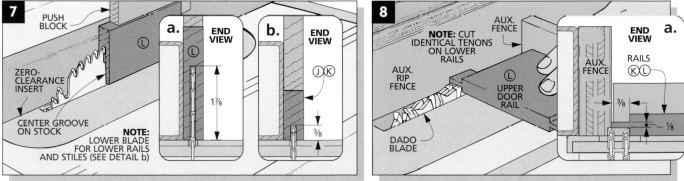

extra deep (1⅞") so you don't have to cut an arched panel. This way, the panel's square upper corners will fit up into the extra-deep grooves *(Fig. 6)*.

After the grooves are cut in the upper rails, you can lower the blade and cut ⅜"-deep grooves in the door stiles and lower door rails *(Fig. 7b)*.

**STUB TENONS.** All that's left now is to cut stub tenons on the upper and lower door rails to fit the grooves in the door stiles. I decided to cut each tenon cheek in a single pass using my dado blade buried in an auxiliary rip fence *(Fig. 8)*. To support these short rail pieces, you'll also want to attach an auxiliary fence to your miter gauge.

**ARCH.** The door stiles and lower door rails can be set aside for now so the arches can be cut in the upper door rails. I used a half-pattern to trace them out *(Fig. 9)*. (It's full-size so you can trace it or photocopy it at 100%.) To make sure the shape of both rails ends up identical, I used carpet tape to hold them together *(Fig. 10)*. Then I carefully drew the curve, working from the center line out to the edge of each rail.

Cutting the arch is a two-step process. First, the curve needs to be roughed out using a band saw *(Fig. 11)*. In other words, don't try to cut right up to the

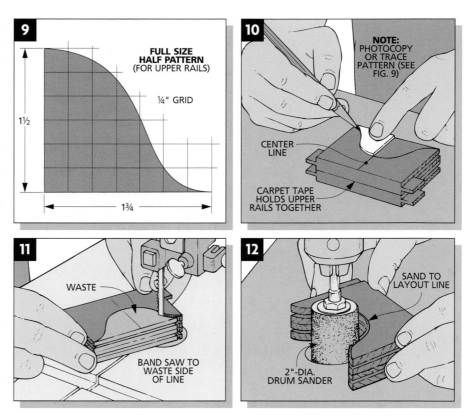

line. That's because the second step is to sand up to this line using a drum sander chucked in the drill press *(Fig. 12)*.

**DOOR PANELS AND ASSEMBLY.** Now that the frame pieces are complete, they

can be dry-assembled. This way, you can cut the plywood door panels (I) to fit into the grooves of the door stiles and rails *(Fig. 6)*. Then the door panels and frames can be glued together.

# DESIGNER'S NOTEBOOK

*Figured veneer gives the doors a new look with just a little effort.*

## VENEER PANEL DOORS

■ Dress up this project by adding figured veneer to the door panels. Figured veneer's irregular grain makes it more prone to wrinkling and splitting — so it's more work to flatten it.

■ The solution is to buy veneer that's already flattened and glued to a thin backer so it's easily glued to the panel.

■ To glue it to the door panel, I like to use contact cement. Since the veneer will adhere on contact, I use waxed paper to prevent it from sticking prematurely while I rolled it down in place *(Fig. 1)*.

■ When the glue has dried, trim the veneer *(Fig. 2)*. Start with light scoring passes, then cut the excess veneer away.

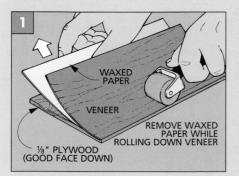

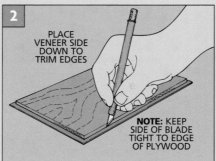

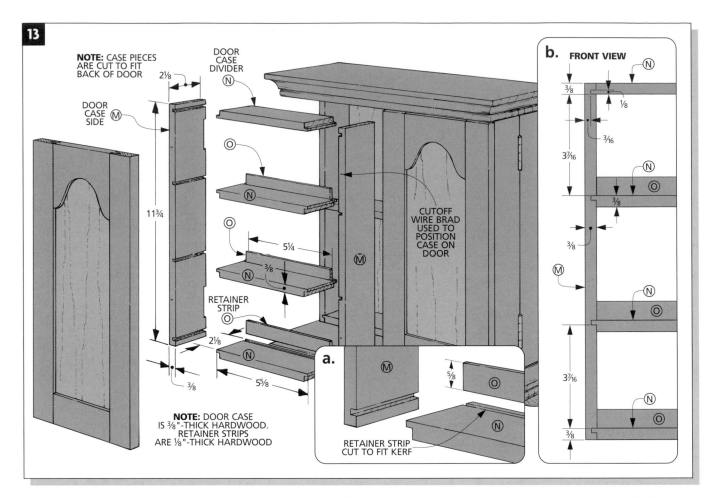

**13**

NOTE: CASE PIECES
ARE CUT TO FIT
BACK OF DOOR

DOOR
CASE
DIVIDER
N

$2\frac{1}{8}$

DOOR
CASE
SIDE M

$11\frac{3}{4}$

O

N

O

$5\frac{1}{4}$

$\frac{3}{8}$

N

RETAINER
STRIP
O

$2\frac{1}{8}$

N

$\frac{3}{8}$

$5\frac{5}{8}$

NOTE: DOOR CASE
IS $\frac{3}{8}$"-THICK HARDWOOD.
RETAINER STRIPS
ARE $\frac{1}{8}$"-THICK HARDWOOD

CUTOFF
WIRE BRAD
USED TO
POSITION
CASE ON
DOOR

M

**a.**

M

O

$\frac{5}{8}$

N

RETAINER STRIP
CUT TO FIT KERF

**b.** FRONT VIEW

N

$\frac{3}{8}$ $\frac{1}{8}$

$\frac{3}{16}$

$3\frac{7}{16}$

N

O

$\frac{3}{8}$

$\frac{3}{8}$

M

N

O

N

$3\frac{7}{16}$

N

O

$\frac{3}{8}$

## DOOR CASE

Even though the doors are assembled, they're not ready to be attached to the case. That's because the second (front) half of the case needs to be built and then glued to the doors *(Fig. 13)*.

The procedures you will use here are much the same as the ones used for the back half of the case you built earlier. Except this time, you'll be building two small sections (instead of one large one), and they'll need to be sized to match the doors. Plus, since these cases are designed to hold smaller spice containers, there's also an extra shelf in each.

**CUT TO SIZE.** Like the case in back, the door case is built from $\frac{3}{8}$"-thick stock *(Fig. 13)*. The door case sides (M) are cut to length to match the height of the doors. The four door case dividers (N) that form the top, bottom, and shelves of the case equal the width of the doors, minus $\frac{3}{8}$" for the dado and tongue joinery.

**DADOES AND TONGUES.** The joinery on the door case is identical to the case built earlier. The first thing you need to to do is cut four $\frac{1}{8}$"-wide dadoes on the case sides *(Figs. 13b and 14)*. To make the $\frac{1}{8}$" tongues that fit into the dadoes, a rabbet is cut on each end of each divider *(Figs. 13a and 13b)*.

**GROOVES FOR RETAINERS.** Before you glue the case together, you'll want to grab three of the dividers and cut a groove in the same face as the tongue *(Fig. 15)*. Later, these grooves will hold retainer strips that will keep the spices from falling out of the door cases.

**DOOR CASE ASSEMBLY.** The two door cases are ready to be assembled at this point. The important thing to check here is not so much that each case is square, but that each case matches the door it will be glued to. So when clamping up the workpieces, I set the door on the assembly to see how well they matched. You'd be surprised how much difference

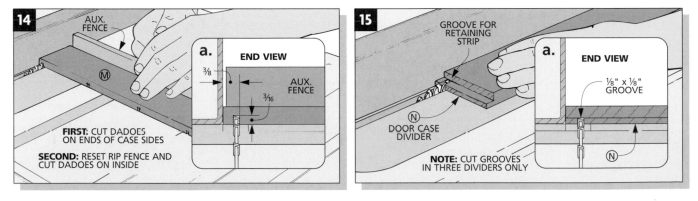

**14**

AUX.
FENCE

M

**a.** END VIEW

$\frac{3}{8}$

AUX.
FENCE

$\frac{3}{16}$

**FIRST:** CUT DADOES
ON ENDS OF CASE SIDES

**SECOND:** RESET RIP FENCE AND
CUT DADOES ON INSIDE

**15**

GROOVE FOR
RETAINING
STRIP

**a.** END VIEW

$\frac{1}{8}$" x $\frac{1}{8}$"
GROOVE

N

DOOR CASE
DIVIDER

N

**NOTE:** CUT GROOVES
IN THREE DIVIDERS ONLY

just repositioning a clamp or two can make to the case's final shape.

Now the assembled cases can be glued to the doors. (Keep in mind that the grooves for the retainer strips should end up on the inside of the cabinet, not next to the door.) The trick here is keeping the edges aligned as the clamps are applied. The solution is the same one you used to attach the molding pieces earlier — wire brads with their heads snipped off *(Fig. 13)*. However, when applying the glue, be careful not to overdo it. Any glue squeezed out on the inside of the case will be hard to get to.

**FIT DOORS.** You may find you need to do a little sanding to get the edges of the case and door flush. Plus, the inside edges of the doors need to be sanded to create the $1/16$" gap between them. (To help keep these edges flat while sanding, lay a strip of adhesive-backed sandpaper down on your table saw.)

**RETAINER STRIPS.** Now the case is ready for retainer strips (O). These strips are cut to fit into the grooves in the case. You don't need a thickness planer to get them down to $1/8$" thick. It's quicker to cut them with the table saw. (See the Shop Tip below for more on this procedure.)

**MOUNT DOORS.** After the retainer strips have been glued into their grooves, the doors are ready to be mounted to the case *(Fig. 17)*. The first step to doing this is to cut the mortises for the hinges.

To keep things easy, I mortised the hinges in the door cases only *(Fig. 16)*. There is just one mortise to cut for each hinge. Another benefit is that the mortise can be cut on the table saw *(Fig. 16a)*. The mortise is cut just short of the full depth of the hinge barrel *(Fig. 16b)*. Make sure you don't push the case all

the way through the blade. You only want to cut the mortises on the outside edge.

It's a good idea to apply the finish now. (I used a couple of coats of a wipe-on finish.) The doors are hung once the

brass knobs are added to the inside rail of each door *(Figs. 17 and 17b)*.

To hold the doors closed I installed a simple brass hook, aligning it with the upper rails *(Fig. 17a)*. ■

---

**16**

**a.** END VIEW

HINGES MORTISED INTO DOOR CASE ONLY

DADO BLADE

WASTE

1 — 1½ — MORTISE FOR HINGE

**b.**

MORTISE SLIGHTLY LESS THAN FULL THICKNESS OF HINGE

SECTION VIEW

HINGE

**17**

NOTE: HOOK LINES UP WITH UPPER RAILS (SEE DETAIL a)

**a.** FRONT VIEW

BRASS HOOK

ALIGN HOOK WITH RAIL

#4 x ³⁄₈" Rh SCREWS

**b.** SIDE SECTION VIEW

³⁄₄" x ³⁄₄" BRASS KNOB

8-32 x ³⁄₄" MACHINE SCREW

BRASS HOOK AND SCREWS

³⁄₄"-DIA. BRASS KNOB

1½" x ⁷⁄₈" BRASS HINGE

DOORS SANDED TO CREATE ¹⁄₁₆" GAP

---

**SHOP TIP** .......................... *Retainer Strips*

The retainer strips are very small pieces, so to cut them safely I used my table saw to sneak up on the thickness. Start by setting the rip fence so the blade is near the center of the piece. After making an initial pass on each face, just nudge the rip fence away from the blade until you've reached the desired thickness. Then adjust the fence and cut the strips to width.

# Glass-Front Breadbox

*The reeded glass in the door of this breadbox give it a nostalgic look suitable for an old-fashioned kitchen. But it's still a practical storage solution for eliminating clutter from your counter top.*

There's something I like about an old-fashioned breadbox. It reminds me of the days when the house was full of the aroma of fresh-baked bread.

Though you don't see them in many kitchens today, breadboxes are still a great place to keep bread. The loaves are close at hand without leaving the kitchen counter looking cluttered.

**GLASS FRONT DOOR.** This breadbox has a simple frame and panel door that lifts up and slides out of the way. But other than the knob, you won't see any hardware because the door slides on "invisible" steel pins. What you *do* see is a reeded glass panel. This glass gives

the box an old-fashioned look and feel. (For an alternative to the glass panel, see the Designer's Notebook on page 37.)

**CONSTRUCTION.** There's nothing fancy about the construction of the box and building it is a snap. Besides the door, the only parts are two side panels, a top, a bottom, and a narrow apron.

**MATERIALS.** The breadbox is made from red oak. I used a straight-grained quartersawn (or riftsawn) red oak. It's commonly used for kitchen cabinets, but you could use almost any hardwood, then stain and finish it to fit your own decor.

**CUTTING BOARD.** I want to mention one other option that will make this Glass-

Front Breadbox unique. It seemed to me that a breadbox should also have some kind of cutting board handy (inset photo).

So I removed the apron to create some space under the bottom of the case. Then I made a hard maple cutting board that would slide into this space. To make it look like it's "floating," the cutting board rests on four nylon chair glides. And to make it a little less conspicuous, I simply added oak edging (and a brass knob) to the panel. To see how it's built, see the Designer's Notebook on page 39.

## EXPLODED VIEW

**OVERALL DIMENSIONS:**
17W x 10¼D x 11H

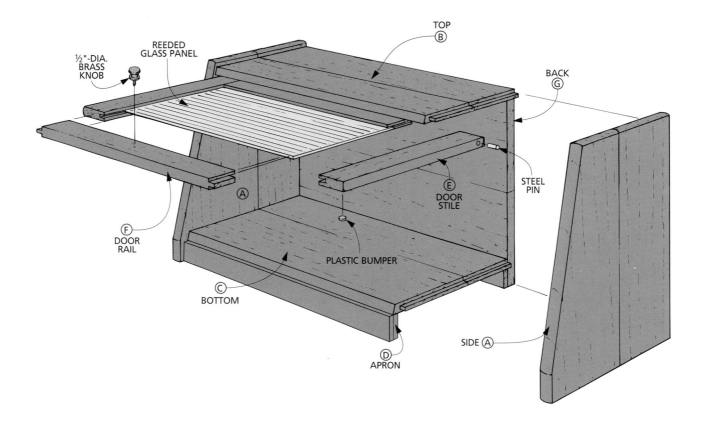

½"-DIA. BRASS KNOB

REEDED GLASS PANEL

TOP
Ⓑ

BACK
Ⓖ

STEEL PIN

Ⓔ
DOOR STILE

SIDE Ⓐ

Ⓐ

Ⓕ
DOOR RAIL

PLASTIC BUMPER

Ⓒ
BOTTOM

Ⓓ
APRON

## MATERIALS LIST

### WOOD
| | | |
|---|---|---|
| **A** | Sides (2) | ½ x 10¼ - 11 |
| **B** | Top (1) | ½ x 7⅝ - 16½ |
| **C** | Bottom (1) | ½ x 8¹⁵⁄₁₆ - 16½ |
| **D** | Apron (1) | 1 x 1¼ - 16 |
| **E** | Door Stiles (2) | ½ x 1½ - 9⅜ |
| **F** | Door Rails (2) | ½ x 1½ - 13⁷⁄₁₆ |
| **G** | Back (1) | ½ x 10½ - 16 |

### HARDWARE SUPPLIES
(4) No. 6 x 1" Fh woodscrews
(4) ¼"-dia. x ¾" steel pins
(1) Reeded glass panel, 6¹³⁄₁₆" x 13⅜"
(2) ¹⁄₁₆"-thick plastic bumpers
(1) ½"-dia. brass knob

## CUTTING DIAGRAM

½ x 5½ - 96 RED OAK (Two Boards @ 1.8 Sq. Ft. Each)

E    F

| A | A | C | B | G | E | D |
|---|---|---|---|---|---|---|

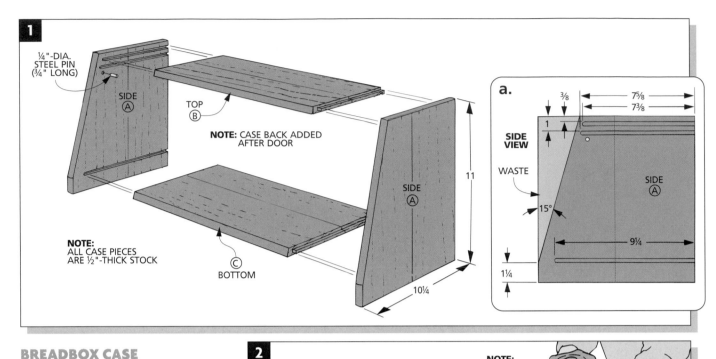

**1**

¼"-DIA. STEEL PIN (¾" LONG)

SIDE Ⓐ

TOP Ⓑ

**NOTE:** CASE BACK ADDED AFTER DOOR

SIDE Ⓐ

**NOTE:** ALL CASE PIECES ARE ½"-THICK STOCK

BOTTOM Ⓒ

11

10¼

**a.**

3/8    7⅝
       7⅜

1

SIDE VIEW

WASTE

SIDE Ⓐ

15°

9¼

1¼

## BREADBOX CASE

There's not much to the case of this breadbox: just two side panels and a top and bottom *(Fig. 1)*. (A back will also be added to the case later.)

Before getting started, let me mention something about the wood. Since this project is rather small, I didn't want the grain pattern to "overpower" the look of the breadbox. So I used quartersawn (or riftsawn) red oak. It has a tight, straight grain pattern that's easy to stain and finish. Although it may be a little hard to find in your area, it's a good choice for this project.

**GLUE UP PANELS.** The case is built with ½"-thick stock *(Fig. 1)*. And since the sides (A) are over 10" wide, it's a good idea to glue up each from two pieces so they'll be less likely to warp.

The key to this case is a series of stopped dadoes that are routed in the side pieces. Two dadoes will hold the top and bottom panels. A third creates a channel to guide and support the door as it's opened and closed.

**LAY OUT DADOES.** The sides "mirror" each other, and anytime you need to cut a mirrored set of dadoes, it's easy to get confused. But I find it helps if I lay out each dado *(Fig. 1a)*. (Drawing the taper on the front edges also helps.) This way, I can "see" what I'm doing a little better.

**ROUT DADOES.** When cutting stopped dadoes, I also like to use a hand-held router. This way, I can see the layout lines and the dado being cut while I'm pushing the router along the panel. (That's

**2**

**NOTE:** ALL DADOES ¼" WIDE, ¼" DEEP

FASTEN PANELS TO SCRAP PIECE WITH CARPET TAPE

SIDES SET BACK TO BACK

**SAFETY NOTE:** MOVE ROUTER LEFT TO RIGHT

ROUTING DIRECTION

EDGE GUIDE (SEE SHOP JIG ON PAGE 35)

because the panel's not face down as it would be on a router table.)

However, I did do one thing out of the ordinary. Instead of clamping each panel to the bench, they're set back-to-back and attached to a long scrap piece using some double-sided carpet tape *(Fig. 2)*. It's this scrap piece that's clamped down. This way, each pair of dadoes is routed in one pass, and no clamps get in the way. Plus, it's no trouble to flip the scrap piece (and panels) around to rout the dadoes on the opposite edges.

**ROUTER EDGE GUIDE.** I haven't mentioned yet that to make these dadoes, you'll need an edge guide for your router. An edge guide is a pretty common accessory, but if you don't have one, it doesn't take much to make one. All you need for one is some ¼"-thick hardboard, a short piece of ¾"-thick scrap for a fence, and a little hardware. (See the Shop Jig box on the next page to learn how I made mine.)

All three dadoes are routed the same. After the edge guide is set, simply turn on the router and lower the bit into the wood near the left mark, carefully holding the guide against the panel *(Fig. 2)*. Now, slowly "creep" the router back to the layout line and then push the router across both panels until the bit reaches the layout line on the right.

**CUT TAPER.** After all the dadoes are routed, the next step is to taper the front edges of the case sides *(Fig. 3)*. I did this on the table saw, and since a shallow taper can't be cut easily with the miter gauge, I used a piece of scrap hardboard.

The hardboard is simply a sled that rides between the fence and the blade. And as you can see, the side is attached with carpet tape to the sled at an angle so the waste hangs over the edge *(Fig. 3)*. But you don't have to work with one piece at a time. I used carpet tape to temporarily fasten the sides together (inside face to

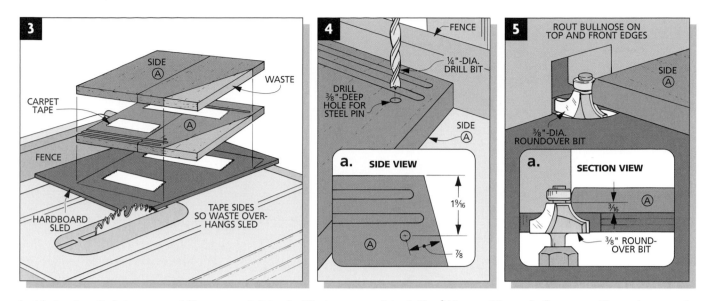

inside face) so their tapers would be easy to cut and end up identical.

**PILOT HOLE AND BULLNOSE PROFILE.** The sides of the case are almost complete, but there are still a couple of things left to do. First, you need to drill a $3/8$"-deep hole in each side for a steel pin that will be added later *(Fig. 4)*.

**Note:** The pin will hold the door in position at the top of the case.

Then a bullnose profile can be routed on the top and front edges *(Fig. 5)*. To do this, use a roundover bit in a router table. Make a pass on one edge, then flip the workpiece and make a second pass.

---

# SHOP JIG ............................... *Router Edge Guide*

When using a hand-held router, an edge guide is great for routing dadoes, grooves, or profiles near the edge of a piece (see photo at right). Most router manufacturers offer an edge guide as an accessory, but it's no trouble at all to build your own. An edge guide is just a replacement base with an adjustable fence (see drawing).

**HARDBOARD BASE.** Start by removing the existing base from your router. Then cut the base of the edge guide from a piece of $1/4$"-thick hardboard. Its size isn't all that important. I made mine big enough to give me "solid" support, but not so big as to be cumbersome (6" x 12").

In the center of the base, you'll need clearance for the router bit. And the larger the hole, the easier it'll be to see what you're routing. (In my base, I drilled a $1 1/4$"-dia. hole with a spade bit.)

Finally, cut two slots to hold the fence (and allow it to be adjusted easily). And use the manufacturer's base plate to add mounting holes for your router.

**HARDWOOD FENCE.** When making the fence, what you want is a straight, smooth edge to slide against the piece. (My fence is hard maple, but I check it often to make sure it hasn't warped.) To attach the fence to the base, I used carriage bolts, washers, and wing nuts (detail 'a').

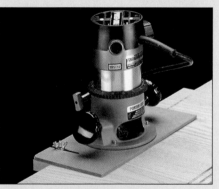

**Stopped Dadoes.** *Cutting a stopped dado near the edge of a workpiece is no problem when using a hand-held router and a shop-made edge guide.*

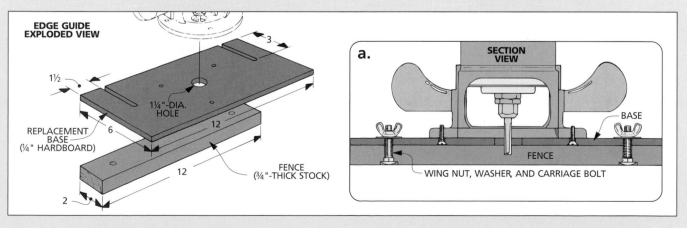

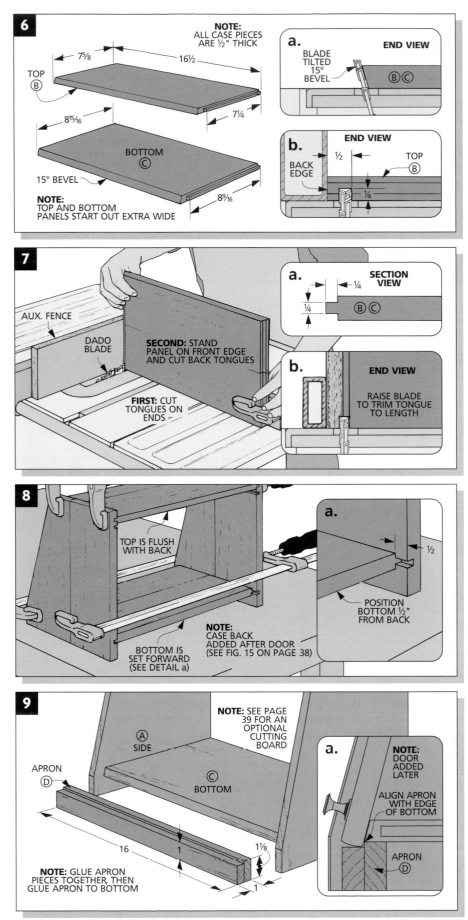

**6**

NOTE: ALL CASE PIECES ARE ½" THICK

TOP (B)

7⅝   16½
7¼

8¹⁵⁄₁₆

BOTTOM (C)

15° BEVEL

8⁹⁄₁₆

NOTE: TOP AND BOTTOM PANELS START OUT EXTRA WIDE

**a.**   END VIEW

BLADE TILTED 15° BEVEL

(B)(C)

**b.**   END VIEW

BACK EDGE   ½   TOP (B)

¼

**7**

AUX. FENCE

DADO BLADE

SECOND: STAND PANEL ON FRONT EDGE AND CUT BACK TONGUES

FIRST: CUT TONGUES ON ENDS

**a.**   SECTION VIEW

¼

¼

(B)(C)

**b.**   END VIEW

RAISE BLADE TO TRIM TONGUE TO LENGTH

**8**

TOP IS FLUSH WITH BACK

NOTE: CASE BACK ADDED AFTER DOOR (SEE FIG. 15 ON PAGE 38)

BOTTOM IS SET FORWARD (SEE DETAIL a)

**a.**

½

POSITION BOTTOM ½" FROM BACK

**9**

NOTE: SEE PAGE 39 FOR AN OPTIONAL CUTTING BOARD

(A) SIDE

(C) BOTTOM

APRON (D)

16   1   1⅛

1

NOTE: GLUE APRON PIECES TOGETHER, THEN GLUE APRON TO BOTTOM

**a.**

NOTE: DOOR ADDED LATER

ALIGN APRON WITH EDGE OF BOTTOM

APRON (D)

## TOP & BOTTOM

Now that the sides are complete, most of the hard work is over. Next you need to make a top and bottom for the case. You'll also need to make a small apron that hides the space below the case bottom.

The top (B) and bottom (C) are simple to build *(Fig. 6)*. What you want to end up with are ½"-thick panels with a 15° bevel on their front edges *(Fig. 6a)*. But the bevel shouldn't be ripped until after the tongues on the ends are cut.

**TONGUES.** Cutting the tongues is a two-step process, but both are done on the table saw with a dado set.

The first step is to cut the tongues all the way across the ends *(Fig. 7a)*. The second step is to cut back the front edges of the tongues. The fence won't change, but this time the panels are stood on edge *(Figs. 7 and 7b)*. Simply raise the blade until the length of the tongue is a little shorter than the stopped dado. (This way, you don't have to worry about fitting the square tongues on the panel into the round ends of the dadoes.)

**TOP GROOVE.** With the dado set still mounted in the saw, I also cut a small groove in the bottom face of the top panel *(Fig. 6b)*. This groove will hold the top of the case back later.

**BEVELED PROFILE.** To complete the top and bottom panels, their front edges are beveled 15° *(Fig. 6a)*.

**Note:** This bevel matches the taper cut earlier on the front edges of the sides.

**ASSEMBLY.** With only four pieces, there isn't much to assembling this breadbox case *(Fig. 8)*. But the bottom panel is a little unusual. When you glue up the case, you'll need to leave some room for the back piece that's added later. So the bottom is located ½" from the back edge of the sides *(Fig. 8a)*.

And while the glue is drying, you can mix up some epoxy and glue the steel pins into the sides.

**APRON.** Finally, I made the apron (D). It's just two pieces of ½"-thick stock that have been ripped to width and glued together *(Fig. 9)*. Then the apron is cut to length to fit between the sides and glued in place *(Figs. 9 and 9a)*.

**Note:** It occured to me after I finished building the breadbox that the space below the bottom of the breadbox is a perfect place to store a maple cutting board. A hardwood cutting board comes in handy after you've just baked a loaf of home-made bread. (To learn how to build the cutting board, see the Designer's Notebook on page 39.)

If you build the cutting board as an accessory, you can skip adding the apron pieces to the bottom of the case.

## DOOR & CASE BACK

The breadbox door is a frame and panel assembly that slides in and out on two steel pins. What makes it unique is its reeded glass panel. (I ordered mine from a local glass shop.) Reeded glass is thicker than regular glass, so I bought the glass before starting on the door. If you prefer a wood panel for your breadbox, see the Designer's Notebook below.

**STILES AND RAILS.** With the glass in hand, I cut the door stiles (E) and rails (F) to size from 1/2"-thick stock *(Fig. 10)*. The goal here is a frame that holds the glass panel and fits between the case sides with about a 1/32" gap on each side. (The height is easy. I made mine 9 3/8" tall.)

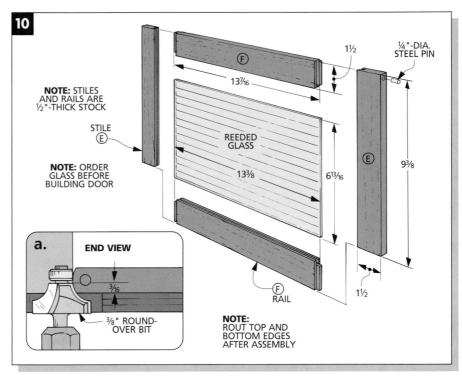

**10**

NOTE: STILES AND RAILS ARE 1/2"-THICK STOCK

STILE
E

NOTE: ORDER GLASS BEFORE BUILDING DOOR

F

REEDED GLASS

13 7/16

1 1/2

1/4"-DIA. STEEL PIN

E

9 3/8

13 3/8

6 13/16

1 1/2

F
RAIL

NOTE: ROUT TOP AND BOTTOM EDGES AFTER ASSEMBLY

**a.**   END VIEW

3/16

3/8" ROUND-OVER BIT

# DESIGNER'S NOTEBOOK

*With a plywood door panel — instead of reeded glass — the breadbox contents stay out of sight.*

## CONSTRUCTION NOTES:

■ The reeded glass front on the breadbox gives it an old-fashioned look. This translucent glass was used on breadboxes, and even cabinet doors, in many early 20th-century homes. (See the Hoosier-Style Cabinet on page 90 and the Oak Icebox on page 124.) But what if your kitchen decor leans more toward contemporary? Don't worry. It's just as easy to replace the glass with a simple plywood panel (see drawing).

■ There's another benefit to using plywood for the door panel — it hides the contents of the box. This is a real bonus if you want to keep a couple of bags of chips handy, but out of sight.

■ I made the panel (H) from a piece of 1/4" oak plywood. Cut it to the same size as the glass (6 13/16" x 13 3/8"). Then cut the door stiles (E) and rails (F) to size as before.

■ I stained my panel before I assembled the door pieces. This way you won't see any unstained strips of wood during expansion and contraction as a result of seasonal changes in humidity.

**Note:** There won't be much, if any, shrinkage of the plywood panel. But the hardwood for the door stiles and rails

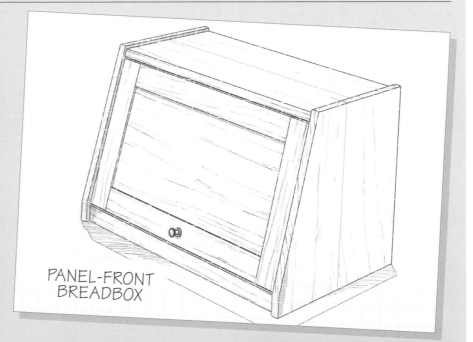

PANEL-FRONT BREADBOX

will most likely shrink a little across the grain, leaving visible strips that will stand out if the entire panel isn't pre-stained.

■ Finally, add the tenons and grooves to the rails and stiles and install the panel.

| MATERIALS LIST | |
| --- | --- |
| **NEW PART** | |
| H   Door Panel (1) | 1/4 ply - 6 13/16 x 13 3/8 |

*The breadbox door is built with common frame and panel construction. But the panel is a piece of reeded glass.*

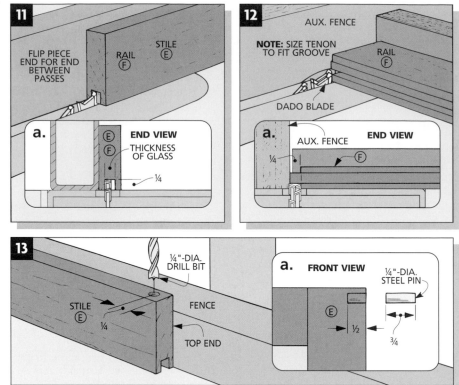

**GROOVES FOR GLASS.** Now the grooves that hold the glass in the frame can be cut along the inside edges of the door rails and stiles *(Fig. 11)*. And it's a good idea to sneak up on the width of these grooves so the glass doesn't rattle as the door is opened and closed.

Stub tenons are cut on the ends of the rails (F) next *(Fig. 12)*. There's nothing tricky here. The tenons are sized to fit in the grooves you just cut.

**ASSEMBLY.** There's one more thing to do before assembling the door. To hold a steel pin, a hole is drilled in the edge of each stile *(Fig. 13)*. Then the rails and stiles can be glued around the glass (refer to *Fig. 10* on page 37).

To complete the door, first rout a bull-nose on its top and bottom edges (once again, refer to *Fig. 10a* on page 37). Then epoxy the steel pins in their holes and slide the door in place. Now to cushion

the door as it's closed, I added a couple of plastic bumpers *(Fig. 15b)*.

With the glass door in place, the back (G) can be added. It's just a ½"-thick panel with a rabbet cut on its back edge *(Figs. 15 and 15a)*. (This creates a tongue that fits the groove in the case top.) To hold the back in place, I screwed it to the edge of the case bottom.

**APPLY FINISH AND HARDWARE.** Before adding the hardware to the glass door, I taped off the glass and finished the project with a thin wiping oil. Then I added the brass knob to the door. ∎

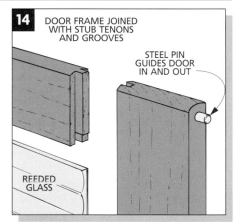

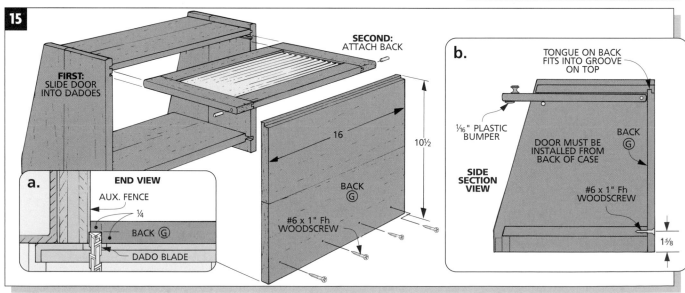

# DESIGNER'S NOTEBOOK

*To make the breadbox even more versatile, you can easily add a functional feature like a cutting board. It's made with strips of edge-glued hard maple and trimmed in oak for a long-lasting, durable surface.*

## CONSTRUCTION NOTES:

■ The only change to the original breadbox is to leave off the apron at the front. This creates a space under the bottom panel for the cutting board to slide into *(Fig. 1)*.

■ For the cutting board, I chose hard maple since it has tight, smooth grain with no open pores. And the surface is edge grain, which makes for a durable cutting board *(Fig. 1a)*.

■ To make this surface, rip the strips (H) from the edge of $3/4$"-thick stock *(Fig. 2)*. Then turn the pieces so the edge grain faces up and glue them into a panel.

■ Once the glue is dry, sand the panel smooth and add a skirt to the front and back edges *(Fig. 3)*. These oak strips of front and back edging (I) match the breadbox, and they're a little taller ($7/8$") than the maple panel *(Fig. 3)*. This way,

they'll hide the nylon chair glides (added later) with a $1/16$" gap on each side.

■ With the oak strips added to the maple panel, you can cut it to size *(Fig. 3)*.

■ Then slide the board under the case bottom to make sure its front edge is flush

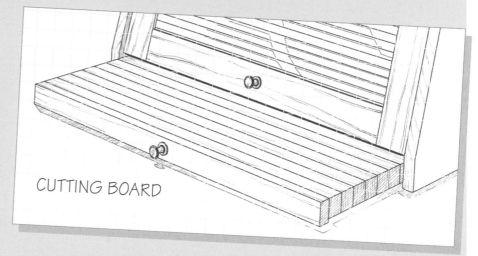

CUTTING BOARD

with the door *(Fig. 1)*. It's likely, though, that you'll need to add a spacer (J) to the back panel. Mine was $3/8$" wide.

■ Before adding the hardware, I finished the cutting board with a thin wipe-on finish, since it's bound to be scratched up and cut with use.

■ Finally, add a brass knob, and to "lift" the board off the edging, add nylon chair glides under the maple panel *(Fig. 1a)*.

## MATERIALS LIST

**NEW PARTS**

| | | |
|---|---|---|
| **H** | Strips (11) | $3/4 \times 3/4$ - $15 7/8$ |
| **I** | Front/Back Edging (2) | $1/2 \times 7/8$ - $15 7/8$ |
| **J** | Spacer (1) | $1/2 \times 3/8$ - 16 |

**Note:** Do not need part D.

**HARDWARE SUPPLIES**

(4) Nylon chair glides
(1) $1/2$"-dia. brass knob

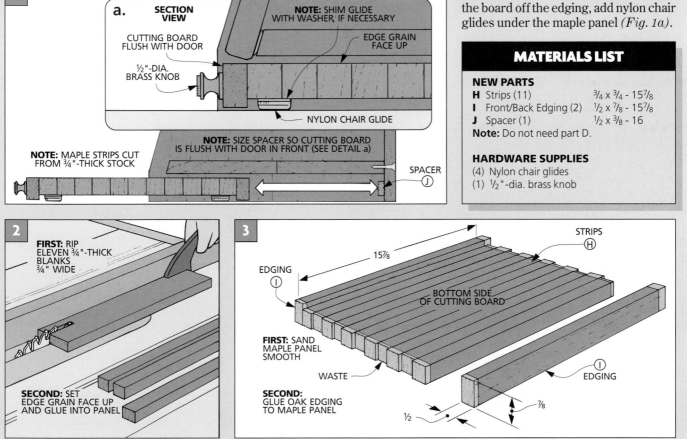

**1**

**a.** **SECTION VIEW**

CUTTING BOARD FLUSH WITH DOOR

$1/2$"-DIA. BRASS KNOB

**NOTE:** SHIM GLIDE WITH WASHER, IF NECESSARY

EDGE GRAIN FACE UP

NYLON CHAIR GLIDE

**NOTE:** MAPLE STRIPS CUT FROM $3/4$"-THICK STOCK

**NOTE:** SIZE SPACER SO CUTTING BOARD IS FLUSH WITH DOOR IN FRONT (SEE DETAIL a)

SPACER J

**2**

**FIRST:** RIP ELEVEN $3/4$"-THICK BLANKS $3/4$" WIDE

**SECOND:** SET EDGE GRAIN FACE UP AND GLUE INTO PANEL

**3**

STRIPS H

$15 7/8$

EDGING I

BOTTOM SIDE OF CUTTING BOARD

**FIRST:** SAND MAPLE PANEL SMOOTH

WASTE

**SECOND:** GLUE OAK EDGING TO MAPLE PANEL

EDGING I

$1/2$    $7/8$

# DINING ROOM

Enjoying an atmosphere of comfort and warmth in your home is important, especially after a long day. From the storage space of the classic sideboard to the colored stain on the country harvest table, these projects will complement your home's decor and your lifestyle.

# Plate Shelf

*Usually, molding is the last item added to a project to provide a finishing touch. But with this shelf, the first thing you do is make one of the moldings. Then the rest of the shelf is built to fit it.*

This shelf is meant to display plates, so it has to look nice to complement them. At the same time, it shouldn't call undue attention to itself. With its spindled rail and architectural-style moldings, it accomplishes both.

**MOLDINGS.** The dentil molding is the key to building the shelf. To look right, the molding needs a full block (dentil) at each corner. So instead of building the shelf and then trimming it with the molding, I cut the dentil molding first, then sized the other pieces to fit it.

Just above the dentil molding is a layer of thick crown molding. It's built up in layers. So to create the profile all you need are a couple of common router bits. The trick is finding the pieces of wood that blend together seamlessly. (The Shop Tip on page 45 shows how.)

**JIGS.** Building the Plate Shelf requires some precise, repetitive work. And for some of these jobs, a jig can prevent a lot of headaches. For example, the dentil molding has raised fields exactly the same length as the space between them. That doesn't mean there's a lot of tedious layout and fiddling to cut this molding. Instead, an indexing jig for the table saw makes the spacing automatic.

The other place where you need precision is when drilling the holes for the spindles in the shelf and rail. The holes must be spaced exactly the same in both pieces for the spindles to align. This time it's not a jig, but some careful layout that guarantees the spindles will stand at attention like a row of soldiers.

**A PLACE FOR PLATES.** The shelf has several features that will keep your collectibles safely on display. First, there are a couple of grooves in the shelf. The rear groove holds the rims of plates and shallow dishes, while the front one is meant to hold the rim of deeper items like bowls. And a hanging cleat makes easy work of mounting the shelf to the wall so it's level and secure.

## EXPLODED VIEW

OVERALL DIMENSIONS:
36W x 6¼D x 5¼H

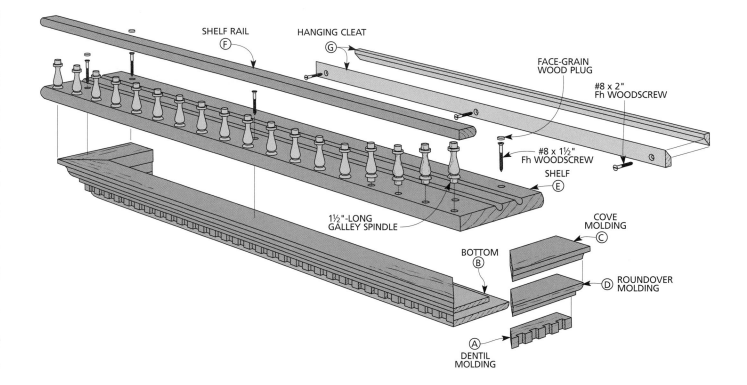

SHELF RAIL
F

HANGING CLEAT
G

FACE-GRAIN
WOOD PLUG

#8 x 2"
Fh WOODSCREW

#8 x 1½"
Fh WOODSCREW

SHELF
E

1½"-LONG
GALLEY SPINDLE

COVE
MOLDING
C

ROUNDOVER
MOLDING
D

BOTTOM
B

DENTIL
MOLDING
A

## CUTTING DIAGRAM

¾ x 7 - 72  (3.5 Bd. Ft.)

E

B

G

¾ x 7 - 60  (2.9 Bd. Ft.)

C

D

F

A

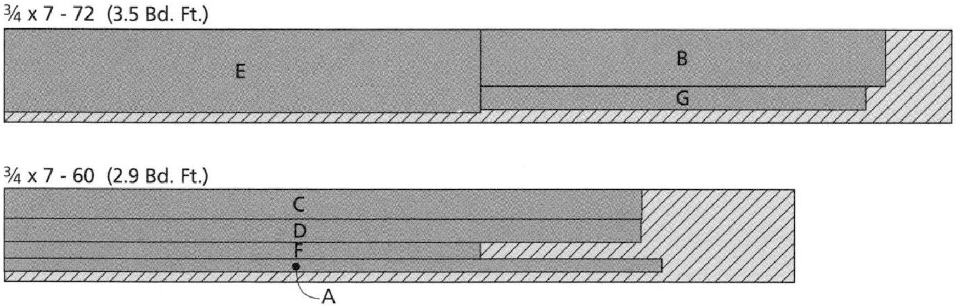

**NOTE:** PARTS A, F, AND G ARE RESAWN TO ½" THICK

## MATERIALS LIST

### WOOD

| | | |
|---|---|---|
| **A** | Dentil Molding (1) | ½ x 1- 42 rough |
| **B** | Bottom (1) | ¾ x 4¼ - 31 |
| **C** | Cove Molding (1) | ¾ x 2¼ - 40 rgh. |
| **D** | Roundover Mldg. (1) | ¾ x 1¾ - 40 rgh. |
| **E** | Shelf (1) | ¾ x 6¼ - 36 |
| **F** | Shelf Rail (1) | ½ x 1¼ - 36 |
| **G** | Hanging Cleat (1) | ½ x 1⅜ - 29½ |

### HARDWARE SUPPLIES

(5) No. 8 x 1½" Fh woodscrews
(3) No. 8 x 2" Fh woodscrews
(5) ⅜" face-grain wood plugs
(18) 1½"-long galley spindles

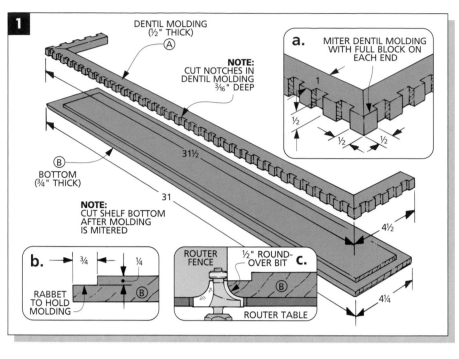

**1**

DENTIL MOLDING (½" THICK) Ⓐ

NOTE: CUT NOTCHES IN DENTIL MOLDING ³⁄₁₆" DEEP

**a.** MITER DENTIL MOLDING WITH FULL BLOCK ON EACH END

1

½  ½  ½

31½

Ⓑ
BOTTOM (¾" THICK)

31

4½

4¼

NOTE: CUT SHELF BOTTOM AFTER MOLDING IS MITERED

**b.** ¾  ¼

RABBET TO HOLD MOLDING

Ⓑ

ROUTER FENCE

½" ROUND-OVER BIT **c.**

Ⓑ

ROUTER TABLE

## MOLDINGS & BOTTOM

The base of the shelf is built around the dentil molding, so I made it first *(Fig. 1)*. But I didn't worry about cutting it to an exact dimension. That's because it's more important to end up with a full dentil block at each corner for the best appearance *(Fig. 1a)*. (As construction goes on, the other base pieces are sized to fit this piece of molding.)

All the dentil molding (A) starts out as a single ½"-thick blank *(Fig. 1)*. (My blank was about 48" long.) Then to cut the dentil blocks, I used a simple shop-made jig. (See the Shop Jig box below for details about building and using the jig.)

Once the dentil blocks are cut, the blank can be mitered to create a three-sided frame. The back end of each side piece is crosscut square, but remember to leave a full block here too *(Fig. 1)*.

## SHOP JIG ................................. Dentil Molding Jig

The key to cutting dentil molding is to get the width of the "blocks" the same as the spacing between the blocks. You could lay out each block on the blank, then line up the layout marks with the blade for each cut. But there's a much easier and more precise method.

I used a simple shop-built jig that guarantees the spacing between the blocks is the same size as the blocks. The jig is just a ¾"-thick auxiliary fence that's attached to the miter gauge on the table saw. Then a small pin is mortised into the bottom edge of the fence.

**MAKING THE JIG.** To make the jig, start by cutting a shallow notch in the fence that's the same width you want the dentil

blocks to be (in my case, this was ½") *(Figs. 1 and 1a)*. The dentil blocks will end up protruding ³⁄₁₆", but I cut the notch only ⅛" deep. This way, with the pin installed, the molding will rest flat on the top of the table saw.

With the notch cut, make the pin so it fits snug and glue it in place *(Fig. 2a)*.

**SET UP.** To set up the jig, clamp it to your miter gauge temporarily. Again, the goal is to make the blocks and the space between them the same. To do this, make sure the distance from the pin to the dado blade is *exactly* the same as the width of the pin (½"). (Make sure you measure to the edge of a tooth, not to the plate of the blade.) Take your time as you set up

the jig, because getting it positioned correctly is critical. Once it is set properly, screw the jig to the miter gauge and remove the clamp.

The next step is to raise the dado blade to the correct height for the notches (in my case, ³⁄₁₆") and cut a second notch in the auxiliary fence *(Figs. 2 and 2a)*.

**CUTTING DENTIL.** Now that the jig is set up, you're ready to cut the dentil molding. Start by butting the end of your blank against the side of the pin and make a pass over the dado blade *(Fig. 3)*. Now place this notch over the pin and make your second pass. By repeating this sequence, all the dentil blocks can be cut along the full length of the blank.

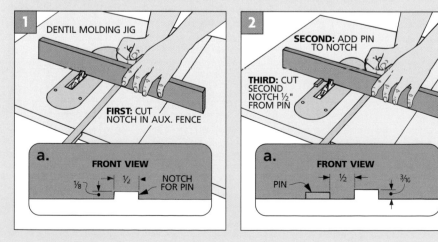

**1** DENTIL MOLDING JIG

**FIRST:** CUT NOTCH IN AUX. FENCE

**a.** FRONT VIEW

⅛  ½  NOTCH FOR PIN

**2** SECOND: ADD PIN TO NOTCH

THIRD: CUT SECOND NOTCH ½" FROM PIN

**a.** FRONT VIEW

PIN  ½  ³⁄₁₆

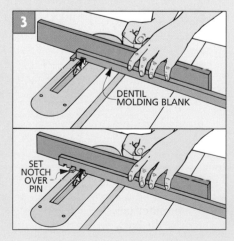

**3** DENTIL MOLDING BLANK

SET NOTCH OVER PIN

**BASE BOTTOM.** The pieces of dentil molding will be glued together at the same time they are glued to the bottom. So I cut the 3/4"-thick bottom (B) to size so the dentil overhangs it 1/4" at the front and sides *(Fig. 1)*.

To cradle the molding, I cut a 1/4"-deep rabbet around the bottom *(Fig. 1b)*. (The rabbet along the back provides clearance for a hanging cleat added later.) The rabbet is sized so the molding pieces fit together and are flush at the back edge. To allow me to sneak up on their final width, I cut the rabbets on the table saw with a dado blade.

Now, before gluing the molding in place, I routed 1/2" roundovers on the bottom of the front and ends *(Fig. 1c)*. (The back edge remains square.)

**CROWN MOLDING.** The next piece to add to the Plate Shelf is a crown molding above the dentil molding *(Fig. 2)*. While it may look like one solid piece of stock, this 1 1/2"-thick molding is actually built up from two 3/4"-thick pieces — a cove molding (C) and a roundover molding (D) *(Fig. 2a)*. And as with the dentil molding, I made one long blank that was then mitered to fit under the shelf.

**Note:** The idea here is to make the crown molding look like one thick piece, so you'll want to choose your stock carefully (see the Shop Tip at right).

But before you laminate the pieces, rout a profile on each one *(Fig. 2a)*. On the cove molding, I routed a 1/2" cove, leaving a 1/4" shoulder on the top. The roundover molding gets a 1/2" roundover with a 1/4" shoulder on the bottom.

Next, glue the two pieces of molding together. Keep an eye on the profiles as you glue them up. The curves should flow together smoothly without a "step" at the joint line. (If the pieces do end up slightly uneven, just sand them smooth.)

When the glue is dry, miter the blank into three pieces. What you want is for the bottom shoulder of the molding to extend 1/4" beyond the dentil molding *(Fig. 2b)*.

**SHELF.** That's all there is to the base, so now you can concentrate on the shelf. The shelf (E) is a 3/4"-thick blank cut to finished size of 6 1/4" x 36" *(Fig. 3)*.

Then to hold the plates, I took the shelf to the router table and routed two 1/4"-deep grooves using a core box bit *(Fig. 3a)*. Once that was completed, I added a bullnose profile to the front and sides with a 1/2" roundover bit raised 3/8" above the router table *(Fig. 3b)*. (Here again, leave the back edge square.)

## SHOP TIP ...... *Matching Grain*

To make the cove molding for the Plate Shelf, I laminated two 3/4"-thick pieces together. But I wanted to match the grain so these pieces still look like one thick blank.

The problem is you can't see the grain you'll be matching until after the profiles are routed. So how do you choose the boards in the first place?

The solution is to look at the end grain. Try to find two boards of similar color that also have end grain that runs in roughly the same direction *(Fig. 1)*. If they don't, the joint line will be obvious *(Fig. 2)*.

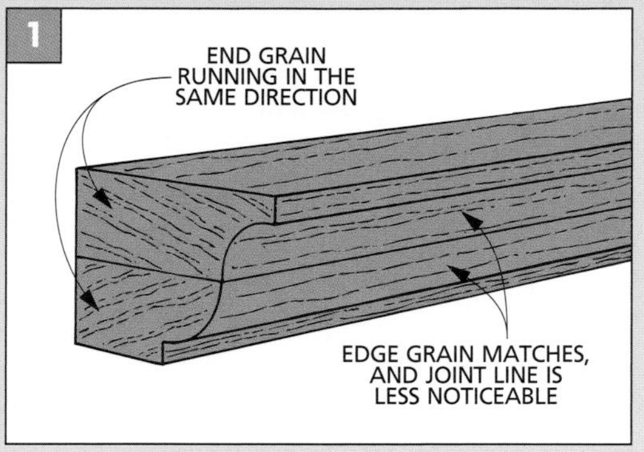

1
END GRAIN RUNNING IN THE SAME DIRECTION
EDGE GRAIN MATCHES, AND JOINT LINE IS LESS NOTICEABLE


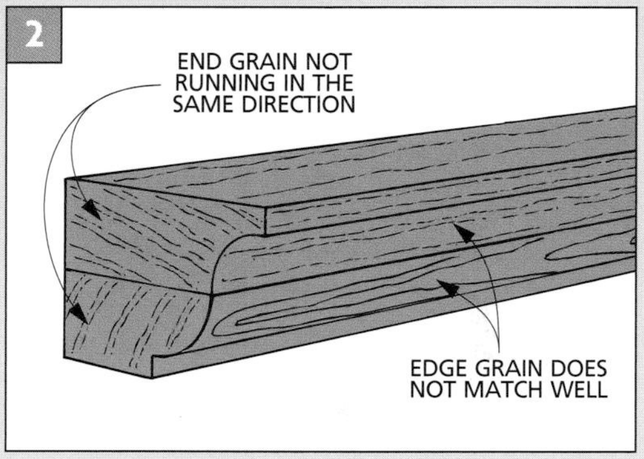

2
END GRAIN NOT RUNNING IN THE SAME DIRECTION
EDGE GRAIN DOES NOT MATCH WELL


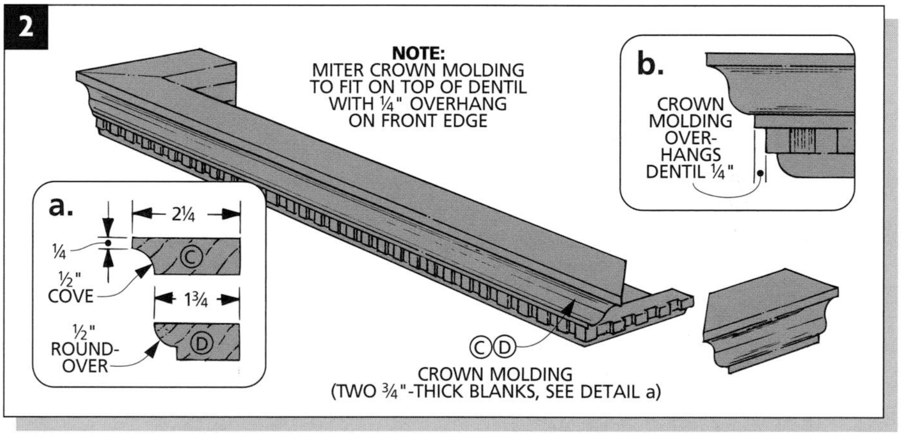

2
NOTE: MITER CROWN MOLDING TO FIT ON TOP OF DENTIL WITH 1/4" OVERHANG ON FRONT EDGE
b.
CROWN MOLDING OVER-HANGS DENTIL 1/4"
a.
2 1/4
1/4
1/2" COVE
C
1 3/4
1/2" ROUND-OVER
D
C D
CROWN MOLDING (TWO 3/4"-THICK BLANKS, SEE DETAIL a)


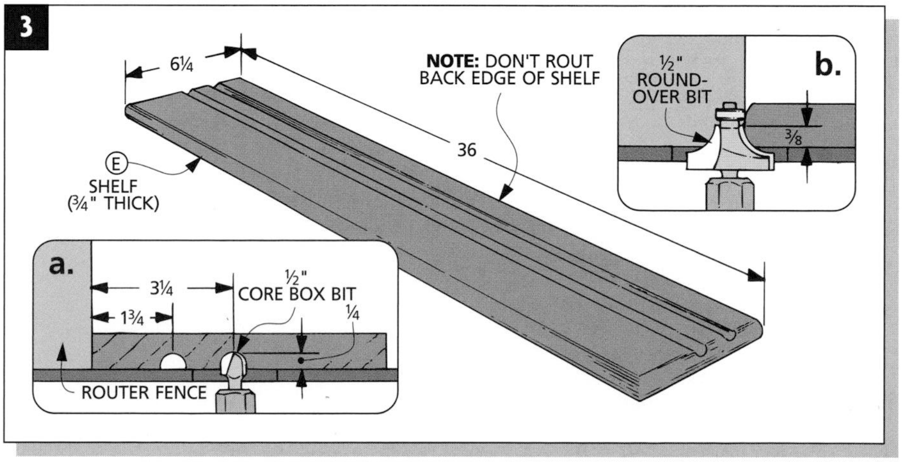

3
6 1/4
NOTE: DON'T ROUT BACK EDGE OF SHELF
36
E
SHELF (3/4" THICK)
b.
1/2" ROUND-OVER BIT
3/8
a.
3 1/4
1 3/4
1/2" CORE BOX BIT
1/4
ROUTER FENCE

**SHELF RAIL.** Next, I added a shelf rail (F) *(Fig. 4)*. After cutting it to size from $\frac{1}{2}$"-thick stock, I routed a bullnose profile on all its edges. But this time, I used a $\frac{3}{8}$" roundover bit *(Fig. 4a)*.

To join the rail to the shelf, I purchased $1\frac{1}{2}$"-long galley spindles from a craft store *(Figs. 4 and 4b)*.

**Note:** Including the lengths of the tenon on each end, the spindles are actually 2" long. Some mail order sources for them are listed on page 126.

To install the spindles, I had to drill 18 holes in each piece. And if just one hole is off, at the least you'll have a spindle that leans. At worst, the assembly won't even go together. So to make sure the holes aligned properly, I clamped the rail and the shelf together edge to edge *(Fig. 5)*. Then I used a try square to lay out the locations on both pieces at the same time.

After gluing the rail and spindles in place, I drilled five counterbored pilot holes in the shelf (two on each end and one in the middle) *(Figs. 6 and 6a)*. You'll need these for screwing the shelf to the base. (Gluing the shelf wouldn't allow the wood to expand.)

Once the shelf and base are screwed together, plugs can be glued into the counterbores (see the Shop Tip below for more about this). Then the plugs can be trimmed with a hand saw or chisel and sanded flush.

**HANGING CLEAT.** Finally, to hang the shelf, I used a hanging cleat (G). This is a remarkably simple system that keeps the shelf (and your treasured plates) securely on the wall. All you need to do is rip a $\frac{1}{2}$"-thick blank in two with the blade set at 45° *(Fig. 7)*. Then screw the wider piece to the wall (make sure you screw into studs) and glue the other portion of the cleat inside the shelf. Then just lift the shelf onto the wall cleat. ∎

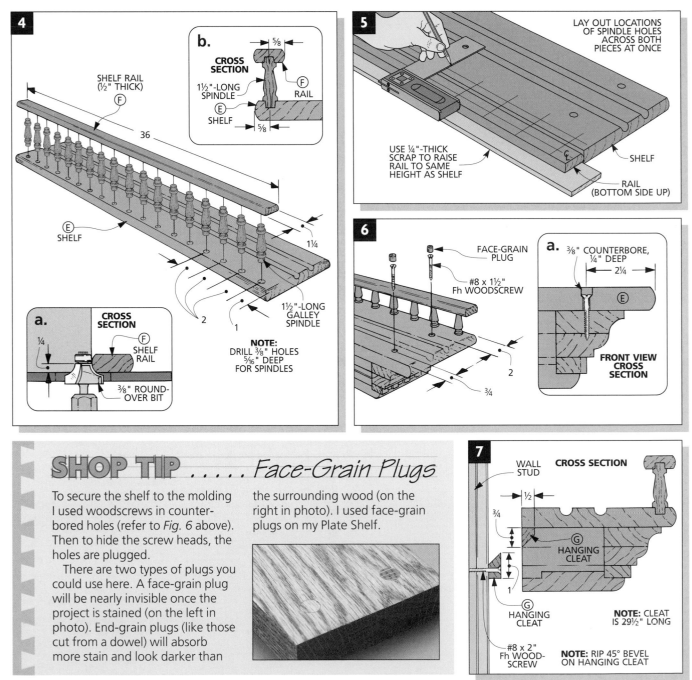

**SHOP TIP ..... Face-Grain Plugs**

To secure the shelf to the molding I used woodscrews in counterbored holes (refer to *Fig. 6* above). Then to hide the screw heads, the holes are plugged.

There are two types of plugs you could use here. A face-grain plug will be nearly invisible once the project is stained (on the left in photo). End-grain plugs (like those cut from a dowel) will absorb more stain and look darker than the surrounding wood (on the right in photo). I used face-grain plugs on my Plate Shelf.

# DESIGNER'S NOTEBOOK

*Take the same moldings and rearrange them to build this shelf for displaying smaller collectibles. It's handsome enough to hang alone or use it as a companion piece with the Plate Shelf.*

## CONSTRUCTION NOTES:

■ This shelf is meant for displaying smaller items so it's a little shallower than the Plate Shelf, although it's the same length. To provide a clear view of the items on the shelf, there's no rail, so you won't need the galley spindles.

■ Although this shelf is different from the Plate Shelf, it also complements it. That's because the same types of moldings are used, just stacked in a different order. That way the shelves could sit near each other on a wall as part of a grouping.

■ As before, I started by cutting the dentil molding to length and sizing the rest of the pieces to match it. The front piece of dentil molding is 32½" long. The side pieces are 3½" long (see drawing).

■ Next, I made the cove and roundover moldings (C, D). These are the same as the moldings stacked up to form the crown molding on the Plate Shelf. But this time, one is above the dentil molding and one is below the dentil molding.

■ The cove molding (C) starts as a 1¼"-wide piece of stock. The ½" cove routed in it has a ¼" shoulder (see drawing).

■ The roundover molding (D) is 2¼" wide. It has a ½" roundover with a ¼" shoulder (see drawing).

■ Next, the cove molding is mitered to fit below the dentil molding. What you want is for the dentil to overhang the cove by ¼" on each side (see drawing).

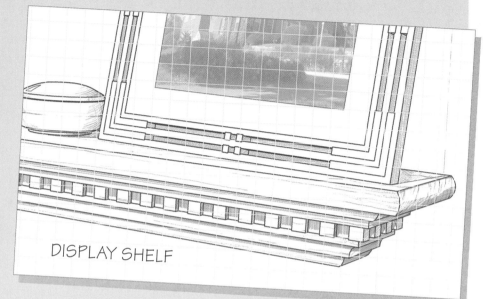

DISPLAY SHELF

■ Once the cove is mitered to length, you can determine the size of the bottom (B). As before, the bottom has rabbets cut around the top face to accept the molding. (The cove molding in this case.)

■ After the rabbets are cut in the bottom, glue the cove molding in place. Then glue the dentil molding in place on top of it. Finally, the roundover molding can be mitered to overhang the dentil by ¾" and glued in place (see drawing).

■ Now cut the shelf (E) to size and rout a bullnose around the front and sides before screwing it in place.

■ Finally, cut a hanging cleat (G). Glue half the cleat under the shelf (E) and screw the mating half to the wall.

### MATERIALS LIST

**CHANGED PARTS**

| | | |
|---|---|---|
| A | Dentil Molding (1) | ½ x 1½ - 44 rgh. |
| B | Bottom (1) | ¾ x 2½ - 30½ |
| C | Cove Molding (1) | ¾ x 1¼ - 40 rgh. |
| D | Roundover Mldg. (1) | ¾ x 2¼ - 40 rgh. |
| E | Shelf (1) | ¾ x 5¼ - 36 |

**Note:** Do not need part F or galley spindles.

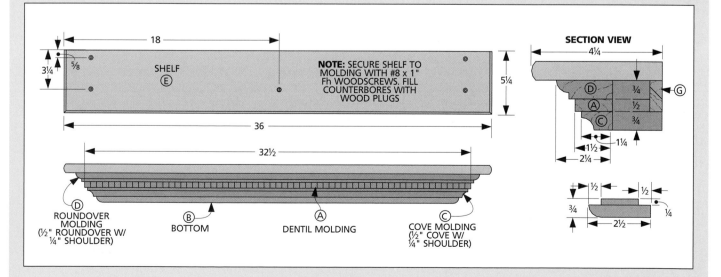

18

3¼  ⅝

SHELF
Ⓔ

NOTE: SECURE SHELF TO MOLDING WITH #8 x 1" Fh WOODSCREWS. FILL COUNTERBORES WITH WOOD PLUGS

5¼

36

32½

ROUNDOVER MOLDING (½" ROUNDOVER W/ ¼" SHOULDER)  Ⓓ

BOTTOM  Ⓑ

DENTIL MOLDING  Ⓐ

COVE MOLDING (½" COVE W/ ¼" SHOULDER)  Ⓒ

**SECTION VIEW**

4¼

Ⓓ  ¾
Ⓖ
Ⓐ  ½
Ⓒ  ¾

1½  1¼

2¼

½  ½

¾  ¼

2½

# Round Dining Table

*The pedestal base makes it easy to seat four people around this table. And when the occasion calls for more places, the table slides open easily to accept a leaf. The secret is ready-made wood slides.*

One of the projects that had been on my "someday" list for quite a while was a Round Dining Table. As I thought about it, I focused in on the features I wanted. The two biggest were a pedestal in the center, so there is "knee room" no matter where you sit, and the table had to open so a leaf could be added to allow more people to be seated.

**SPLIT TABLE TOP.** A table top that opens poses some interesting design challenges. Like finding a way to "split" the pedestal so there will be legs under each half of the table when the leaf is inserted. And the leaf has to be secure in the table so it doesn't slide out. Plus, I had to come up with a device that holds the halves of the table together while it also allows them to slide apart. (This part was pretty easy — in a catalog, I found ready-made wood slides for just this purpose.) But all told, this project isn't that complicated.

**BORDER.** The round top has a solid-wood border (mahogany) surrounding an insert. (More about the insert in a moment.) The border is built first, then the insert is sized to fit inside.

The border starts out as an octagon. Eight mitered pieces are joined with splines to reinforce the joint. Then the border is cut to a circular shape using a router on a shop-made trammel.

**INSERT.** There are a couple of options for the insert in the center of the table. You could use hardwood plywood. But I couldn't find plywood with the quarter-sawn oak veneer I wanted. So I made my own by applying veneer to a particle-board substrate. (There's a veneering article on page 66.)

Another benefit of using sheet goods for the insert instead of solid wood is that I didn't have to worry about wood expansion across the 46"-wide table top.

**MISSION-STYLE OPTION.** With the addition of just a few pieces to the base, the table takes on a Mission look. Details about this option are on page 57.

# EXPLODED VIEW

**OVERALL DIMENSIONS:**
46D x 29H
(46D x 64W WITH LEAF)

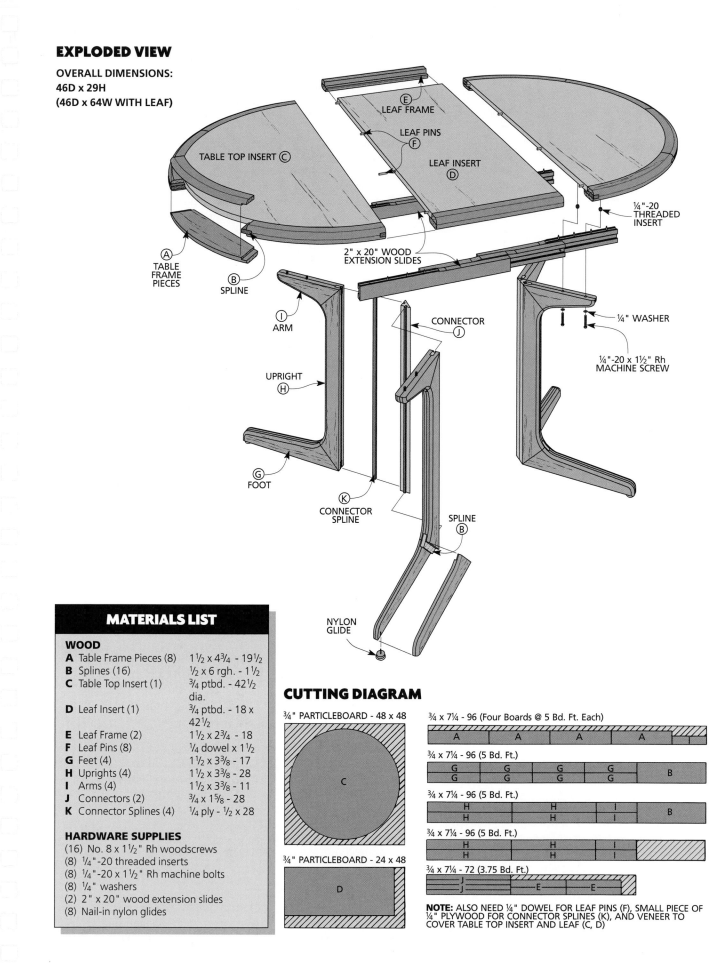

TABLE TOP INSERT Ⓒ

LEAF FRAME

LEAF PINS Ⓕ

LEAF INSERT Ⓓ

Ⓐ TABLE FRAME PIECES

Ⓑ SPLINE

¼"-20 THREADED INSERT

2" x 20" WOOD EXTENSION SLIDES

Ⓘ ARM

CONNECTOR Ⓙ

¼" WASHER

¼"-20 x 1½" Rh MACHINE SCREW

UPRIGHT Ⓗ

Ⓖ FOOT

Ⓚ CONNECTOR SPLINE

SPLINE Ⓑ

NYLON GLIDE

## MATERIALS LIST

### WOOD

| | | |
|---|---|---|
| **A** | Table Frame Pieces (8) | 1½ x 4¾ - 19½ |
| **B** | Splines (16) | ½ x 6 rgh. - 1½ |
| **C** | Table Top Insert (1) | ¾ ptbd. - 42½ dia. |
| **D** | Leaf Insert (1) | ¾ ptbd. - 18 x 42½ |
| **E** | Leaf Frame (2) | 1½ x 2¾ - 18 |
| **F** | Leaf Pins (8) | ¼ dowel x 1½ |
| **G** | Feet (4) | 1½ x 3⅜ - 17 |
| **H** | Uprights (4) | 1½ x 3⅜ - 28 |
| **I** | Arms (4) | 1½ x 3⅜ - 11 |
| **J** | Connectors (2) | ¾ x 1⅝ - 28 |
| **K** | Connector Splines (4) | ¼ ply - ½ x 28 |

### HARDWARE SUPPLIES

(16) No. 8 x 1½" Rh woodscrews
(8) ¼"-20 threaded inserts
(8) ¼"-20 x 1½" Rh machine bolts
(8) ¼" washers
(2) 2" x 20" wood extension slides
(8) Nail-in nylon glides

## CUTTING DIAGRAM

¾" PARTICLEBOARD - 48 x 48

C

¾" PARTICLEBOARD - 24 x 48

D

¾ x 7¼ - 96 (Four Boards @ 5 Bd. Ft. Each)

| A | A | A | A | |

¾ x 7¼ - 96 (5 Bd. Ft.)

| G | G | G | G | |
| G | G | G | G | B |

¾ x 7¼ - 96 (5 Bd. Ft.)

| H | H | I | |
| H | H | I | B |

¾ x 7¼ - 96 (5 Bd. Ft.)

| H | H | I | |
| H | H | I | |

¾ x 7¼ - 72 (3.75 Bd. Ft.)

| J | | | |
| J | E | E | |

**NOTE:** ALSO NEED ¼" DOWEL FOR LEAF PINS (F), SMALL PIECE OF ¼" PLYWOOD FOR CONNECTOR SPLINES (K), AND VENEER TO COVER TABLE TOP INSERT AND LEAF (C, D)

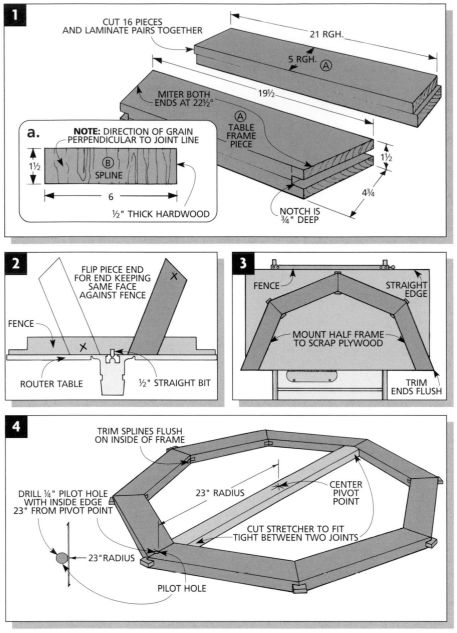

**1** CUT 16 PIECES AND LAMINATE PAIRS TOGETHER

21 RGH.

5 RGH. Ⓐ

MITER BOTH ENDS AT 22½°

19½

Ⓐ TABLE FRAME PIECE

**a.** **NOTE:** DIRECTION OF GRAIN PERPENDICULAR TO JOINT LINE

1½

Ⓑ SPLINE

6

½" THICK HARDWOOD

1½

4¾

NOTCH IS ¾" DEEP

**2** FLIP PIECE END FOR END KEEPING SAME FACE AGAINST FENCE

FENCE

X

X

ROUTER TABLE     ½" STRAIGHT BIT

**3** FENCE     STRAIGHT EDGE

MOUNT HALF FRAME TO SCRAP PLYWOOD

TRIM ENDS FLUSH

**4** TRIM SPLINES FLUSH ON INSIDE OF FRAME

DRILL ¼" PILOT HOLE WITH INSIDE EDGE 23" FROM PIVOT POINT

23" RADIUS

CENTER PIVOT POINT

CUT STRETCHER TO FIT TIGHT BETWEEN TWO JOINTS

23" RADIUS

PILOT HOLE

## BORDER FRAME

The outside border of the table top starts out as a giant octagonal (eight-sided) frame. (I used Honduras mahogany.) To get the thickness I wanted for the border, I rough-cut 16 pieces of ¾" stock and laminated pairs together to form the eight table frame pieces (A) *(Fig. 1)*.

When the glue is dry, trim the eight pieces to a final width of 4¾". Then cut 22½° miters on both ends of each piece so that the final length is 19½" from long point to long point.

**GROOVES.** The eight pieces are joined by cutting grooves through each mitered end and then gluing hardwood splines into the grooves.

To cut the grooves, I used a router table and a ½" straight bit *(Fig. 2)*. Adjust the router table fence so the bit is centered on the thickness of the stock. Then mark the face (top) side of each piece and keep this side against the fence. (This ensures that the top sides of all pieces will be flush when the splines are inserted.)

**SPLINES.** Next, eight splines (B) are cut to fit the grooves. (I used mahogany to match the frame, but you could use a contrasting wood.) The splines should be long enough to stick out both ends of the grooves. (They'll be trimmed later.)

**ASSEMBLY.** Trying to join all eight pieces at one time (while making sure all the joint lines meet perfectly) can be a nightmare. Instead, I glued pairs

together, and then glued these assemblies to form two halves of the frame.

Then to make sure the two half-frames fit together without a gap at the joint line, I trimmed the open ends so they formed a straight line. To do this, tack each half-frame to a piece of plywood so that the open ends just barely hang over the edge, and run them through the saw *(Fig. 3)*.

Finally, glue the two halves together to form the eight-sided frame. (I used a band clamp to pull the halves together.)

## ROUTING THE FRAME

Once the glue has dried, the frame can be routed into its final (circular) shape using a trammel. (If you don't have a trammel, refer to the Shop Jig article on page 53.)

**PIVOT POINT.** To provide a pivot point for the trammel, I cut a stretcher (with pointed ends) to fit tight between two opposing joints of the frame *(Fig. 4)*.

**Note:** For the stretcher to fit, the splines inside the frame must be pared off with a chisel. Don't worry about the outside face. Those splines will be trimmed off when the frame is cut to shape.

To find the pivot point, place the stretcher inside the frame. Then place a straightedge on each set of opposing joint lines and mark lines on the stretcher *(Fig. 4)*. Where these lines intersect is the center of the frame (the pivot point).

Later in this process, you'll need to have pivot points on both the top and bottom sides of the stretcher. So drill a hole the same size as the trammel pivot pin straight down through the stretcher to mark both sides.

**PILOT HOLE.** Before routing the outside edge of the frame, I drilled a pilot hole so the router bit had a place to start. The *inside* edge of this hole should be 23" from the center of the pivot point *(Fig. 4)*.

**OUTSIDE CIRCUMFERENCE.** To rout the outside edge, I used a ¼" straight bit set to a depth of ¼" for the first pass.

After the first pass is made, lower the bit and make successively deeper passes until you're about halfway through the thickness of the frame. Then remove the router trammel, flip over the entire assembly (the frame and the stretcher), and rout the other side until the outside waste breaks free *(Fig. 5a)*.

**INSIDE RABBET.** Next, the inside edge of the frame is routed to form a rabbet to hold the table top's circular insert. To make this rabbet, the first step is to rout a groove around the inside edge of the frame. This groove should be about $1/32"$ deeper than the thickness of the insert. (Later, the frame will be sanded down flush with the insert.)

But there's just one problem. Before you can rout this groove, you have to know the thickness of the insert. My insert was made from a veneered piece of particleboard. So I had to build the insert first (page 52) before routing the rabbet.

Once you've determined the thickness of your insert (and the depth of the rabbet), drill a pilot hole to this depth with its *outside* edge $21^{1}/_{4}"$ from the center of the trammel pivot *(Fig. 5b)*.

Now just reposition the trammel so the bit fits into the pilot hole and rout the groove to final depth in several passes. Finally, to remove the waste sections between the groove and the inside of the frame, just reposition the router along the trammel as needed.

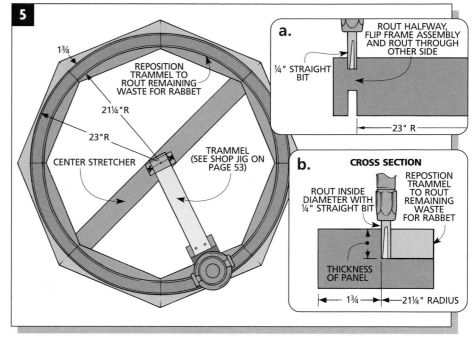

**5**

1¾

REPOSITION TRAMMEL TO ROUT REMAINING WASTE FOR RABBET

21¼"R

23"R

CENTER STRETCHER

TRAMMEL (SEE SHOP JIG ON PAGE 53)

**a.**
ROUT HALFWAY, FLIP FRAME ASSEMBLY AND ROUT THROUGH OTHER SIDE

¼" STRAIGHT BIT

23" R

**b.** CROSS SECTION

ROUT INSIDE DIAMETER WITH ¼" STRAIGHT BIT

REPOSTION TRAMMEL TO ROUT REMAINING WASTE FOR RABBET

THICKNESS OF PANEL

1¾ — 21¼" RADIUS

---

# TECHNIQUE . . . . . . . . . . . . . . . . . . . . . . . . . . . . . . . *Splined Miters*

**M**iters are attractive because no end grain shows, but they need some reinforcement. For the dining table, I used splines to "beef up" each joint.

## CUTTING MITERS

Although cutting miters seems like a simple operation, there's really more to it than just cutting the workpiece at the correct angle. In fact, even when the angle is set correctly, the cut can still be off. The problem is that the saw blade can either pull or push the workpiece.

**CREEPING.** The easiest way to prevent the workpiece from creeping is to attach a plywood fence to the miter gauge to support the workpiece all the way to the blade. Then clamp a stop block to the fence so the workpiece can be pressed against it *(Fig. 1)*. (Gluing a piece of sandpaper to the face of the fence will also help keep the workpiece from slipping.)

**CUT MITERS.** To cut the mitered pieces, I use the following procedure: first I cut each of the pieces for the frame to rough length (about 1" longer than needed).

Then I've found it's best to sneak up on the miter by making two cuts. The first cut clears away most of the waste. Next, a trim cut is made which just barely skims off the end of the miter. This way there's much less chance of the blade pulling or pushing the workpiece out of line.

## GROOVES

After the miters are cut, the pieces are joined with the use of splines that fit into grooves in the miters. To keep the pieces aligned, these grooves must be the same distance from the face side of each piece.

For the frame of the table, I cut the pieces on the router table, keeping the top face of each piece against the fence (refer to *Fig. 2* on facing page).

## SPLINES

Of course, once the grooves are cut, the splines have to be cut to match. The key here is to cut the splines so the frame pieces fit together perfectly.

If the splines are solid wood, they should be cut so the grain is running across the joint line for greatest strength (*Fig. 2* below and refer to *Fig. 1a* on opposite page). This requires two cuts. The first cut is made by setting the rip fence the "proper distance" from the blade. This distance is equal to the width of the groove in the mitered pieces. Then raise the blade $1^{1}/_{2}"$ above the table.

For the second cut, set the rip fence about $1/32"$ beyond the bottom of the first cut, and guide the workpiece with the miter gauge to make two shallow cuts (*Fig. 2*). Then simply snap off the splines and sand off the ragged edge.

**GLUE UP.** If the spline fits well, the mitered pieces can be glued together without clamping. Hand pressure alone will produce a good, tight joint. This is because the strength of a spline joint is between the face grain of the spline and the sides of the grooves — not between the end grain of the mitered edges.

Just hold the joint together for a minute or so, and then set it down on a flat surface to dry completely.

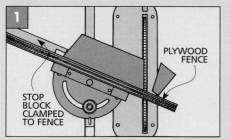

**1**

PLYWOOD FENCE

STOP BLOCK CLAMPED TO FENCE

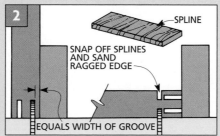

**2**

SPLINE

SNAP OFF SPLINES AND SAND RAGGED EDGE

EQUALS WIDTH OF GROOVE

# CIRCULAR INSERT

There are two choices for the table top's center insert. The easiest way to make it is to use ³⁄₄" hardwood plywood.

But since I wanted quartersawn white oak for the top (which I couldn't find in plywood), I bought a 36" x 96" piece of flexible veneer and mounted it to a couple of pieces of particleboard.

**VENEERING.** To make the veneered table top, I glued two 24" x 48" pieces of veneer to the particleboard *(Fig. 6)*. (The leftover veneer will be used for the table leaf.) The Technique article on page 66 will walk you through veneering so you get a joint line that's almost invisible.

**ROUT INSERT.** Whether you use plywood or veneered particleboard, you should have a 48" x 48" workpiece for the table top insert (C). To turn this square into a circle, draw diagonal lines on the back side to locate the pivot point for the trammel *(Fig. 7)*. Drill a hole for the pivot pin at this point. (Don't drill through the insert.) Next, set the trammel to the radius of the rabbeted area on the frame (21¹⁄₄"), and make a *shallow* cut on the back side of the insert.

Check this cut by laying the border frame over the scored insert. The shoulder of the rabbet in the frame should touch the outside edge of the scored groove *(Fig. 7a)*. Then just adjust the trammel so that the outside edge of the groove is a hair less than the rabbet.

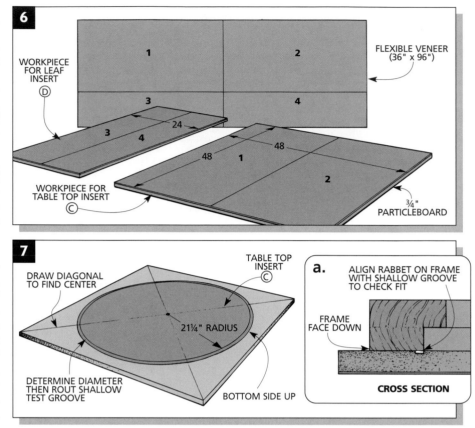

When you've got the right diameter for the groove, drill a ¹⁄₄"-dia. pilot hole on the edge of the trial groove and rout the insert. (When you're done, save the outer waste piece. It will be used later.)

**ASSEMBLY.** After the insert is routed to shape, spread glue in the rabbet in the frame and clamp the insert in place. For the best appearance, be sure to align the grain of the insert with two opposing joint lines on the frame.

After the glue has dried completely, sand the frame so it ends up flush with the face of the insert.

---

# SHOP JIG .................... *Large Sled*

**B**ecause I wanted to add a leaf to the Round Dining Table, I had to cut the top into two halves. To do this, I used the outer waste piece left over from routing the circular insert as a sled to carry the table top past the saw blade.

Start by marking lines on this waste piece to divide it in half *(Fig. 1)*. Then tack the table top to the waste piece so that two opposing joint lines of the frame are aligned with the lines marked on the waste piece *(Fig. 1)*.

**Note:** Tack from the bottom and sink the heads below the surface *(Fig. 1a)*.

**CUT IN HALF.** This whole setup can now be ripped in half on a table saw. Set the fence so the blade splits the marked lines on the waste piece *(Fig. 2)*.

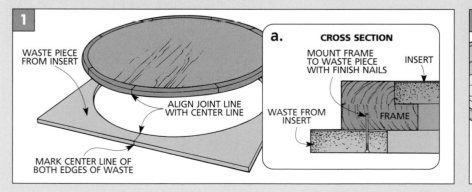

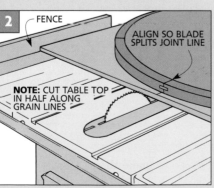

# SHOP JIG .......... Router Trammel

**C**utting circles is easy if you have a trammel to attach to your router. And the simple design of this shop-built trammel solves two problems I've always had with large trammels.

First, it's lightweight but still strong. And second, you can quickly and accurately set the size of the radius.

This jig consists of three pieces: a base for your router, an aluminum ruler for a trammel arm, and a pivot block you can adjust to change the size of the circle.

**Note:** The 36" aluminum ruler is inexpensive and can be found at hardware stores or art supply stores.

**BASE.** To build the base, start with a rectangular piece of 1/4"-thick hardboard *(Fig. 2)*. The idea here is to center the router on the base 6" from the back edge.

First, measure from the back edge and mark a centerpoint. Then use a compass to draw a diameter the same size as your router base. Now use the existing router base as a template to mark and drill the mounting holes and clearance hole for the bit. Finally, cut and sand the base to its finished shape.

To complete the base, a mounting block is glued and screwed to the back edge *(Fig. 1)*. This is just a 3/4"-thick piece of hardwood (maple) with a wide dado cut in the top to accept the ruler. To be safe, I started with an extra-long blank then cut off the 2"-long block.

**Note:** Save the rest of the blank. It's used in the next step.

**PIVOT BLOCK.** All that's left to finish the jig is to make the pivot block. The 2"-long piece left over from the base blank is perfect for the bracket. Then add a base and pin *(Fig. 1)*. The pin fits in the center hole of your circle.

What makes this pivot block especially handy is an acrylic plastic indicator on top *(Fig. 1a)*. This indicator has a scribed line that serves as a pointer to help you set the radius of the jig accurately. A pair of threaded knobs (or wing nuts) locks the pivot block to the trammel arm once the size of the radius is set.

**ASSEMBLY.** With the pivot block and base complete, you can assemble the jig and calibrate it for accuracy. This is simply a matter of attaching the trammel arm to the mounting block on the base with a couple of screws *(Fig. 1)*.

But to make the jig accurate when using the indicator, you'll have to use the same dimension that was used to center the router on the base earlier. Since I centered the router at 6", I aligned the 6" mark on the ruler with the back edge of the mounting block and screwed it in place. Finally, cut off the end of the trammel arm that sticks out past the mounting block *(Fig. 1)*.

**Note:** Keep in mind that the jig measures the cut to the center of your bit. Bits of different sizes will alter the measurement indicated on the ruler slightly.

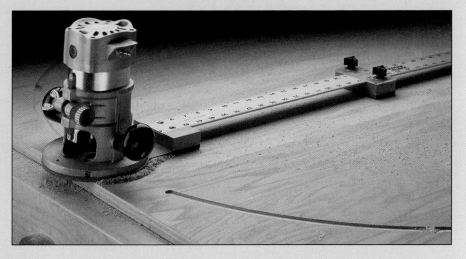

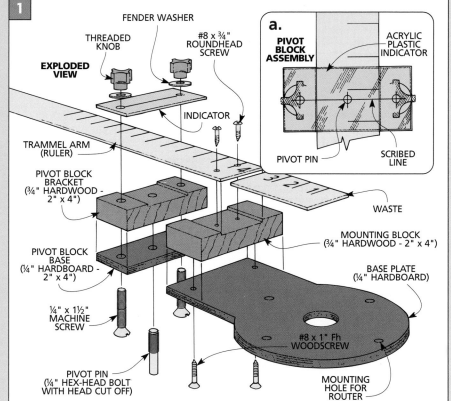

**1** EXPLODED VIEW

FENDER WASHER
THREADED KNOB
#8 x 3/4" ROUNDHEAD SCREW
INDICATOR
TRAMMEL ARM (RULER)
PIVOT BLOCK BRACKET (3/4" HARDWOOD - 2" x 4")
PIVOT BLOCK BASE (1/4" HARDBOARD - 2" x 4")
1/4" x 1 1/2" MACHINE SCREW
PIVOT PIN (1/4" HEX-HEAD BOLT WITH HEAD CUT OFF)
WASTE
MOUNTING BLOCK (3/4" HARDWOOD - 2" x 4")
BASE PLATE (1/4" HARDBOARD)
#8 x 1" Fh WOODSCREW
MOUNTING HOLE FOR ROUTER

**a.** PIVOT BLOCK ASSEMBLY
ACRYLIC PLASTIC INDICATOR
PIVOT PIN
SCRIBED LINE

**2** BASE LAYOUT

1/4" OPENING FOR ALIGNING ROUTER
1" OPENING FOR ROUTER BITS

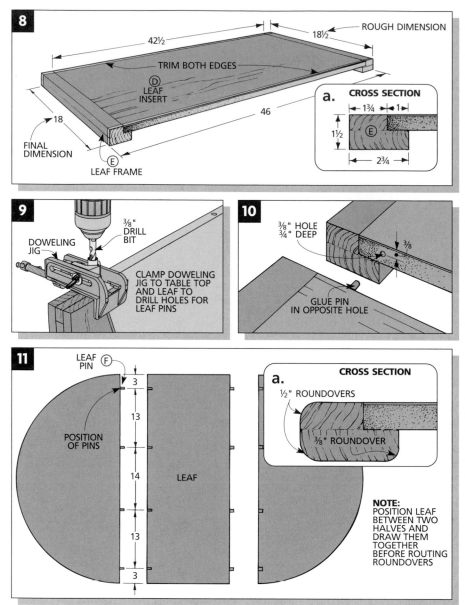

Adding a leaf (D) to this table is easy. Rip a piece of veneered particleboard (or plywood) to a width of $18\frac{1}{2}$" and to length to match the diameter of the insert.

**BORDER.** This leaf has a laminated frame similar to that of the table top. First, cut four pieces of $\frac{3}{4}$" stock 3" wide, and laminate them to form the two leaf frames (E). When the glue is dry, trim them to final width *(Fig. 8a)*. Then cut a 1"-wide rabbet on one edge of each piece.

Glue and clamp the leaf into the rabbets of these pieces. Then rip the entire leaf to final width of 18". (Here it's best to rip an equal amount from both edges so you have two parallel edges.)

**LEAF PINS.** Since the table top is split in half, some provision must be made to align the two halves, and also to align the leaf (when it's used) with the table top. To accomplish this, I used wooden pins mounted in holes.

Start by laying out four holes on each exposed edge of the table top and the leaf *(Fig. 11)*. (There are 16 holes in all.) To drill the holes, I used a hand-held drill with a doweling jig *(Fig. 9)*.

Next, cut leaf pins (F) from a $\frac{1}{4}$" dowel to fit the holes. Glue four of these pins into the holes on one edge of the table top (to align the two halves of the table), and glue the other four pins into the holes in one edge of the leaf (to align it when it's used). Then I sanded a slight chamfer on the end of each pin so it would slide into the opposing hole easily.

**ROUND EDGES.** To complete the table top, I rounded all the edges. Position the

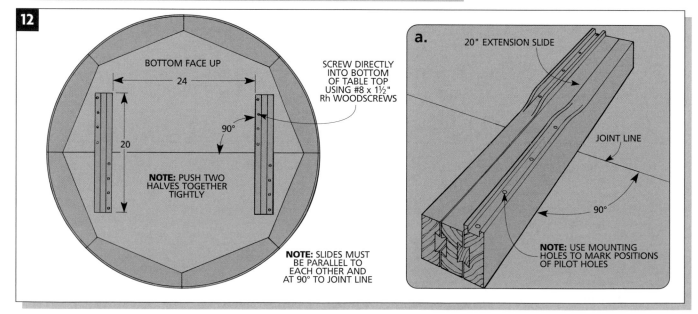

leaf between the two halves of the table and draw them together. Then lay this assembly face down on a work surface.

Now rout a $3/8$" roundover on the inside edge of the frame *(Fig. 11a)*. Next, switch to a $1/2$" roundover bit to round over the outside edge of the frame. Then flip the table top over and rout a $1/2$" roundover on the top edge of the frame.

## EXTENSION SLIDES

The last step on the table top is to mount the extension slides. I used a set of manufactured wooden slides *(Fig. 12a)*. (For sources of these slides, see page 126.)

To mount the extension slides, place the two halves of the table top face down on a work surface and push them together. Then align the slides so they're 24" apart and exactly perpendicular to the joint line *(Fig. 12)*.

The slides I bought have pre-drilled mounting holes. I marked their positions on the bottom of the table top, drilled pilot holes, and then screwed the extension slides in place *(Fig. 12a)*.

**Note:** As the slides are screwed in place, be sure they're parallel and exactly 90° to the joint line. If the slides are out of kilter, they will bind as the table halves are pulled apart. As a final check, insert the leaf and close the table halves. I had to adjust the slides a little to get the top halves to close tight against the leaf.

## BASE

Once the table top is complete, all it needs is a base to rest on. The challenge here is to construct a pedestal base that can be separated when the table top is pulled apart (for the leaf).

The base I made consists of four C-shaped leg units that are joined together in pairs and then attached to the two halves of the table top (refer to *Fig. 18* on page 56). When the table top is pushed together, the legs form a four-leg pedestal. And when the table top is separated to insert the leaf, the legs also separate to support the extended version of the table.

**C-FRAMES.** To build this double-duty base, I made four C-frames. Each C-frame consists of three parts: a foot (G), an upright (H), and an arm (I) *(Fig. 13)*. The $1/2$"-thick blanks for these pieces are laminated from two pieces of $3/4$"-thick stock *(Fig. 13b)*.

**CUT MITERS.** After all the pieces are laminated, trim them to a final width of

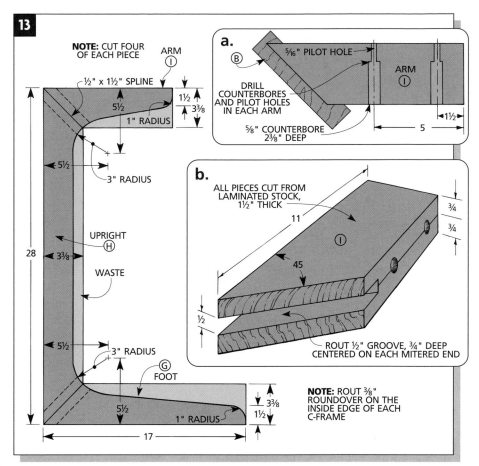

$3^3/8$". Next, cut a 45° miter on only one end of each arm and foot. And finally, crosscut the other end so the final length of each arm is 11" *(Fig. 13b)* and each foot is 17" *(Fig. 13)*. (Measure each piece to the long point of the miter.)

For the uprights, cut 45° miters on both ends so the final length is 28" from long point to long point.

**GROOVES AND SPLINES.** To assemble the C-frames, the mitered ends of the arms and legs are joined to the uprights with splines. To do this, first cut $1/2$"-wide through grooves centered on the mitered ends of each piece. Once again, I marked the face side of each piece, then cut the grooves on a router table with the marked face against the fence. Then splines (B) are cut to fit the grooves *(Fig. 13)*.

**HOLES IN ARMS.** Before assembling the C-frames, I drilled counterbored holes in the arms for $1^1/2$" machine screws and washers *(Fig. 13a)*. (Later, threaded inserts are installed in the table top so the machine screws can be screwed through the base and into the table top.)

**ASSEMBLY.** Now the C-frames can be assembled. The important thing here is to make sure the arms and feet are parallel. So I cut a spacer piece to fit between

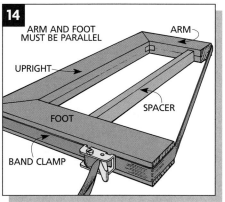

the arm and leg and used a band clamp to pull the pieces together *(Fig. 14)*.

**CUT LEGS TO SHAPE.** After the glue is dry on the four leg units, I cut them to their final profile. This is simply a matter of rounding the inside corners (where the splines are) to a radius of $3^1/2$", and then tapering the arms and feet down to a width of $1^1/2$" *(Fig. 13)*.

To ensure all four C-frames are the same, draw the profiles on cardboard, cut out the patterns, and trace them on each C-frame. Then cut the shape on a band saw and sand the edges smooth. And finally, rout a $3/8$" roundover on the inside of each C-frame.

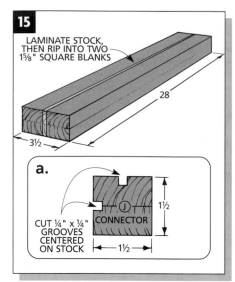

**15**
LAMINATE STOCK, THEN RIP INTO TWO 1⅝" SQUARE BLANKS

28

3½

**a.**
CUT ¼" x ¼" GROOVES CENTERED ON STOCK

CONNECTOR (J)

1½

1½

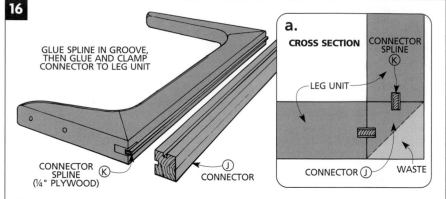

**16**
GLUE SPLINE IN GROOVE, THEN GLUE AND CLAMP CONNECTOR TO LEG UNIT

CONNECTOR SPLINE (K) (¼" PLYWOOD)

CONNECTOR (J)

**a.**
CROSS SECTION

CONNECTOR SPLINE (K)

LEG UNIT

CONNECTOR (J)

WASTE

## CONNECTING LEG UNITS

Now comes the tricky part. The leg units are joined together in pairs to form two 90° assemblies. This is accomplished with a long, square connector piece between each pair of C-frames.

**CONNECTORS.** To make the connectors (J), laminate two pieces of ³/₄"-thick stock to make a blank 3½" wide and 28" long *(Fig. 15)*. Then rip this laminated piece into two 1½"-square blanks.

**JOIN TO C-FRAMES.** Each connector is joined to two C-frames with splines to

help align the pieces. Because these splines are so long, I used ¼" plywood instead of hardwood.

So the first thing to do is to cut grooves centered on two faces of each connector *(Fig. 15a)*. And remember, ¼" plywood is usually just under ¼" thick, so cut the grooves to match the actual thickness of the plywood. Then cut matching grooves centered on the edge of the upright on each C-frame *(Fig. 16)*.

**SPLINES.** Once the grooves were completed, I cut connector splines (K) to fit the grooves. Then glue and clamp two C-frames to each connector *(Fig. 16a)*. Make sure the C-frames are 90° to each other, and the top edges of the arms and bottom edges of the feet are flush.

**BEVEL EDGE.** The next step is to bevel rip the connectors at 45°. This requires the use of an auxiliary fence.

This long, L-shaped fence is clamped to the rip fence *(Fig. 17)*. The fence provides clearance for the saw blade and a surface for the upright to ride against.

After the auxiliary fence is attached, tilt the blade to 45° and position the rip fence so the blade just touches the corners of the uprights *(Fig. 17)*. Then bevel rip each of the connectors.

**GLIDES.** There's one last thing to do before attaching the legs to the table. That is to add a couple of nylon glides to the bottom of each foot *(Fig. 18a)*. These make the feet slide easily when you need to open up the table to insert the leaf.

**ATTACH LEGS.** Now the two leg assemblies can be joined to the table top. With the table top upside down and the two halves pushed together tightly, center the two leg units on each half of the top. Then mark the position of the mounting holes that were drilled in the arms earlier *(Fig. 18)*. Remove the leg units and drill holes for ¼" threaded inserts *(Fig. 18b)*. After installing the inserts, mount the leg units to the top with 1½" machine bolts and washers.

## FINISHING

I used a tung oil/polyurethane mixture to finish the table top and base. If there are small voids between the tabletop's border frame and the insert, they can be filled with a mixture of fine sawdust (from sanding) and the tung oil/polyurethane finish. Then I applied three coats of finish to the entire table according to the instructions on the can. ■

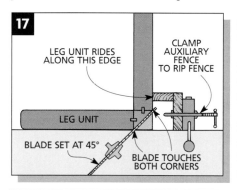

**17**
LEG UNIT RIDES ALONG THIS EDGE

CLAMP AUXILIARY FENCE TO RIP FENCE

LEG UNIT

BLADE SET AT 45°

BLADE TOUCHES BOTH CORNERS

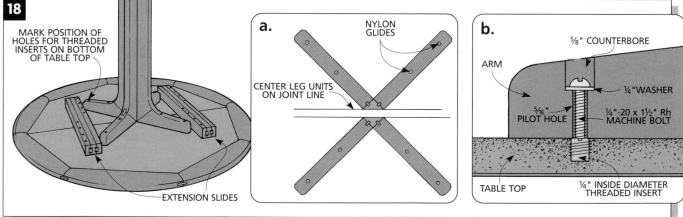

**18**
MARK POSITION OF HOLES FOR THREADED INSERTS ON BOTTOM OF TABLE TOP

EXTENSION SLIDES

**a.**
NYLON GLIDES

CENTER LEG UNITS ON JOINT LINE

**b.**
⅝" COUNTERBORE

ARM

¼" WASHER

⁵/₁₆" PILOT HOLE

¼"-20 x 1½" Rh MACHINE BOLT

TABLE TOP

¼" INSIDE DIAMETER THREADED INSERT

# DESIGNER'S NOTEBOOK

*It's easy to change the look of the table from contemporary to Mission-style by changing a few profiles, then making some simple cuts and adding two narrow uprights to each C-frame.*

## CONSTRUCTION NOTES:

■ First, after building the table top and insert, rout $\frac{1}{8}$" roundovers along the edges instead of $\frac{1}{2}$" roundovers.

■ Two uprights added to each C-frame give the table its Mission look. Glue up eight blanks for the narrow uprights (L) and cut them to finished width and thickness and to rough length *(Fig. 2)*.

■ When it's time to build the base, you need to make a few cuts in the arms and feet before assembling the C-frames. First, laminate the blanks for the arms and feet. Then miter one end of each blank at 45° as before.

■ Next, two dadoes are cut in the inside edge of each arm and foot *(Fig. 2a)*. These accept the narrow uprights.

■ To cut these dadoes, I attached a tall auxiliary fence with a stop block to my miter gauge *(Fig. 1)*. Then I set up a $\frac{3}{4}$" dado blade in the table saw. With the mitered end of each piece against the stop block, make a pass to cut the inside shoulder of the inside dado on each piece.

Then reposition the stop block and cut the dadoes to finished width. Repeat this process to cut the outside dadoes.

■ Now cut a 3" radius at the end of each foot and a $\frac{3}{8}$" radius on the end of each arm. Then drill a counterbored shank hole in each arm *(Fig. 2a)*.

■ The next step is to dry-assemble the C-frames and measure between the dadoes

ROUND MISSION TABLE

to find the length of the narrow uprights. Also drill shank and pilot holes for the screws that hold the narrow uprights.

■ Cut the narrow uprights to length and glue and screw the frames together.

■ After the base has been glued up, ease the sharp edges of the C-frames and narrow uprights with sandpaper.

■ Finally, position the base on the bottom of the table top and mark the locations for the threaded inserts.

## MATERIALS LIST

**NEW PART**

L   Narrow Uprights (8)   $1\frac{1}{2}$ x $1\frac{1}{2}$ - $23\frac{1}{4}$

**HARDWARE SUPPLIES**

(16) No. 8 x 3" Fh woodscrews
(4) $\frac{1}{4}$"-20 threaded inserts
(4) $\frac{1}{4}$"-20 x $1\frac{1}{2}$" Rh machine bolts
(4) $\frac{1}{4}$" washers

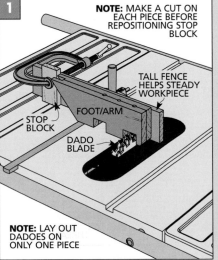

**1**

**NOTE:** MAKE A CUT ON EACH PIECE BEFORE REPOSITIONING STOP BLOCK

TALL FENCE HELPS STEADY WORKPIECE

FOOT/ARM

STOP BLOCK

DADO BLADE

**NOTE:** LAY OUT DADOES ON ONLY ONE PIECE

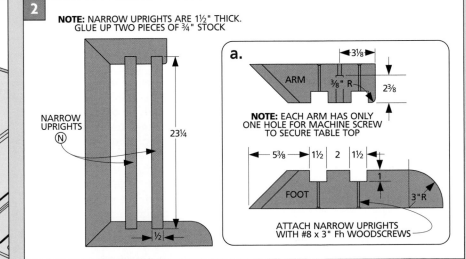

**2**

**NOTE:** NARROW UPRIGHTS ARE $1\frac{1}{2}$" THICK. GLUE UP TWO PIECES OF $\frac{3}{4}$" STOCK

NARROW UPRIGHTS (N)

$23\frac{1}{4}$

$\frac{1}{2}$

**a.**

$3\frac{1}{8}$

ARM   $\frac{3}{8}$" R   $2\frac{3}{8}$

**NOTE:** EACH ARM HAS ONLY ONE HOLE FOR MACHINE SCREW TO SECURE TABLE TOP

$5\frac{3}{8}$   $1\frac{1}{2}$   2   $1\frac{1}{2}$

FOOT   1   3" R

ATTACH NARROW UPRIGHTS WITH #8 x 3" Fh WOODSCREWS

# Classic Sideboard

*Start with tapered legs, and dovetailed drawers with antiqued brass pulls. Add twin mortise and tenon joinery and wrap it in curly maple veneer. All the details you'd expect in an heirloom piece are here.*

**S**trolling past an antique store one day, I spotted a sideboard that was the inspiration for this piece. While I picked up many of the details from the original (dovetailed drawers, traditional wooden drawer guides, tapered legs, and brass drawer pulls), I also made a change that makes it easier to build.

The change was using veneered plywood panels instead of solid wood. I did this for two reasons. First, using plywood eliminates concerns about wood movement. And second, this is a perfect project for highlighting a curly maple veneer.

**NATURAL VENEER.** The veneer I chose was a "natural" veneer. This means it was just the veneer, without the paper backing that I was used to. So the veneer tends to be wrinkled before it's applied.

Now all I needed was to figure out how to apply the veneer. I was a little worried that it would be tricky to apply this much natural veneer to a project. But it's actually easier when you know the right steps to take. (The Technique article on page 66 will walk you through it.)

Still, just getting the veneer on didn't necessarily mean the sideboard would look good — or authentic. What it needed was a special finish.

**FINISH.** The finishing process took three steps. First, the color had to be just right. To give the sideboard an antique feel (like aged shellac), I stained it with aniline dyes. But finding the right mixture took some time and experimentation.

The next step was to brush on several coats of varnish and rub them out smooth. (This is all detailed on page 72.)

My last authentic detail was to darken the shiny, new brass drawer pulls so they had the patina of much older hardware.

**MISSION OPTION.** With straight legs, a change in hardware, and quartersawn white oak veneer, the sideboard takes on a Mission style. This version also features doors instead of the larger drawers. Details are on page 65.

# EXPLODED VIEW

**OVERALL DIMENSIONS:**
**48W x 16D x 36H**

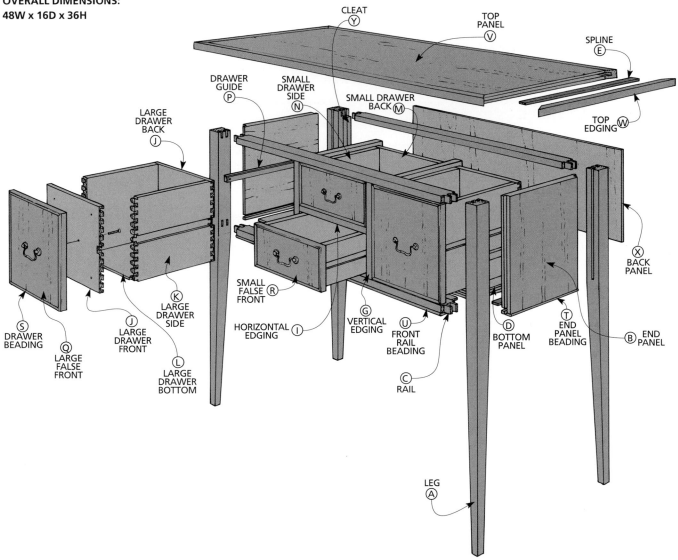

## MATERIALS LIST

### WOOD

| | | |
|---|---|---|
| **A** | Legs (4) | 1¾ x 1¾ - 35¼ |
| **B** | End Panels (2) | ¾ ply - 12 x 12 |
| **C** | Rails (4) | ¾ x 1¾ - 42 |
| **D** | Bottom Panel (1) | ¾ ply - 11½ x 42 |
| **E** | Splines | ¹¹⁄₁₆ x ¼ - 232 rgh. |
| **F** | Vertical Dividers (2) | ¾ ply - 14 x 10½ |
| **G** | Vertical Edging (2) | ¾ x ¾ - 10½ |
| **H** | Horizontal Divider (1) | ¾ ply - 14 x 15¾ |
| **I** | Horizontal Edging (1) | ¾ x ¾ - 15 |
| **J** | Lg. Drawer Fr./Bk. (4) | ½ x 9⅝ - 11½ |
| **K** | Lg. Drawer Sides (4) | ½ x 9⅝ - 12¾ |
| **L** | Lg. Drawer Btm. (2) | ¼ ply - 12½ x 11 |
| **M** | Sm. Drwr. Fr./Bk. (4) | ½ x 4⅜ - 14½ |
| **N** | Sm. Drawer Sides (4) | ½ x 4⅜ - 12¾ |
| **O** | Sm. Drawer Btm. (2) | ¼ ply - 12½ x 14 |
| **P** | Drawer Guides (8) | ¾ x ½ - 13¼ |
| **Q** | Large False Fronts (2) | ¾ ply - 9⅞ x 11⅜ |
| **R** | Sm. False Fronts (2) | ¾ ply - 4¼ x 14⅜ |
| **S** | Drawer Beading (4) | ¼ x ⅞ - 48 rough |
| **T** | End Pnl. Beading (2) | ¼ x ⅞ - 12 rough |
| **U** | Fr. Rail Beading (1) | ¼ x 1⅞ - 41 rough |
| **V** | Top Panel (1) | ¾ ply - 46½ x 14½ |
| **W** | Top Edging (2) | ¾ x ¾ - 128 rgh. |
| **X** | Back Panel (1) | ¼ ply - 40½ x 11½ |
| **Y** | Cleats (2) | ¾ x ½ - 10½ |

### HARDWARE SUPPLIES

(22) No. 6 x ½" Fh woodscrews
(32) No. 8 x 1" Fh woodscrews
(8) No. 8 x 1¼" Fh woodscrews
(8) No. 8 x 2" Fh woodscrews
(10 sq. ft.) Curly maple veneer
(4) Swan neck brass pulls w/ screws

## CUTTING DIAGRAM

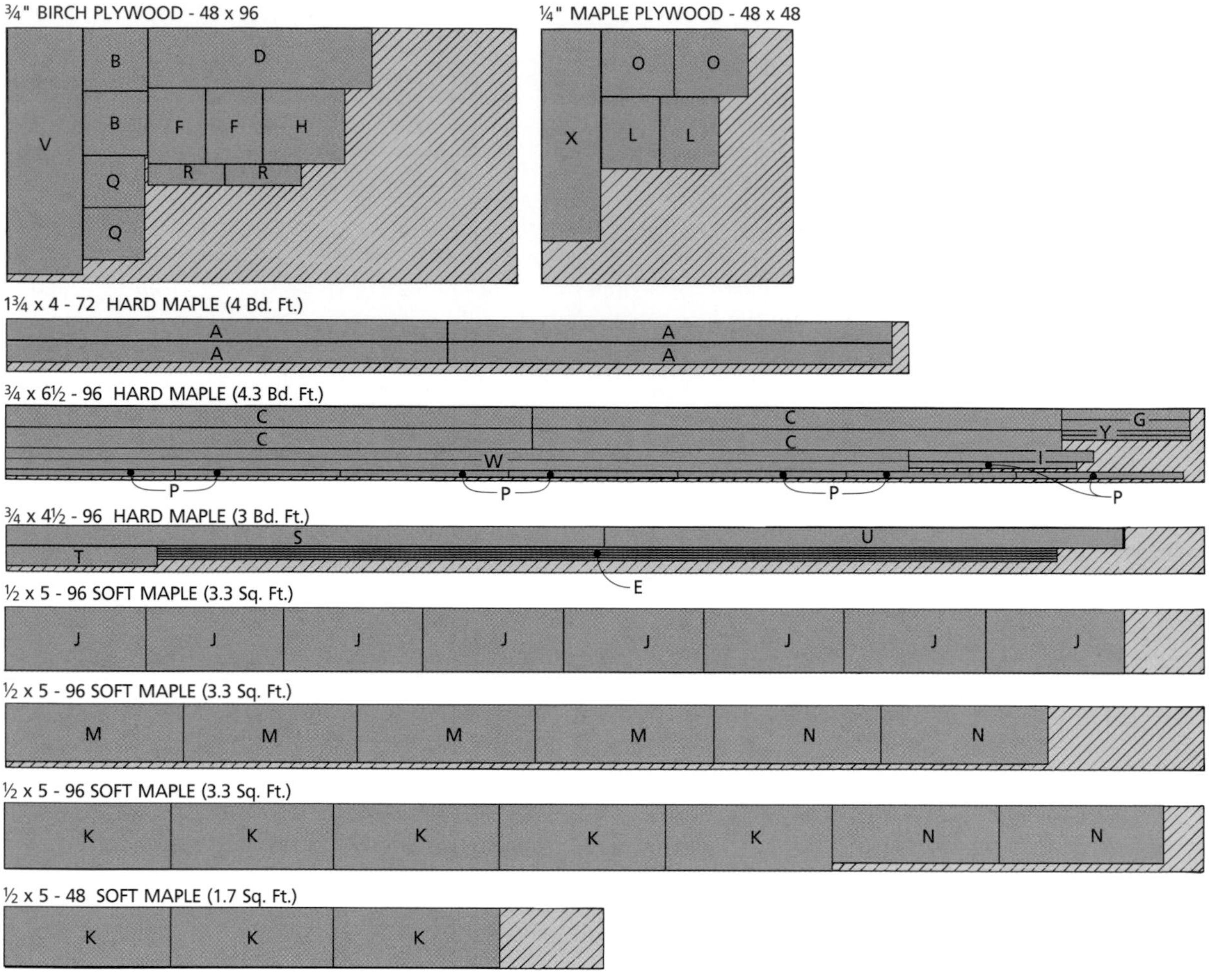

¾" BIRCH PLYWOOD - 48 x 96
V
B
B
Q
Q
D
F
F
H
R
R
¼" MAPLE PLYWOOD - 48 x 48
X
O
O
L
L
1¾ x 4 - 72 HARD MAPLE (4 Bd. Ft.)
A
A
A
A
¾ x 6½ - 96 HARD MAPLE (4.3 Bd. Ft.)
C
C
C
C
G
Y
W
I
P
P
P
P
¾ x 4½ - 96 HARD MAPLE (3 Bd. Ft.)
S
U
T
E
½ x 5 - 96 SOFT MAPLE (3.3 Sq. Ft.)
J J J J J J J J
½ x 5 - 96 SOFT MAPLE (3.3 Sq. Ft.)
M M M M N N
½ x 5 - 96 SOFT MAPLE (3.3 Sq. Ft.)
K K K K K N N
½ x 5 - 48 SOFT MAPLE (1.7 Sq. Ft.)
K K K


**1**

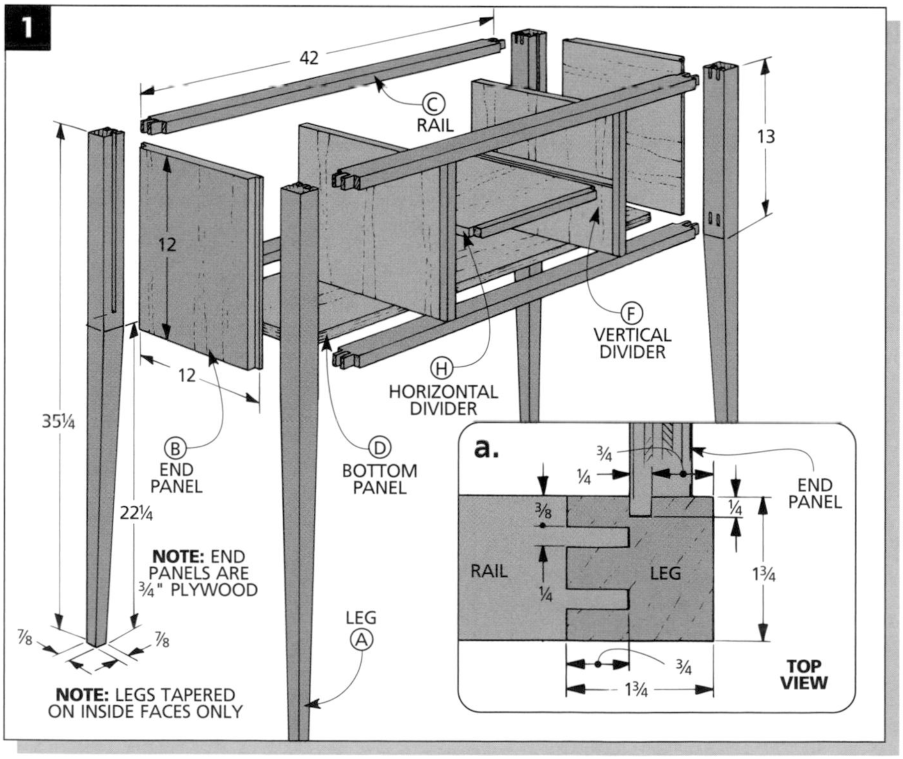

42
C RAIL
13
12
12
35¼
22¼
F VERTICAL DIVIDER
H HORIZONTAL DIVIDER
B END PANEL
D BOTTOM PANEL
NOTE: END PANELS ARE ¾" PLYWOOD
LEG A
⅞
⅞
NOTE: LEGS TAPERED ON INSIDE FACES ONLY
a.
¾
¼
⅜
¼
¼
END PANEL
RAIL
LEG
1¾
¾
1¾
TOP VIEW


## CASE

Think of a sideboard as a cross between a side table and a cupboard — it's a small storage case on legs. The legs are joined with end panels, rails, and a bottom panel *(Fig. 1)*. This forms the case that holds the drawers. Later, dividers are added to create the spaces for the drawers.

**LEGS.** I began the case by building the legs (A). They're cut to size from 1$^3/_4$" square blanks *(Figs. 1 and 1a)*. There are two sets of mortises for each leg *(Fig. 2)*. One is simply a long groove that holds the end panels. (These grooves should stop exactly 12" from the top.) To make them, I drilled overlapping holes and squared the ends and sides with a chisel.

The other set of mortises joins the rails and the legs. This time, I used twin mortises. Though they might sound more complicated, making twin mortises really isn't any harder than making a single mortise (see the step-by-step article on page 62).

The real trick is remembering which face gets which mortise. So to help me keep everything straight, I laid out the mortises on the top ends of all the leg pieces before I started drilling (*Fig. 1a*).

**TAPERS.** After cutting the mortises at the top of the legs, I turned my attention to the lower part of the legs.

If left as is, the legs would look heavy and "blocky." So I tapered them. But not every face. That would make the case look a bit bow-legged. Instead, I tapered the inside faces only (the same faces that have the mortises) (*Fig. 1*).

**Note:** I tapered the legs using a shop-built taper jig (see the box below).

**END PANELS.** To connect the legs at the sides of the case, I made two end panels. The end panels (B) are first cut 12" wide (*Fig. 3*). Then they are cut to match the length of the long grooves that were cut in the legs (12") (*Fig. 3*).

**Note:** If you plan to veneer the panels, do this before cutting them to size (refer to page 66). And make sure the grain direction of the *veneer* runs vertically.

To hold the legs together, each end panel has tongues that fit the grooves in

the legs (*Fig. 3a*). These tongues are formed by cutting a rabbet on the outside edges of each panel (*Fig. 3*).

**RAILS.** Four long rails (C) join the legs at the front and back (*Fig. 4*). Twin tenons are cut on the ends of each to fit the twin mortises in the legs (*Fig. 4a*).

When the twin tenons on the rails fit the mortises in the legs, the rails are almost complete. All that's left is to cut a small 1/4" x 1/2" rabbet on the rails at the back of the case (*Figs. 4 and 4a*). (These rabbets are for a plywood back that will be added later.)

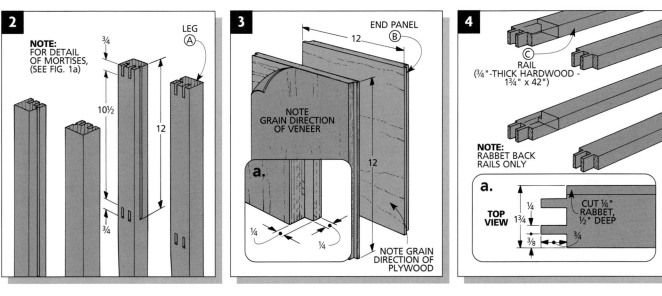

**2** NOTE: FOR DETAIL OF MORTISES, (SEE FIG. 1a) — 3/4 — 10½ — 12 — 3/4 — LEG Ⓐ

**3** END PANEL Ⓑ — 12 — NOTE GRAIN DIRECTION OF VENEER — a. — 1/4 — 1/4 — 12 — NOTE GRAIN DIRECTION OF PLYWOOD

**4** Ⓒ RAIL (3/4"-THICK HARDWOOD - 1¾" x 42") — NOTE: RABBET BACK RAILS ONLY — a. — TOP VIEW — 1/4 — 1¾ — 3/8 — 3/4 — CUT 1/4" RABBET, 1/2" DEEP

# SHOP JIG .................................... Leg Tapering Jig

With a formal project like the sideboard, the legs look better if they're tapered, rather than square. The fastest and easiest way to do this is with a table saw and a taper jig. I made this simple jig from a couple of pieces of scrap wood.

Start with a piece of plywood the same length as the tapered section on the actual leg (22¼") (*Fig. 1*). The width isn't that

critical. What's important is the amount the jig tapers from top to bottom (7/8").

I used the band saw to cut the taper on the plywood, then sanded the cut edge smooth. Finally, to hold the workpiece in the jig, I screwed a stop block to the wide end of the plywood.

**USING THE JIG.** To use the jig, first mark the width of the taper (7/8") on the

bottom end of the leg (*Fig. 2*). Then position the table saw rip fence so the blade aligns to the waste side of the mark. (Once the fence is set, leave it in place until all the legs have been tapered.)

Now taper the leg by sliding both the jig and the workpiece along the fence.

To cut the second taper, just roll the workpiece 90° and repeat the cut (*Fig. 3*).

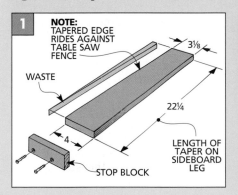

**1** NOTE: TAPERED EDGE RIDES AGAINST TABLE SAW FENCE — 3⅛ — WASTE — 22¼ — 4 — LENGTH OF TAPER ON SIDEBOARD LEG — STOP BLOCK

**2** 7/8 — RIP FENCE — WASTE SIDE — ALIGN BLADE TO LAYOUT MARK ON END OF LEG

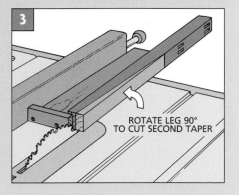

**3** ROTATE LEG 90° TO CUT SECOND TAPER

**B**igger isn't always better. Take a mortise and tenon joint, for instance. Instead of one large mortise and tenon, it may be better to cut two small tenons that fit in two small mortises (see photo). Why? It all has to do with the orientation of the workpiece that fits into the mortises (the piece with the tenons).

**VERTICAL RAILS.** With most projects (like tables, for instance) the rails or stretchers are joined to the legs vertically. That is, they're oriented up and down (*Fig. 1*). With this joint, there's a lot of good face grain to face grain gluing surface on the long cheeks of the tenon.

**HORIZONTAL RAILS.** But the rails on the sideboard are different. They face down, so they sit horizontal, not vertical (*Fig. 1*). This creates an opening for the drawers. But this orientation also creates a problem. Instead of one wide rail with good gluing surface, what you end up with are two thin rails with poor gluing surface. The faces on the top and bottom of the tenon are glued to end grain — not a strong glue joint.

**SOLUTION.** The solution to this problem is to cut two mortises and two tenons (*Fig. 2*). While this may look like it weakens the joint because the parts of the joint are smaller, that's not the case.

What the twin tenons do is increase the glue surface. Doubling the mortises and tenons adds two more cheeks inside the joint. So there is twice as much good gluing surface that's available.

**MORE WORK?** Okay, a twin mortise and tenon joint is a good choice for joining legs to narrow (thin) rails. But isn't cutting two mortises and two tenons going to be twice the work of a traditional (single) mortise and tenon joint?

Well, there are twice the usual number of cuts. But that doesn't mean there are twice as many setups. In fact, the number of setups is practically the same.

For the Classic Sideboard, the rails and legs are designed to be identical in width. This means the outside cheeks of each mortise (and each tenon) can be the same distance from the edges of the workpiece. So the two mortises on each leg (and the two outside cheeks of the tenons) can be cut with one setup each. You just flip the workpiece around.

**SEQUENCE.** As with any mortise and tenon joint, I prefer to cut the mortises first (see below). All this requires is just one setup on the drill press. Then the walls and ends of the mortises can quickly be cleaned up with a chisel.

Later, the tenons can be cut slightly oversize on a table saw. And finally, to achieve a perfect fit, they're trimmed with a chisel (see the step-by-step sequence on the facing page).

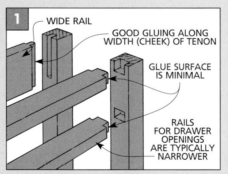

**1** WIDE RAIL
GOOD GLUING ALONG WIDTH (CHEEK) OF TENON
GLUE SURFACE IS MINIMAL
RAILS FOR DRAWER OPENINGS ARE TYPICALLY NARROWER

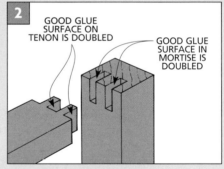

**2** GOOD GLUE SURFACE ON TENON IS DOUBLED
GOOD GLUE SURFACE IN MORTISE IS DOUBLED

## TWIN MORTISES

There's nothing unusual about drilling twin mortises. It's very similar to drilling a single mortise. The process takes just three simple steps.

First, the mortises are laid out in the desired locations on each leg (refer to *Step 1* at right and *Figs. 1a and 2* on pages 60 and 61).

**Note:** For the sideboard, the mortises are $\frac{1}{4}$" wide, $\frac{3}{4}$" deep, and $\frac{3}{4}$" long. And remember to lay out the open mortises at the top of each leg.

Second, a fence is clamped to the drill press table and is used to position the leg for drilling the first mortise. After drilling the first mortise, the piece is flipped end for end for the second mortise (*Step 2*). Because the outside cheeks of

the mortises are the same distance from the outside edges of the leg, every mortise can be drilled using this setup.

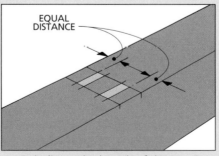

EQUAL DISTANCE

**1** *To indicate the length of the mortises, lay out the top and bottom of all the mortises on each workpiece. Then lay out the four sides to indicate the width.*

The third step (not shown) is to use a chisel to clean up the sides of each mortise and to square up the ends.

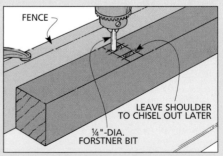

FENCE
LEAVE SHOULDER TO CHISEL OUT LATER
$\frac{1}{4}$"-DIA. FORSTNER BIT

**2** *Install a Forstner bit in the drill press, then clamp a fence to the table. Now each mortise is drilled with overlapping holes, then cleaned up with a chisel.*

# TWIN TENONS

Just like the mortises, the twin tenons are symmetrical, so there are only two setups. I started with the outside cheeks.

**OUTSIDE CHEEKS.** The first thing to do is to position the table saw rip fence as a stop for cutting the shoulders of the tenon (*Steps 1, 2, and 3* below). This determines the length of the tenon.

Next adjust the height of the blade to establish the cheeks — but don't try to get it perfect the first time. Make a series of overlapping cuts for the first cheek (*Step 1*). Then flip the workpiece over and cut the second cheek (*Step 2*).

Check the overall width of the tenon against the mortises (see photo at right).

Raise the blade and trim a little more off if necessary. But remember, the cheeks will be trimmed later, so don't remove too much wood at this point. In fact, there should be some small ridges for you to clean up later (*Step 3*).

**INSIDE CHEEKS.** The inside cheeks are cut next. I lay them out directly from the mortises. To do this, just set the workpiece over the mortises and make a mark (see photo at right). Like the outside cheeks, the inside cheeks also require only one setup. But this time, the workpiece stands on end (*Steps 4, 5, and 6*).

**TRIM TO FIT.** After both tenons have been roughed out, test their fit in the mortises (*Step 7*). Most likely, the cheeks and shoulders will need to be trimmed for a perfect fit (*Steps 8 and 9*).

**Mark tenons.** *The mortises on the leg can be used to quickly indicate the position of the tenons on the rail.*

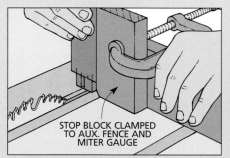

**1** All cuts for the twin tenons can be made on the table saw. An auxiliary fence on the miter gauge prevents chipout on the back side of the cut.

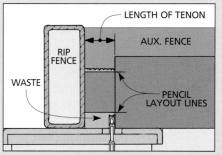

**2** The distance between the rip fence and the outside of the saw blade establishes the length of the tenon. The waste is cleaned out with overlapping cuts.

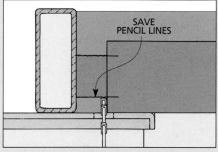

**3** Sneak up on the final size of the cheeks (just below the pencil marks). The small ridges left on the cheeks will be shaved for a perfect fit in the mortises.

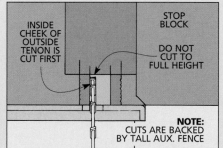

**4** The inside cheeks of the tenons are cut with the workpiece standing on end. A stop block clamped to the auxiliary fence helps support the workpiece.

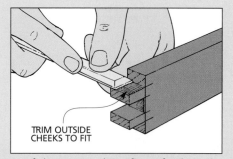

**5** To cut the inside cheeks, first raise the saw blade to just under the shoulder. Then clamp a stop block to the auxiliary fence to cut the inside cheek.

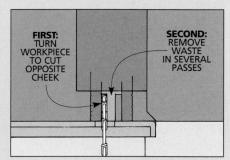

**6** Without changing your setup, turn the workpiece so the opposite edge is against the stop block. Then cut the cheek and remove the waste between the tenons.

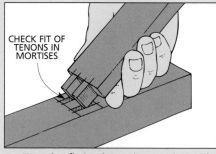

**7** Test the fit in the twin mortises. The cheeks and shoulders will probably have to be shaved for a perfect fit.

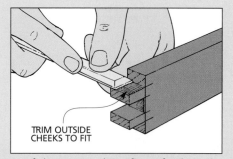

**8** If the tenons don't fit perfectly in the mortise, use a chisel to remove the ridges on the outside cheeks.

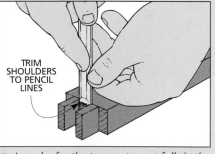

**9** In order for the tenons to seat fully in the mortises, the shoulders of the tenons also need to be slightly back-cut.

**BOTTOM PANEL.** Next, I added a piece of ³/₄"-thick plywood for the bottom panel (D). To determine the size of this panel, simply dry-assemble the case and measure the opening *(Fig. 5)*.

Grooves and hardwood splines hold the bottom in place *(Fig. 6)*. This way, the bottom panel doesn't need to be notched to fit around the legs. And all the ³/₈"-deep grooves can be cut with the same setup (see the Shop Tip at right). When the grooves were routed, I cut ¹¹/₁₆"-wide splines (E). (These are a little narrow to allow room for excess glue.)

**ASSEMBLY.** Now the case is ready to be assembled. First, two end assemblies are made by gluing the end panels between the legs *(Fig. 6)*. When these are dry, all that's left is to connect the end assemblies with the rails and the bottom panel.

**DIVIDERS.** At this point, the outside of the case is complete. The next step is to add the dividers for the drawer openings. Both the vertical and horizontal dividers are plywood with edging strips.

**VERTICAL DIVIDERS.** Start with the two vertical dividers (F) first *(Fig. 7)*. To determine their height (length), measure between the two rails.

**Note:** Measure at the ends of the case, not the center, to get an accurate reading.

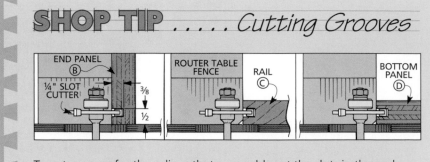

**SHOP TIP ..... *Cutting Grooves***

To cut grooves for the splines that join the bottom panel to the sides and rails, I used a ¼" slot cutter bit in the router table. This way, I could rout the slots in the end panels, rails, and bottom with the same setup. And I didn't have to stand the bottom panel on end.

As for their depth (width), the dividers align with the edge of the rabbet in the back of the rails and are set back ³/₄" from the front *(Fig. 7a)*. This ³/₄" is for a strip of solid wood edging that will cover the plywood edge of the divider.

After the dividers are cut to size, two things must be done before they can be installed inside the case.

First, cut a ³/₈"-deep dado that's centered on the inside face of each vertical divider *(Fig. 7a)*. These dadoes will hold the horizontal divider, which is also a piece of ³/₄"-thick plywood *(Fig. 8)*.

When the dadoes are cut, apply a strip of ³/₄"-wide vertical edging (G) to the front of each divider. Then the dividers can be screwed in the case *(Fig. 7)*.

**Note:** When installing the vertical dividers, it's critical that they're parallel to the sides of the case. Otherwise, you'll have trouble later fitting the drawers.

**HORIZONTAL DIVIDER.** The next to last piece to add to the case is the horizontal divider (H). Just cut the plywood to fit between the dadoes in the vertical divider and glue it in place *(Fig. 8)*. Finally, add a strip of horizontal edging (I).

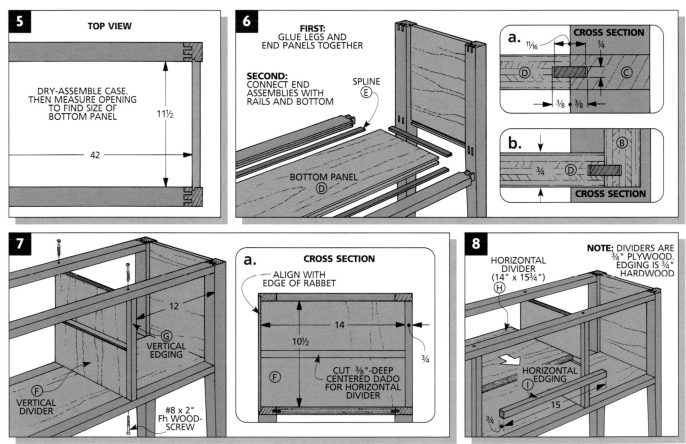

# DESIGNER'S NOTEBOOK

*Straight legs, quartersawn oak and veneer, and a change in hardware make the sideboard into a Mission piece. Replacing the large drawers with doors provides for more versatile storage.*

## CONSTRUCTION NOTES:

■ The legs on this sideboard are not tapered. Otherwise, they are identical to the legs on the Classic Sideboard.

■ When assembling the case, the vertical dividers (F) are positioned to make the outside openings $11\frac{1}{4}$" wide instead of 12" wide *(Fig. 1)*. This means the horizontal divider (H) and horizontal edging (I) need to be longer as well.

■ When building the drawers, note that the fronts and backs (M) are longer *(Fig. 2)*. Also, the outside openings in the case won't need drawer guides.

■ The drawer false fronts (R) are cut to fit the openings with $\frac{1}{16}$" of clearance on all sides. Because they are solid wood, no beading is needed.

■ The doors are typical frame and panel assemblies joined with stub tenons and grooves *(Fig. 3)*. The rails (Z) and stiles (AA) are sized to leave a $\frac{1}{16}$" gap around the doors.

■ Also, mortises for the hinges are cut on the inside door stiles *(Fig. 3)*.

■ The door panels (BB) are solid wood, so to allow for expansion they're $\frac{1}{8}$" narrower than the distance between the grooves *(Fig. 3)*. When you glue up the doors, make sure the panels are not glued into the frame, but float freely.

■ Finally, add the magnetic catches to the cabinet and the pulls to the doors and drawers *(Figs. 1, 2, and 3)*.

MISSION-STYLE SIDEBOARD

## MATERIALS LIST

### CHANGED PARTS

| | | |
|---|---|---|
| H | Horiz. Divider (1) | $\frac{3}{4}$ ply - 14 x $17\frac{1}{4}$ |
| I | Horiz. Edging (1) | $\frac{3}{4}$ x $\frac{3}{4}$ - $16\frac{1}{2}$ |
| M | Drawer Fr./Bk. (4) | $\frac{1}{2}$ x $4\frac{3}{8}$ - 16 |
| O | Drawer Bottoms (2) | $\frac{1}{4}$ ply - $12\frac{1}{2}$ x $15\frac{1}{2}$ |
| P | Drawer Guides (4) | $\frac{3}{4}$ x $\frac{1}{2}$ - $13\frac{1}{4}$ |
| R | False Fronts (2) | $\frac{3}{4}$ x $4\frac{3}{4}$ - $16\frac{3}{8}$ |

### NEW PARTS

| | | |
|---|---|---|
| Z | Door Rails (4) | $\frac{3}{4}$ x 3 - $5\frac{7}{8}$ |
| AA | Door Stiles (4) | $\frac{3}{4}$ x 3 - $10\frac{3}{8}$ |
| BB | Door Panels (2) | $\frac{1}{4}$ x $5\frac{3}{4}$ - $5\frac{1}{8}$ |

### HARDWARE SUPPLIES

(6) $1\frac{1}{8}$" Mission-style square pulls
(2 pr.) $1\frac{1}{2}$" x $1\frac{1}{4}$" brass butt hinges
(2) $\frac{1}{2}$" x $\frac{3}{4}$" x $\frac{7}{8}$" magnetic catches
(7 sq. ft.) Quartersawn white oak veneer

**Note:** Do not need parts J, K, L, Q, S, T, U, brass bail pulls, and maple veneer.

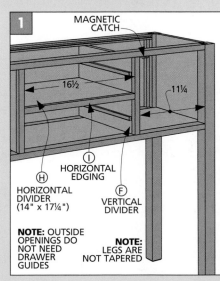

**1** MAGNETIC CATCH

$16\frac{1}{2}$ — $11\frac{1}{4}$

HORIZONTAL EDGING (I)

HORIZONTAL DIVIDER (14" x $17\frac{1}{4}$") (H)

VERTICAL DIVIDER (F)

**NOTE:** OUTSIDE OPENINGS DO NOT NEED DRAWER GUIDES

**NOTE:** LEGS ARE NOT TAPERED

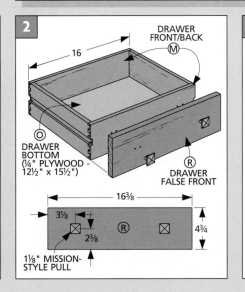

**2** DRAWER FRONT/BACK (M)

16

DRAWER BOTTOM ($\frac{1}{4}$" PLYWOOD - $12\frac{1}{2}$" x $15\frac{1}{2}$") (O)

DRAWER FALSE FRONT (R)

$16\frac{3}{8}$ — $3\frac{1}{8}$ — $2\frac{3}{8}$ — $4\frac{3}{4}$

$1\frac{1}{8}$" MISSION-STYLE PULL

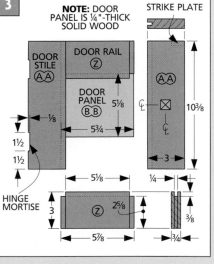

**3** NOTE: DOOR PANEL IS $\frac{1}{4}$"-THICK SOLID WOOD

STRIKE PLATE

DOOR STILE (AA)

DOOR RAIL (Z)

DOOR PANEL (BB)

(AA)

$\frac{1}{8}$ — $5\frac{1}{8}$ — $5\frac{3}{4}$ — $10\frac{3}{8}$

$1\frac{1}{2}$ — $1\frac{1}{2}$ — $5\frac{1}{8}$ — $\frac{1}{4}$ — 3

HINGE MORTISE

3 — (Z) — $2\frac{5}{8}$ — $\frac{3}{8}$

$5\frac{7}{8}$ — $\frac{3}{4}$

# TECHNIQUE ............... *Veneering*

I've worked with veneers quite a bit (mainly the paper-backed variety). So when I came across some large pieces of curly maple veneer, I thought it would be a good chance to try natural veneer.

## PREPARING THE VENEER

Natural, solid-wood veneers are so thin they "memorize" the way they've been stored. So before actually working with veneer, you want to make it as flat as possible. Of course, you might get lucky and find some pretty flat sheets. But many times the pieces of veneer will be curled and cupped, especially the highly figured varieties.

Fortunately, it's not very difficult to flatten veneer. You just have to change its memory. To do that, I use a little water. The key word being "little." Just wipe the back of the veneer with a damp sponge.

The veneer will react almost immediately. But probably not in the way you'd expect. My pieces started to curl and roll like bacon in a hot frying pan. But that's okay. It means the veneer can now be "trained" to lie flat.

To do that, simply sandwich the veneer between two sheets of plywood and weigh down the top *(Step 1)*.

**Note:** To help absorb any excess moisture, I used brown paper (like grocery bags) between the pieces.

**TRUING THE EDGE.** Natural veneer comes in varying widths, usually nothing wider than 12". That means you'll need to join (splice) pieces together to cover wide areas (like the top on the sideboard).

The goal here is to end up with a tight-fitting, nearly invisible seam between the pieces. To do that, you need to square up an edge on each piece of veneer. I tried using a sharp utility knife and a straightedge. But halfway through the cut the knife decided to follow the veneer grain instead of the straightedge.

Then I switched to the jointer. The secret to using this method is making sure the veneer doesn't move during the entire cut. To do that, I used a couple of

scrap 1x6s and clamped the veneer between them *(Step 2)*.

But I couldn't just run the boards through the jointer. The clamps holding the boards together hit the fence. So I fastened an auxiliary fence to the jointer bed to provide clearance *(Step 2)*.

With the auxiliary fence in place, I ran the boards and veneer over the jointer, checking for chipout after each pass. One of my pieces had a small knot located on the jointed edge. So I used a knife to cut off a strip of veneer removing the knot. Then I finished squaring up the pieces on the jointer.

**JOINING THE VENEER.** Once the veneer edges are square, they can be joined together. But there was a problem. I planned on using contact cement, and it bonds immediately. That makes it difficult to butt the pieces together for an invisible seam without getting them stuck to the core. (The core is what the veneer will be glued to.) So I tried something a little different. I edge glued the veneer pieces together first.

The pieces of veneer that I was using were $1/28$" thick. Now I know you're probably thinking that the veneer is too thin to edge glue. But there is a wide enough surface for the yellow glue to hold the pieces together *(Step 3)*. I also used several pieces of tape to hold the seam tight until the glue dried *(Step 4)*. By "walking"

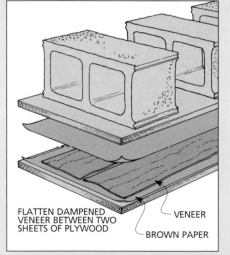

FLATTEN DAMPENED VENEER BETWEEN TWO SHEETS OF PLYWOOD — VENEER — BROWN PAPER

**1** *Lightly dampen the veneer, then press it overnight between two weighted sheets of plywood. Sheets of brown wrapping paper will help absorb the moisture.*

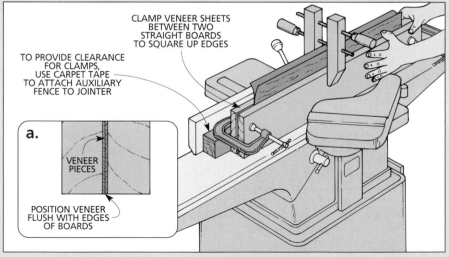

CLAMP VENEER SHEETS BETWEEN TWO STRAIGHT BOARDS TO SQUARE UP EDGES

TO PROVIDE CLEARANCE FOR CLAMPS, USE CARPET TAPE TO ATTACH AUXILIARY FENCE TO JOINTER

a.

VENEER PIECES

POSITION VENEER FLUSH WITH EDGES OF BOARDS

**2** *Straight and square edges are needed to join veneer pieces to get an invisible seam. The edges of the veneer can be trued up on the jointer. First, clamp the veneer between two pieces of scrap with the mating edges down. Then run the assembly across the jointer. Make as many passes as needed until the jointed edges are free from chipout.*

my fingers down the joint, I closed the seam while taping the pieces together.

**Note:** Using clear strapping tape made it easy for me to check for a tight seam.

## PREPARING THE CORE

While the glue on the edges dried, I got the core piece ready. There are several materials that will work for a core. The important thing is that the core is flat, smooth, and stable. (I used birch plywood, but medium density fiberboard or high density particleboard also work.)

To prepare the core, I simply cut it slightly larger than the piece of veneer. But you need to keep one thing in mind. When adding veneer to plywood, what you're really doing is adding another ply. So it's best to cut the plywood core so the grain of the veneer will run across the grain on the plywood when it's glued down. This keeps the panel stable.

**Note:** If your veneered panel won't be held in a frame (like the sides of a cabinet), it's a good idea to veneer both sides so the core won't warp. But if you veneer both sides, you'll have to cut the core to finished size now. The overhanging veneer will be trimmed flush later.

## GLUE UP

At this point, you're ready to glue the veneer to the core. I used a contact adhesive so I could eliminate all the clamps and fixtures that are needed with other kinds of glue. Contact adhesives come in two types: solvent-based and water-based.

I tried the water-based adhesive first. It looked promising: no fumes and easy cleanup. But there was a problem. The water in the adhesive made the veneer expand. Then as the water evaporated and the veneer dried, the pieces shrank back to original size. So my nice tight seam would always open up.

To solve this problem, I switched to a solvent-based contact adhesive. The solvents don't expand the veneer, which eliminates the problem with shrinkage. Applying the adhesive is easy. Just use a foam brush and spread an even coat on both the core and the veneer. After it's dry (usually 15 minutes), I apply a thin second coat over the first.

**INSTALLATION.** Once the second coat of glue is dry, the veneer can be attached to the core. The thing to keep in mind is that contact adhesive bonds instantly. So you want to position the veneer exactly where you want it the first time.

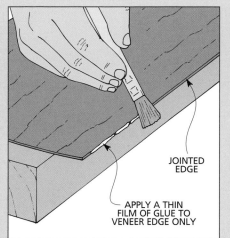

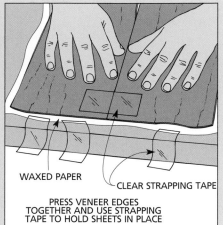

**3** Next, spread a thin film of glue along the jointed edges to hold the veneer pieces together. A brush makes it easier to apply the glue evenly.

**4** Butt the veneer pieces together and use clear strapping tape to hold them together. Waxed paper under the veneer keeps it from sticking to the work surface.

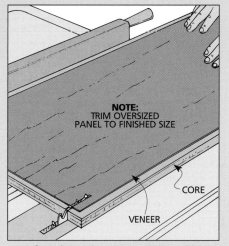

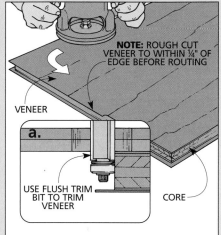

**5** After gluing the veneer to the substrate (I used contact cement), cut the panel to size on the table saw. A fine tooth blade reduces chipout — especially on crosscuts.

**6** Rough-trim the veneer with a razor knife. Then use a flush trim bit to trim the overhanging veneer flush with the core. Rout in a counterclockwise direction.

To help me get things lined up, I put sheets of waxed paper between the veneer and core. That way, you can slide the veneer around until it's in position. Then slip the sheets out from under the veneer as you press it into place.

For a good bond, the veneer needs to be pressed down firmly. I used a hard rubber roller and rolled the entire veneer sheet. By starting at the joint line and working toward the sides, any air bubbles under the veneer get squeezed out.

## TRIM & FINISH

Once the veneer has been attached to the core and rolled down, you can immediately cut the panel to size. I used the table saw to cut my oversize panel to finished size (Step 5). It's best to use a blade with

at least 50 teeth to keep chipout to a minimum. Another way to reduce chipout is to cut the panel with the veneered side up.

**Note:** If both sides of the panel have been veneered, the table saw method won't work. Instead, use a flush trim bit in your router. That way you can trim both sides without breaking the veneer that overhangs the edges (Step 6).

**FINISHING.** The veneer can be finished like solid wood. I sanded my panel first to make sure that any contact adhesive or fingerprints were removed. But remember, don't sand for too long in one spot (especially if you're using a power finish sander). It doesn't take much to sand through the thin veneer.

When the sanding is completed, you can stain and varnish the veneer just like the rest of the project.

With the case complete, work on the drawers can begin. There are two deep drawers and two shallow drawers. All four are made with ½"-thick soft maple and have dovetails at the front and back. And later, false fronts are added.

**DRAWERS.** The dovetails on the drawer pieces were routed with a jig, so the height of each had to be a multiple of ⁷⁄₈". This leaves a half pin at the top and bottom of the drawer *(Fig. 9)*. The large drawer fronts (J), backs (J), and sides (K) are 9⅝" tall (wide). The small drawer fronts (M), backs (M), and sides (N) are 4⅜" tall. As for the width and depth of the drawers, the fronts and backs are ½" narrower than the openings. And the sides are 12¾" long. For the drawer bottoms (L, O), I used ¼"-thick maple plywood set in ¼"-deep grooves. (The tops of these grooves are located ½" from the bottom of each piece.)

**DRAWER GUIDES.** When the drawers are built, the next step is to add the drawer guides (P) to the case. (The false fronts will be added to the drawers later.) These guides are just ¾" x ½" strips of hard maple *(Fig. 10a)*.

Getting the guides positioned correctly can be tricky. There are two things you need to get right. First, the guides have to be mounted parallel to the bottom. A quick and easy way to do this is to make a spacer for each guide to set on *(Fig. 11)*.

Second, the guides have to be set back ¾" to allow for the false drawer fronts. To do this, I simply marked these locations inside the case and lined up the guides with the marks *(Fig. 10a)*.

**FITTING THE DRAWERS.** With the guides in place, it's time to fit the drawers. The goal here is to end up with a snug, smooth fit with no side-to-side movement.

Start by cutting a centered groove in each drawer side *(Figs. 12 and 12a)*. These grooves are cut so the drawers fit over the guides in the case. But to get the drawers to slide in and out easily requires a little custom fitting (refer to the Shop Tip on the next page).

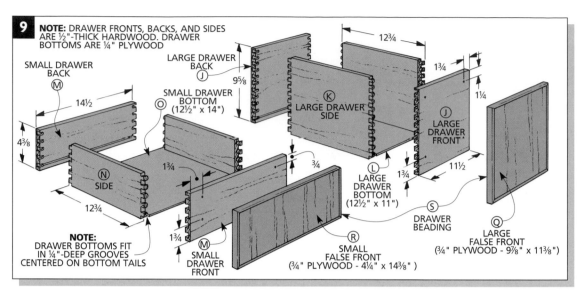

**9** NOTE: DRAWER FRONTS, BACKS, AND SIDES ARE ½"-THICK HARDWOOD. DRAWER BOTTOMS ARE ¼" PLYWOOD

SMALL DRAWER BACK (M)

LARGE DRAWER BACK (J)

SMALL DRAWER BOTTOM (O) (12½" x 14")

LARGE DRAWER SIDE (K)

LARGE DRAWER FRONT (J)

SIDE (N)

NOTE: DRAWER BOTTOMS FIT IN ¼"-DEEP GROOVES CENTERED ON BOTTOM TAILS

SMALL DRAWER FRONT (M)

LARGE DRAWER BOTTOM (L) (12½" x 11")

DRAWER BEADING (S)

SMALL FALSE FRONT (R) (¾" PLYWOOD - 4¼" x 14⅜")

LARGE FALSE FRONT (Q) (¾" PLYWOOD - 9⅞" x 11⅜")

12¾    1¾    1¼    9⅝    14½    4⅜    12¾    1¾    1¾    ¾    11½

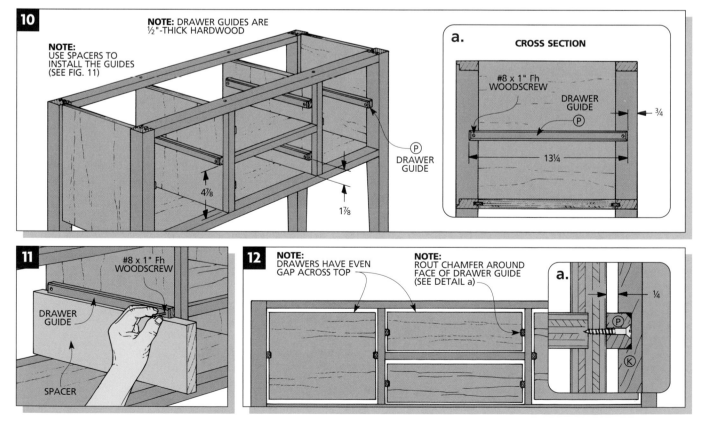

**10** NOTE: DRAWER GUIDES ARE ½"-THICK HARDWOOD

NOTE: USE SPACERS TO INSTALL THE GUIDES (SEE FIG. 11)

DRAWER GUIDE (P)

4⅞    1⅞

**a.** CROSS SECTION

#8 x 1" Fh WOODSCREW

DRAWER GUIDE (P)

¾    13¼

**11** #8 x 1" Fh WOODSCREW

DRAWER GUIDE

SPACER

**12** NOTE: DRAWERS HAVE EVEN GAP ACROSS TOP

NOTE: ROUT CHAMFER AROUND FACE OF DRAWER GUIDE (SEE DETAIL a)

**a.** ¼    (P)    (K)

The drawers in the sideboard ride on simple wood guides. So to get the drawers to slide in and out easily, the grooves need to be sized exactly.

**Note:** Before installing the wood guides, I chamfered their outside edges first *(Fig. 1a)*. This prevents the corners from breaking with use.

Getting all the grooves to fit the guides is a two-step process. First, I cut the grooves so each drawer fit tightly on its guides. Then I sanded the grooves until the drawers slid smoothly.

A dado blade in the table saw works best to cut the grooves. Use a scrap piece to test the width *(Fig. 1)*. Then set the rip fence so the grooves are centered on the sides of the drawers.

Now the depth of the grooves needs to be established. The goal here is a tight fit with no side-to-side movement. The best way to do this is to sneak up on the final depth *(Fig. 2)*. (I started by cutting the grooves just under ¼" deep.)

After making a pass on each side of a drawer, test the fit of the drawer in its opening. If it fits too tight (or doesn't fit at all), raise the blade a hair and cut the grooves again. But remember, you'll be cutting both grooves deeper, so make blade adjustments very small.

When each drawer fits snug in its opening, sand the bottom of the grooves until the drawer slides smoothly *(Fig. 2a)*. But don't sand the full length of the grooves, only the high spots.

Finally, I applied wax to both the grooves and the drawer guides.

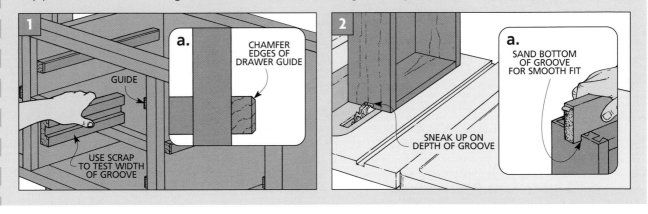

**FALSE FRONTS.** After all the drawers fit into their openings, the last step is to add the false fronts. The large and small false fronts (Q, R) are made from ¾"-thick plywood plus a layer of veneer. Usually, I cut drawer fronts to fit their openings with only a ¹⁄₁₆" gap on each side. But these false fronts are a little different. They're ⁵⁄₁₆" short on each side *(Fig. 13)*. In addition to the ¹⁄₁₆" gap, this extra ¼" allows for strips of beading to cover the edges of the plywood *(Fig. 14)*.

**BEADING.** To make the drawer beading (S), I started with overwidth blanks that have a ¹⁄₈" radius routed on all the edges (see the Shop Tip on page 70). This way I could get two strips from each blank.

To add the beading, I mitered each piece to length, then glued and clamped them to the false fronts *(Fig. 14a)*.

**ADDING THE FALSE FRONTS.** Now that the false fronts are complete, they can be mounted to the drawers *(Fig. 15)*. To do this, put some carpet tape on the back of each false front. Then center a false front in each opening and stick it to the drawer front. (Make sure there's an even gap all the way around.) Now, drill shank and pilot holes, remove the carpet tape, and screw the false fronts to the drawers.

To mount the brass pulls, drill two holes through both the false fronts and the drawer fronts *(Fig. 15a)*. These holes should be centered top-to-bottom and side-to-side. (Mine were 3" apart.) Finally, screw the pulls in place.

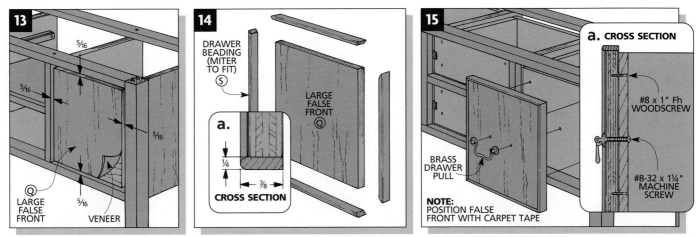

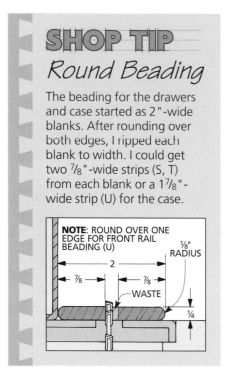

## SHOP TIP
### Round Beading

The beading for the drawers and case started as 2"-wide blanks. After rounding over both edges, I ripped each blank to width. I could get two $7/8$"-wide strips (S, T) from each blank or a $1\,7/8$"- wide strip (U) for the case.

**NOTE:** ROUND OVER ONE EDGE FOR FRONT RAIL BEADING (U)

$1/8$" RADIUS

2

$7/8$     $7/8$

WASTE

$1/4$

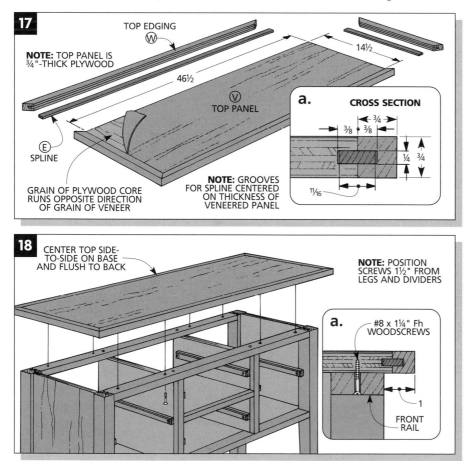

(SEE DETAIL b)

(U) FRONT RAIL BEADING (SEE DETAIL c)

END PANEL BEADING (SEE DETAIL a) (T)

**a.** (B) (T) (D) (A) $7/8$

**b.** TOP VIEW $1/8$" RADIUS AT ENDS OF BEADING (U)

**c.** (A) (U) (C) $1\,7/8$

## CASE BEADING

The same beading that surrounds the drawers is also applied to the bottom edges of the case. But here you need two different sizes to match the pieces they're glued to. The beading under the end panels is the same as the beading around the drawers (*Fig. 16a*). But the beading at the front rail is wider (*Fig. 16c*).

Again, I started out with 2"-wide blanks just like the drawer beading (see the Shop Tip above left). The blank for the end panel beading (T) is ripped into two $7/8$"-wide pieces. The blank for the front rail beading (U) is ripped $1\,7/8$" wide.

After the beading strips are cut to length to fit between the legs, they can be added to the case. The end panel beading strips are simply glued on flush with the inside of the end panels (*Fig. 16a*).

But the beading along the front requires another step. Since the rails are flush with the legs, the ends of the beading stick out, creating tiny, sharp corners (*Fig. 16c*). So I sanded a $1/8$" radius on each (*Fig. 16b*). Then I glued the front rail beading in place.

## TOP & BACK

With the drawers in place, the sideboard is just about complete. The top and back are all that still need to be added.

**TOP.** I began with the top. Like the other panels, the top (V) is $3/4$" plywood that's veneered on one face (*Fig. 17*). This means the piece of plywood must be cut with the grain running across the width, not along the length. This allows the veneer to be applied across the grain.

The top needs hardwood strips to cover the edges of the plywood. To do this, I used the same method as on the bottom: grooves and splines (*Fig. 17*). The splines keep the top and the edging

**17** TOP EDGING (W)

**NOTE:** TOP PANEL IS $3/4$"-THICK PLYWOOD

$14\,1/2$

$46\,1/2$

(V) TOP PANEL

(E) SPLINE

GRAIN OF PLYWOOD CORE RUNS OPPOSITE DIRECTION OF GRAIN OF VENEER

**a.** CROSS SECTION

$3/8$  $3/4$  $3/8$

$1/4$  $3/4$

$11/16$

**NOTE:** GROOVES FOR SPLINE CENTERED ON THICKNESS OF VENEERED PANEL

**18** CENTER TOP SIDE-TO-SIDE ON BASE AND FLUSH TO BACK

**NOTE:** POSITION SCREWS $1\,1/2$" FROM LEGS AND DIVIDERS

**a.** #8 x $1\,1/4$" Fh WOODSCREWS

1

FRONT RAIL

The back of the sideboard is secured with over twenty screws, all spaced evenly around the plywood edge. That's a lot of screws to lay out.

To mark all the screw holes the same distance from the edge of the plywood, mount a ruler on a piece of scrap (see photo). This eliminates the need for a tape measure.

First, cut the piece of scrap to match the length of a 12" shop rule (see drawing). Then, cut a shallow rabbet along the edge to hold the rule in position.

Cut the width of the rabbet narrower than the rule. This way it hangs over the edge of the scrap. The amount of overhang should equal the inset of the woodscrews.

To make it even more useful, cut a rabbet on the other three edges of the tool (detail 'a'). This way, the tool can be used to lay out screw holes that require a different inset.

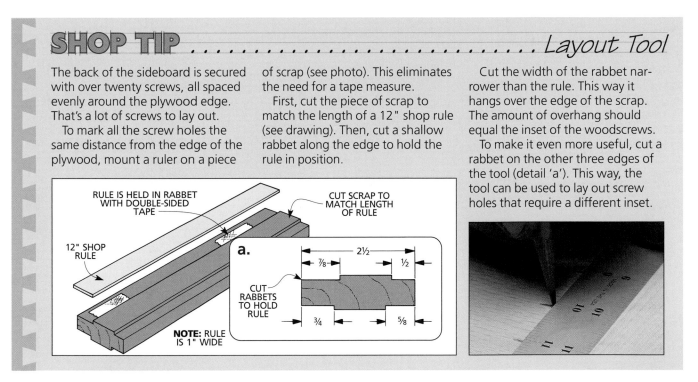

RULE IS HELD IN RABBET WITH DOUBLE-SIDED TAPE

12" SHOP RULE

CUT SCRAP TO MATCH LENGTH OF RULE

**NOTE:** RULE IS 1" WIDE

**a.**

CUT RABBETS TO HOLD RULE

$2\frac{1}{2}$

$\frac{7}{8}$ · $\frac{1}{2}$

$\frac{3}{4}$ · $\frac{5}{8}$

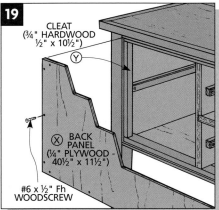

aligned, and no tongue needs to be cut on the plywood panel to fit the groove.

When the top edging (W) had been mitered and glued to the panel, I screwed the top to the case *(Fig. 18)*. (It's centered left to right but is flush at the back.)

**BACK PANEL.** Finally, I added a back panel (X) to the case *(Fig. 19)*. This is simply a $\frac{1}{4}$"-thick piece of maple plywood. This panel fits into the rabbets that have already been cut on the rails at the back of the case.

**Note:** The grain direction of the veneer on this plywood piece is the same as the grain on the end panels. It runs up and down (not lengthwise).

To install the back, I wanted to screw it to the top and bottom rails. That's no problem. These pieces have rabbets for accepting the panel. But to secure the back at the ends, I glued small maple cleats (Y) to the inside face of each back leg (flush with the shoulder of the rabbet) *(Fig. 16)*. Then I screwed the back to the cleats *(Fig. 19)*. This takes a good number of screws, so I came up with a tool to help me lay them all out neatly (see the Shop Tip above). ∎

**19**

CLEAT ($\frac{3}{4}$" HARDWOOD $\frac{1}{2}$" x $10\frac{1}{2}$")

Y

X BACK PANEL ($\frac{1}{4}$" PLYWOOD - $40\frac{1}{2}$" x $11\frac{1}{2}$")

#6 x $\frac{1}{2}$" Fh WOODSCREW

The brass pulls I chose for the sideboard were only available with a bright finish and looked too new (top pull in photo). But you can "instantly" age the pulls with an antiquing solution that darkens brass. (For sources, see page 126.)

Before you can use the solution, you need to remove the protective coating on the hardware. This can be done by soaking the hardware in acetone or lacquer thinner for about three minutes. Then remove the hardware and wipe it dry.

Now you can mix up a batch of antiquing solution. The solution is mildly corrosive. So it's a good idea to cover your work area with a piece of plastic. You should also wear safety goggles and rubber gloves.

First, mix three capfuls of darkening solution in a pint of water. Then place the hardware into the mixture and watch the darkening process begin. It only took about three minutes to get the antique appearance that I was after (bottom pull in photo). Leaving it in longer or using a stronger mixture will turn the brass darker.

When you have the look you want, remove the hardware from

the solution and rinse it with water to stop the darkening process.

Finally, to keep the hardware from darkening further, I applied several light coats of a spray lacquer finish (available at local hardware stores).

Special projects deserve a special finish. That's how I felt after deciding on curly maple veneer for the Classic Sideboard.

A dramatically figured wood like this deserves to be shown off. That's the perfect reason to use an aniline dye to highlight the grain and then top it off with the gloss from several built-up layers of brushing varnish.

Why not just use a wiping varnish? Good question.

Wiping varnish is a great finish for many projects. But for the Classic Sideboard I wanted more protection than you get with a wiping varnish. Also, I wanted a deeper, glossier appearance. Something that would highlight

the interesting grain patterns in the curly maple veneer emphasized by the dye.

**WHAT IT IS.** Wiping varnish and brushing varnish are very similar. But

brushing varnish has a higher concentration of oil and solids. This makes it thicker when it's applied and harder when it dries. It builds up in layers rather than soaking into the wood. Each coat gives you more build-up and also more protection.

**HOW IT WORKS.** But there are drawbacks. More oil and solids make brushing varnishes slower to dry. So drips and brush marks can develop, or dust can settle on the varnish before it dries.

But most of these problems can be prevented with careful preparation of the wood in advance. Or eliminated by following a certain technique for brushing and sanding between coats.

## ANILINE DYE

As I mentioned, I wanted to show off the curly maple figure of the sideboard. But if you're using an off-the-shelf stain, the pigments in them sit on top of the wood. So they tend to cover the grain. The solution is to use aniline dye.

**ANILINE DYES.** Instead of sitting on top of the wood, aniline dyes soak in and actually change the color of the wood. So they don't hide the grain at all. In fact, they enhance it by giving it more depth.

Aniline dyes come in powder form, so you have to mix them yourself. (For sources, see page 126.)

An added benefit to mixing your own stain is that you can control the color. I tried a number of dyes in a number of different combinations and concentrations.

I ended mixing two parts of Moser's Natural Antique Cherry and one part Bright Red Cherry in a pint of water.

**APPLYING THE STAIN.** Because it's mixed in water, the stain is very thin. So to prevent runs, the first thing I did was disassemble the sideboard as much as possible. That way, I could work on sections as they lay flat on a workbench.

To stain a section, flood the wood and keep it wet. If the stain is allowed to dry before you're through, it will leave lap marks. When the section is covered, wipe the stain off as evenly as possible.

Finished aniline stain and unfinished aniline stain are like night and day (see photo). After staining the sideboard, the next step is to apply the varnish.

*Aniline dye and topcoat. Without any top coat an aniline dye will look dull and flat when it dries (left). But don't worry. With the addition of a top coat, the depth of the color returns (right).*

## VARNISHING

When using a wiping varnish, I sand a project up to 220-grit. But for brushing varnish, I usually sand only to 180-grit. That's because the varnish needs something to grab onto.

**DUST-FREE.** When using a slow-drying finish like varnish, your worst enemy is dust. So it pays to think like a surgeon and keep everything clean. Isolate the project from everyday traffic. Give the finishing area a thorough cleaning. Also, give the project itself a good wipe-down with a cloth dampened in mineral spirits.

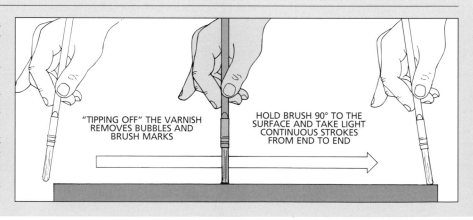

"TIPPING OFF" THE VARNISH REMOVES BUBBLES AND BRUSH MARKS

HOLD BRUSH 90° TO THE SURFACE AND TAKE LIGHT CONTINUOUS STROKES FROM END TO END

**BRISTLE BRUSH.** There's one tool that can make or break a varnish job and that's the brush. In the past I've had good success with a disposable foam brush. But for a larger project, a 2" to 3"-long China bristle is perfect. It will hold more varnish and distribute it more evenly than a nylon bristle or foam brush.

**WASH COAT.** Now a "wash coat" of varnish can be applied. I diluted my varnish with mineral spirits for this. This diluted first coat will penetrate the wood pores and dry faster than a full-strength coat.

To prepare the wash coat, I use a paper strainer (or cheese cloth) to strain some of the varnish into a glass container with an equal amount of mineral spirits. Straining prevents any globs or "skin" in the original container from getting on the brush or the project.

Now, start by flowing the varnish onto the project. The object is to spread the varnish evenly over the entire surface of the project. Use overlapping strokes working in the direction of the grain to spread and level the varnish.

**Note:** It helps to hold the brush at an angle while flowing on the varnish.

Then, to blend in the brush marks and remove air bubbles, hold the brush straight up and down to "tip off" the surface. This involves taking long, light, uninterrupted brush strokes from one end of the piece to the other (see drawing on opposite page). After tipping off the surface, stop brushing — too much will cause more brush marks.

Let the project dry for at least 24 hours (depending on the temperature and humidity in the finish room). The more time the varnish has to cure, the harder it becomes. And the easier it is to sand.

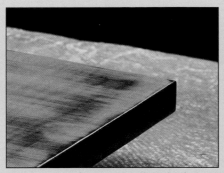

*Low spots. After wet-sanding, high spots on the finish show up as dull areas. Sand until the low shiny areas become dull too.*

**WET SAND.** After the first coat has dried, I like to wet-sand lightly with 400 wet/dry paper (see top photo on the facing page). Again, use a sanding block.

**Note:** If the sandpaper starts to clog up with gummy varnish, allow the varnish to dry some more.

The goal while wet-sanding is to bring down any high spots and remove any bubbles and brush marks (see left photo above). This is the messy part. But it's also one of the most important.

The sanding slurry that develops will even out the surface so the next coat of varnish goes on smoother and flatter.

**Note:** Don't sand too heavily or you may cut through the stain. But don't panic if you do. A small bare spot can always be touched up (right photo above).

Also, while you're sanding check the vertical surfaces for drips and runs. Before sanding them, scrape off the drips with a cabinet scraper.

**TACK CLEAN.** After a quick once-over with the sandpaper, examine the surface. Hold a bright light to the back of the project and sight across the surface from

*Touch-up. When sanding between coats, you might cut through the stain. Use a small sponge "dabber" as a touch-up tool.*

the front. This will highlight the high and low spots. Then use a clean tack cloth to remove the sanding dust.

**ADDITIONAL COATS.** Now begin building up the layers of varnish with several full-strength coats. Here the object is to level out the entire surface and build the depth and protection. You want the varnish to flow on smoothly and build up in consistent, thin layers, with fewer and fewer blemishes.

Now the procedure becomes repetitive. Apply another coat, building up the layers and filling in the low spots. Let dry, sand with wet/dry paper, tack clean, then build up again.

For surfaces that receive little wear, like the base on the sideboard, two full-strength coats is plenty. For heavily used surfaces, like the top, I apply at least four full-strength coats. Sometimes more.

When the varnish dries smooth and flat, I'll put on one last coat. But first do a final sanding with 600 wet/dry paper.

For a deep shine, I use gloss varnish for each coat. Then I rub it out after it has cured for several days (see below).

## RUBBING OUT THE TOP COAT

The goal with any built-up finish is to get closer to perfect with every additional coat. But you have to stop somewhere.

And when you do, there will probably still be some small blemishes. One good reason to "finish the finish."

**PUMICE.** The safest way to remove the few remaining blemishes is to rub out the finish with pumice. Pumice is a finer abrasive than wet/dry sandpaper. It comes in powder form in several grits. (I used 000 on the sideboard.)

Like any fine abrasive, pumice should be used with a lubricant to generate a slurry. (Water works fine.) The best tool for applying the pumice is a felt block (see photo at left). It's soft, flat, and works like a sanding block. (It's sort of like a chalkboard eraser.)

Start by wetting the block. Then sprinkle a little pumice on the surface. Now, rub the pumice into a slurry over every surface of the project. Wipe away the slurry with a clean soft cloth and repeat if any blemishes are still visible.

**ROTTENSTONE.** The second reason to rub out a finish is the shine. After rubbing out the blemishes, the surface of the sideboard looked a bit dull. So I went a step further to bring back an even gloss finish. Rottenstone was the answer.

Rottenstone is a powder finer than pumice. It's used the same way, just with a different felt block. The level of gloss just depends on the number of rubbings.

# Country Harvest Table

*Inspired by tables that seated a dozen hungry farm hands, this scaled-down version is easy to build. But from the tapered legs to the breadboard ends, there's more woodworking here than meets the eye.*

Building this harvest table is in some ways, a lot like taking a road trip. Half the fun is just getting to your destination. It's stopping at the little roadside diners and taking side excursions that make the journey enjoyable.

With this table, the side trips have more to do with the construction. All in all, it's not a difficult or unusual project to build. But there are a few things a bit out of the ordinary that make for some interesting woodworking challenges.

**TAPERED LEGS.** Take the legs for example. They have an unusual double taper profile. But unlike most tapered legs, I didn't cut these on the table saw. Instead I used a different technique that involves a band saw.

**TABLE TOP.** The top of the table is a glued-up panel with breadboard ends. But instead of simply pinning the ends to the top, I came up with a different method that uses some common hardware items. This helps strengthen the joint and allows the ends to be tightened if the wood shrinks over time.

**FINISH.** Finally comes the finish. Normally I don't like to cover up the beauty of natural wood. But this time, I thought I would try using a stain on the base of the table. And I have to say, I was pleased with the results.

The finished product also has some pretty neat features. Like a built-in drawer at each end to store silverware and napkins. And bolt-on legs that come off quickly so the table can be easily stored.

**OPTIONS.** There are several ways to customize this table. As shown on page 77, you can use ready-made turned legs instead of tapered legs. Or if you don't need a table this big, you can make a scaled-down version. I've detailed this (plus how to add a profile to the aprons) in the Designer's Notebook on page 86.

# EXPLODED VIEW

**OVERALL DIMENSIONS:**
36W x 65⅛D x 30¼H

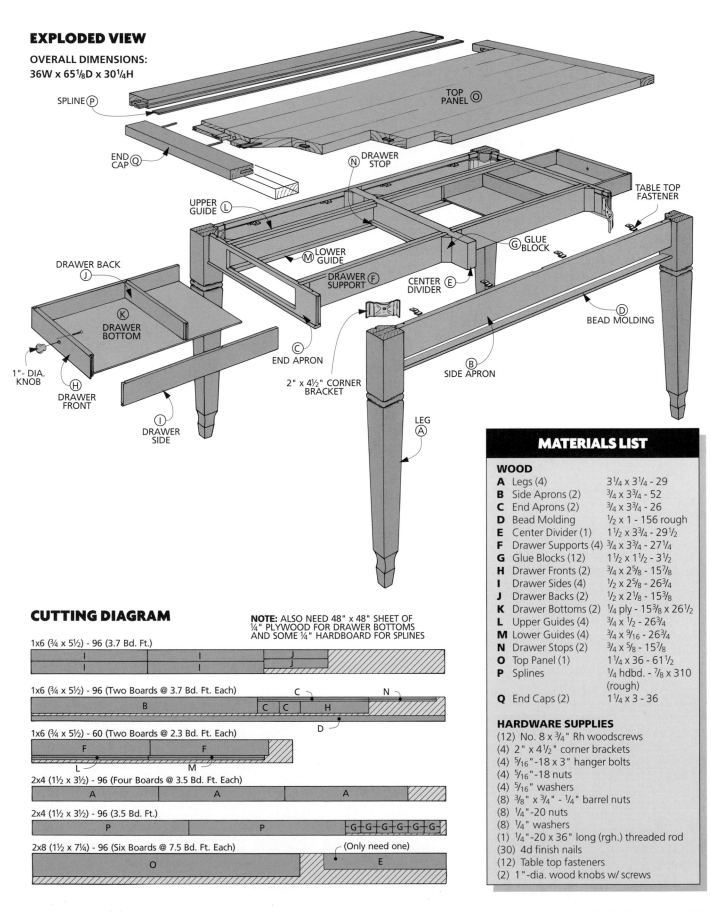

SPLINE (P)

TOP PANEL (O)

END CAP (Q)

DRAWER STOP (N)

UPPER GUIDE (L)

TABLE TOP FASTENER

LOWER GUIDE (M)

GLUE BLOCK (G)

DRAWER BACK (J)

DRAWER SUPPORT (F)

CENTER DIVIDER (E)

DRAWER BOTTOM (K)

1"- DIA. KNOB

DRAWER FRONT (H)

END APRON (C)

2" x 4½" CORNER BRACKET

SIDE APRON (B)

BEAD MOLDING (D)

DRAWER SIDE (I)

LEG (A)

## CUTTING DIAGRAM

**NOTE:** ALSO NEED 48" x 48" SHEET OF ¼" PLYWOOD FOR DRAWER BOTTOMS AND SOME ¼" HARDBOARD FOR SPLINES

1x6 (¾ x 5½) - 96 (3.7 Bd. Ft.)

| I | I | J |
| I | I | J |

1x6 (¾ x 5½) - 96 (Two Boards @ 3.7 Bd. Ft. Each)

C    N

| B | C C | H |
D

1x6 (¾ x 5½) - 60 (Two Boards @ 2.3 Bd. Ft. Each)

| F | F |
L    M

2x4 (1½ x 3½) - 96 (Four Boards @ 3.5 Bd. Ft. Each)

| A | A | A |

2x4 (1½ x 3½) - 96 (3.5 Bd. Ft.)

| P | P | G G G G G G |

2x8 (1½ x 7¼) - 96 (Six Boards @ 7.5 Bd. Ft. Each)

(Only need one)

| O | E |

## MATERIALS LIST

### WOOD

| | | |
|---|---|---|
| **A** | Legs (4) | 3¼ x 3¼ - 29 |
| **B** | Side Aprons (2) | ¾ x 3¾ - 52 |
| **C** | End Aprons (2) | ¾ x 3¾ - 26 |
| **D** | Bead Molding | ½ x 1 - 156 rough |
| **E** | Center Divider (1) | 1½ x 3¾ - 29½ |
| **F** | Drawer Supports (4) | ¾ x 3¾ - 27¼ |
| **G** | Glue Blocks (12) | 1½ x 1½ - 3½ |
| **H** | Drawer Fronts (2) | ¾ x 2⅝ - 15⅞ |
| **I** | Drawer Sides (4) | ½ x 2⅝ - 26¾ |
| **J** | Drawer Backs (2) | ½ x 2⅛ - 15⅜ |
| **K** | Drawer Bottoms (2) | ¼ ply - 15⅜ x 26½ |
| **L** | Upper Guides (4) | ¾ x ½ - 26¾ |
| **M** | Lower Guides (4) | ¾ x 9/16 - 26¾ |
| **N** | Drawer Stops (2) | ¾ x ⅝ - 15⅞ |
| **O** | Top Panel (1) | 1¼ x 36 - 61½ |
| **P** | Splines | ¼ hdbd. - ⅞ x 310 (rough) |
| **Q** | End Caps (2) | 1¼ x 3 - 36 |

### HARDWARE SUPPLIES

(12) No. 8 x ¾" Rh woodscrews
(4) 2" x 4½" corner brackets
(4) 5/16"-18 x 3" hanger bolts
(4) 5/16"-18 nuts
(4) 5/16" washers
(8) ⅜" x ¾" - ¼" barrel nuts
(8) ¼"-20 nuts
(8) ¼" washers
(1) ¼"-20 x 36" long (rgh.) threaded rod
(30) 4d finish nails
(12) Table top fasteners
(2) 1"-dia. wood knobs w/ screws

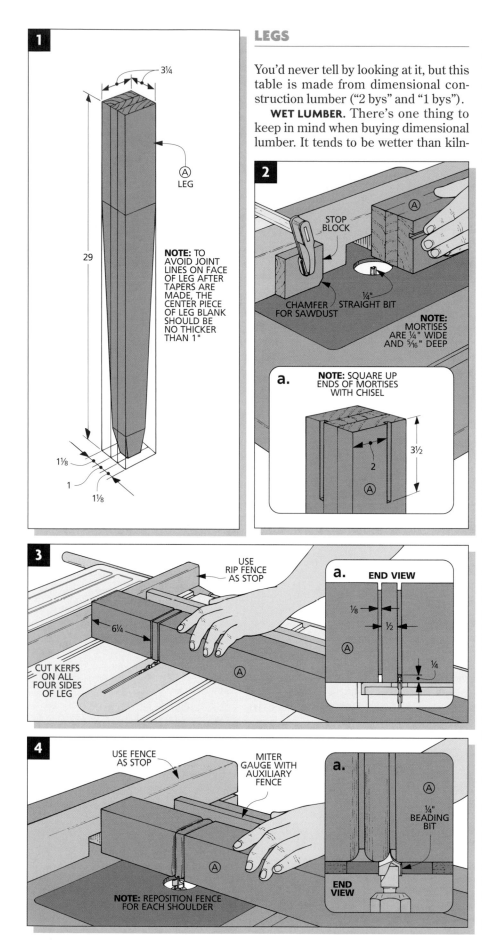

**NOTE:** TO AVOID JOINT LINES ON FACE OF LEG AFTER TAPERS ARE MADE, THE CENTER PIECE OF LEG BLANK SHOULD BE NO THICKER THAN 1"

A LEG

3¼

29

1⅛
1
1⅛

---

**2**

STOP BLOCK

CHAMFER FOR SAWDUST

¼" STRAIGHT BIT

A

**NOTE:** MORTISES ARE ¼" WIDE AND 5/16" DEEP

**a.** **NOTE:** SQUARE UP ENDS OF MORTISES WITH CHISEL

3½

2

A

---

**3**

USE RIP FENCE AS STOP

6¼

CUT KERFS ON ALL FOUR SIDES OF LEG

A

**a.** **END VIEW**

⅛

½

¼

A

A

---

**4**

USE FENCE AS STOP

MITER GAUGE WITH AUXILIARY FENCE

A

**NOTE:** REPOSITION FENCE FOR EACH SHOULDER

**a.**

A

¼" BEADING BIT

**END VIEW**

---

## LEGS

You'd never tell by looking at it, but this table is made from dimensional construction lumber ("2 bys" and "1 bys").

**WET LUMBER.** There's one thing to keep in mind when buying dimensional lumber. It tends to be wetter than kiln-dried hardwoods. So I buy my lumber a couple of weeks before I start construction of a project. That way, it can sit in my shop and dry out a little more.

**DOUBLE TAPERED LEGS.** I began work on this table by making the legs. I wanted them to be strong enough to support the table, but I didn't want them to look too heavy. So I tapered them.

**Note:** If you don't want to make the legs, another option is to purchase turned legs (see the Woodworker's Notebook on the opposite page).

Now, tapering a table leg to make it look more slender certainly isn't a new idea. But the legs on this table actually have a double taper. A long, narrow taper gives the leg its basic shape. Then a short, steeper taper near the bottom creates a "foot" for the leg to stand on *(Fig. 1)*.

The square blanks for the legs (A) are glued up out of three separate pieces. But to avoid cutting through the joint line when tapering the legs, the two outer pieces of the leg are thicker than the center piece *(Fig. 1)*.

Each leg has two mortises near the top to hold the aprons of the table. I found it easiest to make these mortises while the legs were still square. So after squaring up the blanks and cutting them to length, I stepped over to the router table and routed the ¼"-wide mortises *(Fig. 2)*.

**Note:** Using a stop block will ensure that all the mortises are the same length.

Notice that the mortises are open-ended at the top *(Fig. 2a)*. This design allows the legs to be removed from the table if you need to move or store it. (The legs aren't glued in place. Instead they'll be fastened to the aprons with some knock-down hardware.)

**BEAD.** After completing the mortises, the next step is to make the bead detail near the top of each leg. This is done in two stages. First, a pair of kerfs are cut on all four sides of each leg to establish the shoulders of the beads *(Figs. 3 and 3a)*.

Next, the edges of these kerfs are rounded over on a router table, using a special beading bit *(Figs. 4 and 4a)*.

Once this was done, I cut away a small section of the inside corner of each leg *(Fig. 5)*. This is simply to create a flat surface for the leg brackets that will be used to connect the legs to the aprons. I made these cuts on the band saw, using a simple V-block to hold the leg at a 45° angle while making the cut *(Fig. 5a)*.

**TWO TAPERS.** At this point, you're ready to create the tapers on the legs.

This is a two-step process. First, the long slender tapers are laid out and cut. Then you can make the short tapers that create the "foot" of each leg.

Because of the size of these legs, I cut the tapers on a band saw instead of a table saw. To do this, start by laying out the end of the long tapers on the bottom (end) of each leg *(Figs. 6a and 7)*. Then lay out the tapers on one face of the leg.

Now cut along the layout lines, staying just to the waste side *(Fig. 6)*.

Cut the tapers on the other three faces in the same manner, drawing the layout lines on one face at a time and then making the cuts before moving on to the taper on the next face *(Fig. 7)*.

**Note:** You'll want to save one of the waste pieces from tapering the legs. It will be used later when sanding the arcs.

Once I had all the long tapers roughed out, I cleaned up the faces of the legs by sanding down to the layout lines with a stationary belt sander. (You could also use a hand plane.)

# WOODWORKER'S NOTEBOOK
## READY-MADE LEGS

■ If you prefer the look of turned legs, you can build the Country Harvest Table with them, even if you don't own a lathe (see photo).

■ There are a number of mail-order sources that sell turned legs in several styles. (See Sources on page 126.) You'll still have to cut the mortises for the aprons, and shave the inside corner for the knock-down hardware.

■ When ordering your legs, it helps to pay attention to the dimensions. Most table legs are a standard 29" long. But the width can vary. Of the sources I checked, some legs are $3\frac{1}{4}$" square while others are $3\frac{1}{2}$". Either size will work, but the larger leg will stand proud of the aprons a little more than the smaller one.

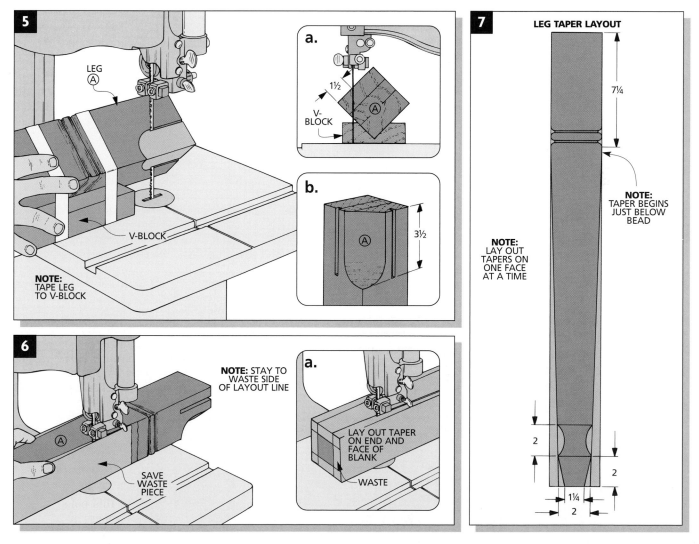

**5**

LEG Ⓐ

V-BLOCK

NOTE: TAPE LEG TO V-BLOCK

**a.** $1\frac{1}{2}$ V-BLOCK Ⓐ

**b.** Ⓐ $3\frac{1}{2}$

**6**

NOTE: STAY TO WASTE SIDE OF LAYOUT LINE

Ⓐ

SAVE WASTE PIECE

**a.** LAY OUT TAPER ON END AND FACE OF BLANK WASTE

**7** LEG TAPER LAYOUT

$7\frac{1}{4}$

NOTE: TAPER BEGINS JUST BELOW BEAD

NOTE: LAY OUT TAPERS ON ONE FACE AT A TIME

2

2

2

$1\frac{1}{4}$

2

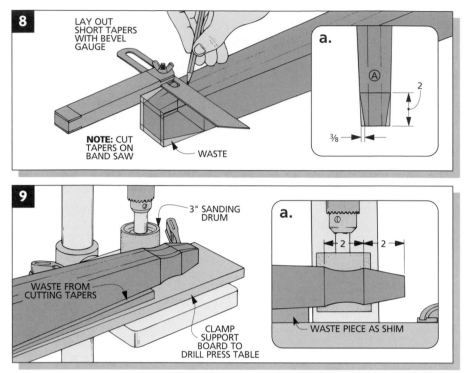

**8** LAY OUT SHORT TAPERS WITH BEVEL GAUGE

**NOTE:** CUT TAPERS ON BAND SAW

WASTE

**a.** Ⓐ  2  3/8

**9** 3" SANDING DRUM

WASTE FROM CUTTING TAPERS

CLAMP SUPPORT BOARD TO DRILL PRESS TABLE

**a.** Ⓒ  2  2

WASTE PIECE AS SHIM

**SHORT TAPERS.** To create a tapered foot at the bottom of each leg, I cut some short tapers, beginning just 2" from the bottom of each leg. These tapers are cut in the same manner as the longer ones — I drew layout lines around each leg and also on the bottom of the leg (*Figs. 8 and 8a*). Then I cut the tapers on the band saw and sanded them smooth.

**ARCS.** To create a softer transition between the two tapers, and to make the tapered foot stand out from the leg a little more, I sanded a shallow arc just above the start of the short taper.

To do this, I started by drawing a line around each leg 2" above the start of the short taper. Then using a 3"-dia. sanding drum on my drill press, I hollowed out the area between the layout line and the start of the taper (*Figs. 9 and 9a*).

And to hold the tapered leg level during sanding, I shimmed the leg using one of the wedge-shaped waste pieces left over from tapering the legs (*Fig. 9*).

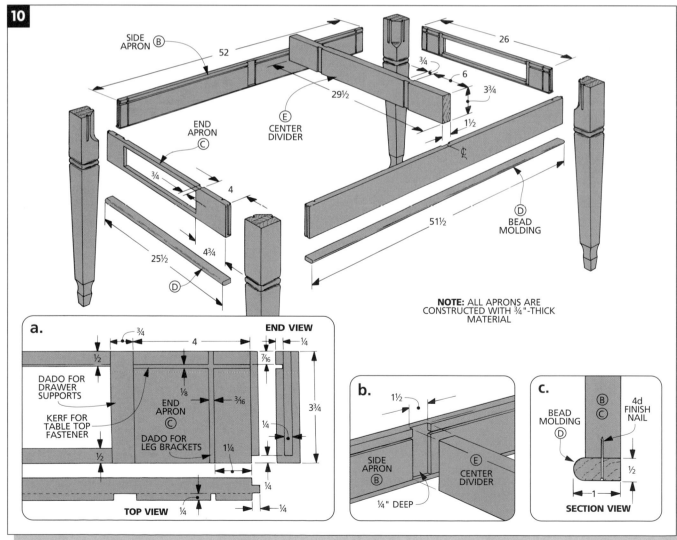

**10**

SIDE APRON Ⓑ  52

END APRON Ⓒ

CENTER DIVIDER Ⓔ

29½

3/4  6  3¾  1½

26

3/4  4

25½  4¾  Ⓓ

51½  BEAD MOLDING Ⓓ

₡

**NOTE:** ALL APRONS ARE CONSTRUCTED WITH ¾"-THICK MATERIAL

**a.** END VIEW

3/4  4  1/4  ½  7/16  1/8  3/16  3¾

DADO FOR DRAWER SUPPORTS

KERF FOR TABLE TOP FASTENER

END APRON Ⓒ

DADO FOR LEG BRACKETS

½  1¼  1/4  1/4  1/4  1/4

TOP VIEW

**b.** 1½

SIDE APRON Ⓑ

CENTER DIVIDER Ⓔ

¼" DEEP

**c.** SECTION VIEW

BEAD MOLDING Ⓓ

Ⓑ Ⓒ

4d FINISH NAIL

½  1

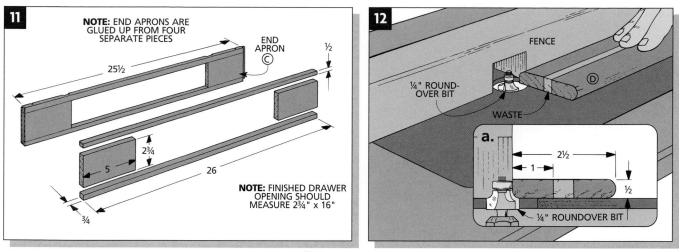

A long board underneath the leg helped support the workpiece.

**SANDING.** Finally, I eased the sharp edges on each leg by sanding them lightly. (Leave the top edges square.)

## APRONS & DIVIDER

The legs of the table are connected by a framework consisting of four aprons and a center divider *(Fig. 10)*. This creates a stable foundation for the top. Later, drawer supports will be added between the end aprons and the center divider.

To make the aprons, I started by cutting the apron blanks to size. For the two long side aprons (B), this is simply a matter of cutting a couple of pieces of $^3/_4$"-thick stock to size *(Fig. 10)*.

But the end aprons (C) are a little different. They have a rectangular opening in the center for a drawer. So to create this opening, I glued up each end apron out of four separate pieces *(Fig. 11)*.

**KERFS.** With the apron blanks cut to size, I cut a kerf on the inside face of each apron near the top edge. This kerf is for the fasteners that will be used to attach the top later *(Fig. 10a)*.

**DADOES.** Next, I cut dadoes in the aprons to hold the center divider, drawer supports, and leg hardware *(Figs. 10a and 10b)*. First, a $^3/_{16}$"-wide dado is cut near the end of each apron to hold the leg bracket *(Figs. 10a and 13)*. This is made in two passes with an ordinary saw blade.

When the table is assembled, a center divider will fit between the two side aprons, preventing them from bowing inward. To help hold this 1½"-thick divider in place, a dado is cut on the inside face of each side apron *(Fig. 10b)*.

While I was at it, I cut similar dadoes on the end aprons. But these dadoes are

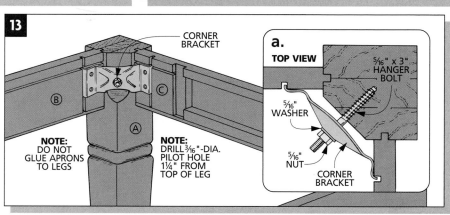

narrower because they're sized to hold the $^3/_4$"-thick drawer supports that are added later *(Fig. 10a)*.

**TENONS.** Once all the dadoes and grooves are cut, you can start cutting a tenon on each end of the aprons to fit the mortises in the legs *(Fig. 10a)*. These tenons don't get glued into the mortises on the legs. Their real purpose is to simply help align the legs with the aprons while the leg bracket hardware is tightened. (This allows the legs to be removed.) Because of this, the tenons are only ¼" long.

**BEAD MOLDING.** To dress up the aprons and support the center divider and drawer supports, I added a bead molding (D) to the bottom edge of the aprons *(Fig. 10c)*. This molding is made by rounding over the edges of a thin piece of stock, then ripping the molding to width *(Figs. 12 and 12a)*.

After cutting it to length, the molding is glued and nailed in place. The inside edges of the apron and molding should be flush *(Fig. 10c)*. Once this is done, you're ready to attach the legs to the aprons.

**HARDWARE.** In order to allow the legs to be removed from the table for moving or storage, the legs are fastened to the aprons with knock-down hardware rather than glue *(Fig. 13)*.

Installing the hardware involves nothing more than screwing a hanger bolt into each leg. (The hanger bolt is installed by threading a nut on one end and then using a wrench to screw it into a hole drilled in the leg.) The bolt fits into a hole in the corner bracket. Then a washer and nut are tightened against the bracket to pull the leg and aprons firmly against each other *(Fig. 13a)*.

**CENTER DIVIDER.** Even with the hardware, the legs and aprons alone don't make for a very steady base. To help strengthen and stiffen the table, as well as provide a means of supporting the top, I added a center divider *(Fig. 10)*.

This center divider (E) is a piece of 1½"-thick stock, cut to fit in the dadoes in the side aprons. (Because this piece won't be seen, this is a good place to use some of the less attractive stock.)

But before it can be installed, two dadoes need to be cut on each side of the divider. These dadoes will hold the drawer supports that are added next, so they should line up with the dadoes in the end aprons. Once this is done, the divider can be glued in place.

14

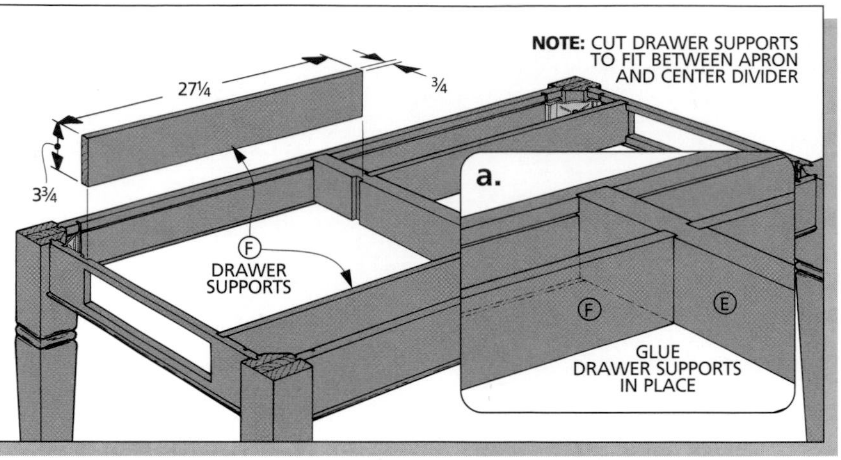
NOTE: CUT DRAWER SUPPORTS TO FIT BETWEEN APRON AND CENTER DIVIDER
27¼
¾
3¾
F
DRAWER SUPPORTS
a.
F
E
GLUE DRAWER SUPPORTS IN PLACE

15

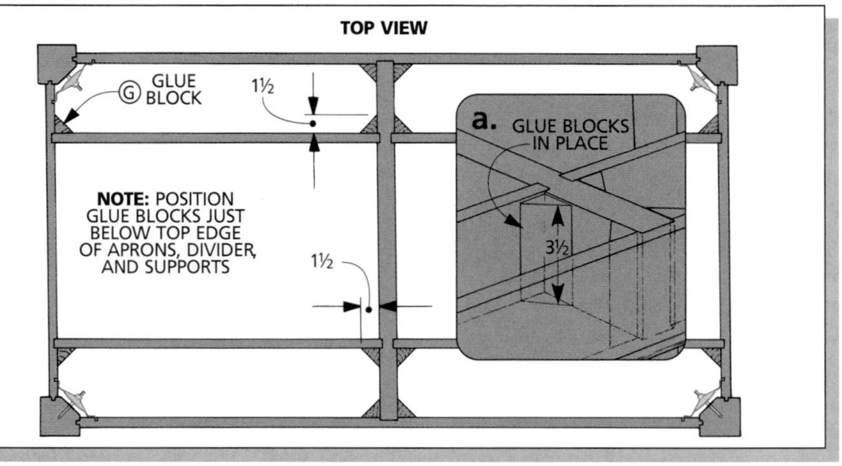
TOP VIEW
G GLUE BLOCK
1½
a. GLUE BLOCKS IN PLACE
NOTE: POSITION GLUE BLOCKS JUST BELOW TOP EDGE OF APRONS, DIVIDER, AND SUPPORTS
1½
3½

16

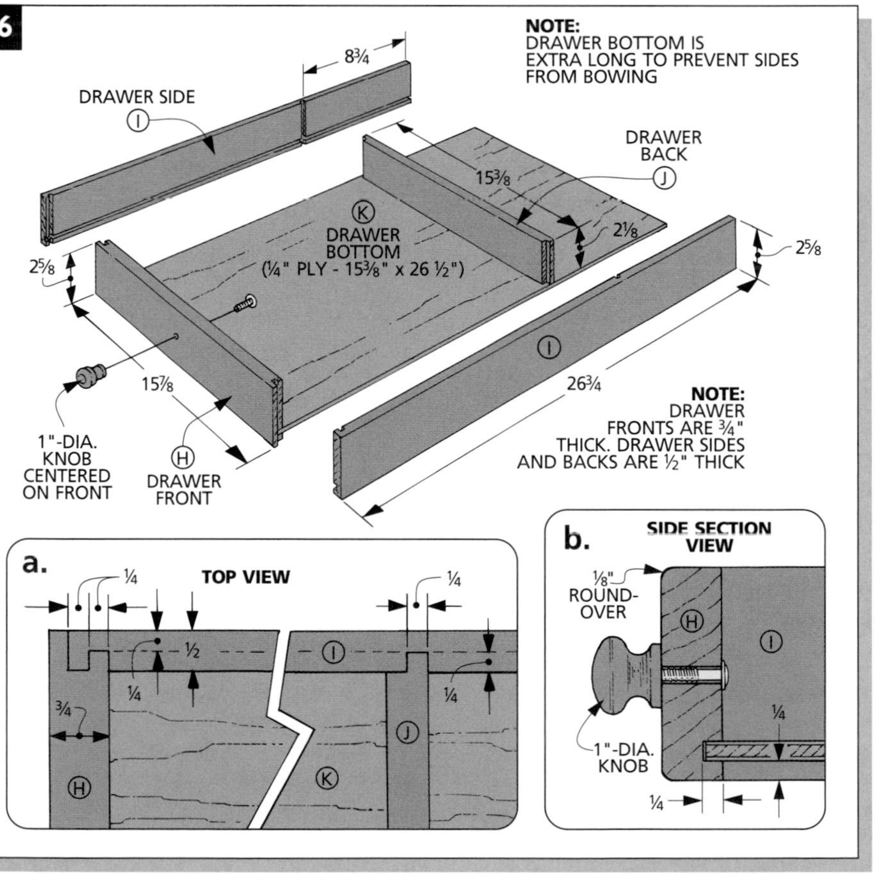
NOTE: DRAWER BOTTOM IS EXTRA LONG TO PREVENT SIDES FROM BOWING
8¾
DRAWER SIDE
I
DRAWER BACK
J
15⅜
K
DRAWER BOTTOM
(¼" PLY - 15⅜" x 26 ½")
2⅛
2⅝
2⅝
I
15⅞
26¾
NOTE: DRAWER FRONTS ARE ¾" THICK. DRAWER SIDES AND BACKS ARE ½" THICK
1"-DIA. KNOB CENTERED ON FRONT
H
DRAWER FRONT
a.
TOP VIEW
¼
¼
½
I
¼
¼
¾
H
K
J
b.
SIDE SECTION VIEW
⅛" ROUND-OVER
H
I
1"-DIA. KNOB
¼
¼

**DRAWER SUPPORTS.** After the center divider is glued in place, you can add the drawer supports (F). These ¾"-thick pieces are cut to fit between the dadoes in the center divider and the end aprons and glued in place *(Figs. 14 and 14a)*.

It's not necessary to clamp the supports since the joints will be reinforced with glue blocks later. So to keep the supports in position while the glue dried, I just turned the table on its side.

**GLUE BLOCKS.** Although the divider and drawer supports are glued into dadoes, the end grain of these pieces doesn't make for a very strong glue joint. So I added glue blocks (G) to each corner *(Figs. 15 and 15a)*. These pieces are nothing more than triangular-shaped blocks that I cut from some scrap.

## DRAWERS

One of the things I really like about this table are the drawers in the ends. They're an ideal place to store napkins, hot pads, or silverware. In fact, seeing how handy they are makes me wonder why more tables don't have this feature.

Putting a drawer in a table does create one problem though. Because of the overhang of the table top, the drawers have to be pulled out extra far in order to get at the contents. To solve this problem, I made the sides of the drawer longer to support the drawer when it's pulled out.

The drawers are sized to fit in the openings in the aprons with a 1/16" gap all around. The drawer front (H) is joined to the drawer sides (I) with a locking rabbet joint *(Fig. 16a)*. (For more on this joint, see the Joinery box on the next page.)

The drawer back (J) is joined to the drawer sides with a tongue and dado *(Fig. 16a)*. Tongues cut on the ends of the drawer back fit into dadoes in the drawer sides. And the plywood drawer bottom (K) simply fits into grooves cut near the bottom edge of the drawer front and drawer sides *(Fig. 16b)*.

Once all the pieces are cut to size and the joinery is completed, you can assemble the drawers. Start by gluing the front, sides, and bottom panel together. Then add the drawer back.

**DRAWER GUIDES.** Before adding the drawers to the table, you'll need to make and install two sets of guides between the center divider and aprons *(Fig. 17)*. The upper guides (L) are glued to the drawer supports so they're flush with the top of the drawer opening *(Fig. 17a)*.

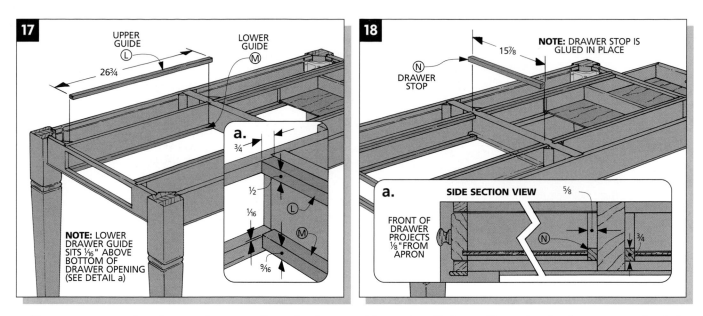

But to prevent the drawer from wearing grooves in the bottom of the drawer opening, the lower guides (M) are positioned so they sit $1/16$" above the bottom of the drawer opening in the end apron (*Figs. 17 and 17a*).

Once the drawer guides are installed, there are just a couple of details to attend to. First, I added a wood knob to each drawer (*Fig. 16b*). These are centered on the drawer fronts and are fastened with a screw from the inside of the drawer.

To make the drawers stand a hair proud from the front of the aprons I added a drawer stop (N) to the back of each drawer compartment (*Figs. 18 and 18a*). These are just pieces of $3/4$"-thick stock glued across the lower drawer runners.

# JOINERY . . . . . . . . . . . . . . . . . . . . . . . . . . . *Locking Rabbet*

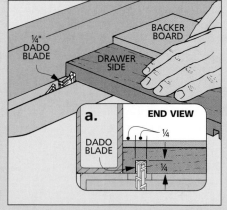

For the drawers on the Country Harvest Table, I used a locking rabbet joint at the front corners (see photo). It's much stronger than a simple butt or rabbet joint, and it's not as difficult as cutting dovetails. In fact, the entire joint can be cut on the table saw.

**Note:** Although I'm showing how to cut the joint on the table saw, the same procedure can be used to cut the joint with a straight bit in the router table.

With a locking rabbet, a groove is cut in each end of the front piece (*Step 1*). The depth of the tongue matches the thickness of the side pieces.

Then the inside tongue of the groove is cut shorter (*Step 2*).

Next, a dado is cut on each side piece to accept this short tongue (*Step 3*). The distance between the dado and the end of the workpiece should equal the width of the dado in the drawer front (see photo).

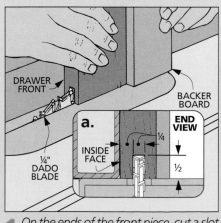

1 On the ends of the front piece, cut a slot to leave a $1/4$"-wide tongue that's as long as the side pieces are thick ($1/2$").

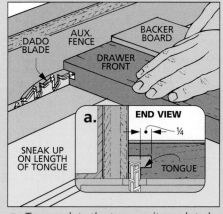

2 To complete the tongue, it needs to be trimmed to length. Sneak up on the cut until the tongue is $1/4$" long.

3 Finally, to hold the tongue on the front, cut a $1/4$" x $1/4$" dado on each side piece. (Check the setup with a test piece.)

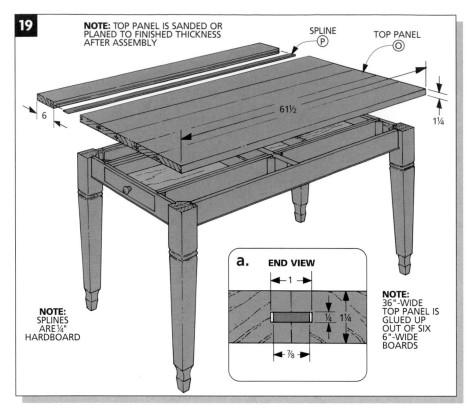

**19**

NOTE: TOP PANEL IS SANDED OR PLANED TO FINISHED THICKNESS AFTER ASSEMBLY

SPLINE
(P)

TOP PANEL
(O)

61½

6

1¼

NOTE: SPLINES ARE ¼" HARDBOARD

**a.** END VIEW

1

¼

1¼

⅞

NOTE: 36"-WIDE TOP PANEL IS GLUED UP OUT OF SIX 6"-WIDE BOARDS

## TOP PANEL

With the base of the table complete, you can now focus on making the top. There are two steps involved here. First, a large panel is glued up. Then, breadboard ends are attached to the ends of the panel.

The top panel (O) is made up of six 6"-wide boards *(Fig. 19)*. I started by planing the stock just enough so that all the pieces were a consistent thickness.

**Note:** Don't get too carried away with the planing. Leave yourself enough material so that you can sand the entire surface flat after assembly and still end up with a top that's about 1¼" thick.

Although the boards for the top are ripped to a width of 6", leave them a little long for now. They'll get trimmed to length after the top is glued up.

**SPLINES.** To help keep all the pieces aligned during the glue-up process, I used hardboard splines *(Fig. 19a and photo on opposite page)*. These fit into grooves routed along the edges of each piece *(Figs. 20 and 20b)*.

## TECHNIQUE ................. *Crosscutting Large Panels*

Whenever I've needed to trim the ends of a long, wide, glued-up panel, I've used either a circular saw or a hand-held router. But to crosscut the top panel for the harvest table, I came up with a different method using my table saw. It takes less time than using a router. And by using my good crosscut blade, I get a clean, square cut with no chipout — much better results than the circular saw.

**RUNNER.** What makes this all work is a temporary runner screwed to the *bottom* face of the top panel. (That way the screw holes won't be seen.) Like the runner on a miter gauge, this hardwood

strip will ride in the slot on the table saw and guide the long panel so the cut will be clean and square *(Fig. 2)*.

To do this, start by making a couple of long runners to fit in your table saw slot. (I made mine out of a ⅜" x ¾" strip of solid wood.) Size the runners carefully — you want a snug fit, but not so tight that it will bind. And they should be longer than the panel is wide *(Fig. 1)*.

**LAYOUT.** Next, I laid out two lines on each end of the panel: a cut line and a line for the runner *(Fig. 1)*. The distance between the cut lines should equal the finished length of the panel (61½"). And the

line for each runner should be located the same distance from the cut line as the saw blade is from the miter gauge slot.

With the lines drawn, the runners can be screwed to the panel. (I used a framing square to align each of them.) And make sure the screw heads are countersunk below the surface of the runners.

**TRIM.** Now with the runners in place, simply flip the panel over and get someone to help support it as you guide it over the saw *(Fig 2)*. Then turn the piece end for end and trim the other end.

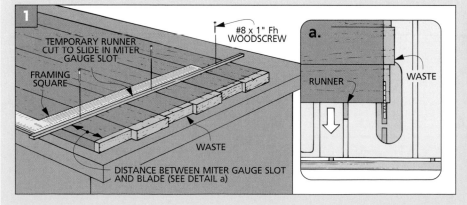

**1**

TEMPORARY RUNNER CUT TO SLIDE IN MITER GAUGE SLOT

#8 x 1" Fh WOODSCREW

FRAMING SQUARE

WASTE

DISTANCE BETWEEN MITER GAUGE SLOT AND BLADE (SEE DETAIL a)

**a.**

RUNNER

WASTE

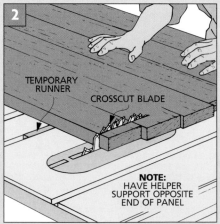

**2**

TEMPORARY RUNNER

CROSSCUT BLADE

NOTE: HAVE HELPER SUPPORT OPPOSITE END OF PANEL

There's a good reason for using a hand-held router instead of the table saw or router table. Even if the board is bowed or twisted slightly, a hand-held router will follow the surface *(Fig. 20a)*. So the groove is always the same distance from the surface of the workpiece.

After the slots have been routed, rip the splines (P) to width from ¼" hardboard. And a tip here — even though the combined depth of the slots is 1", cut the splines about ⅞" wide *(Fig. 19a)*. That way they won't bottom out in the grooves.

Once the splines have been cut to size, the panel can be glued up.

**FLAT TOP.** Even with the splines, there's a pretty good chance that your top panel will still have some uneven

spots (mine did). To get a good, flat surface, I sanded my panel smooth with a belt sander (see the Technique box below). Be careful here — you don't want to remove any more material than is necessary to achieve a flat top.

**TRIMMING THE ENDS.** When it comes to trimming the ends of the top, you have a couple of options. One method is to use a hand-held circular saw with a straightedge for a fence. But I find that the table saw leaves a nicer finished cut with less chipping and less likelihood of burning.

The problem with cutting a piece this wide on the table saw is getting a square cut, since you can't use a miter gauge.

The trick I used was to attach a runner to the bottom of the panel. The runner fits

into the miter gauge slot on my table saw. Then with someone to help support the end of the panel, I simply trimmed each end. (For more on this procedure, see the Technique article on the facing page.)

To keep the surfaces of the boards flush, rout grooves and use hardboard splines. The faces will align automatically.

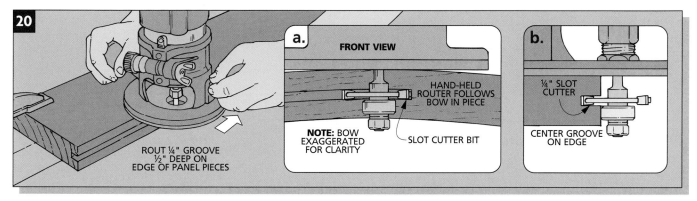

**20** ROUT ¼" GROOVE ½" DEEP ON EDGE OF PANEL PIECES

**a.** FRONT VIEW — HAND-HELD ROUTER FOLLOWS BOW IN PIECE — NOTE: BOW EXAGGERATED FOR CLARITY — SLOT CUTTER BIT

**b.** ¼" SLOT CUTTER — CENTER GROOVE ON EDGE

---

# TECHNIQUE . . . . . . . . . . . . . . . *Flattening a Large Surface*

About the only things you need to flatten a large panel like the table top are a belt sander and a straightedge — and a big can of elbow grease.

**MARK.** I like to start by scribbling a pencil line over the entire surface of the panel so I can check my progress as I go along *(Step 1)*. This helps keep me from getting carried away with the sander.

**SAND.** Then I work the belt sander over the entire top. I run side to side first (cross-grain) to knock down any "ledges" along the joint lines. Then I take a pass *with* the grain *(Step 2)*. Any remaining pencil marks indicate high spots.

I've found that a medium grit belt (100) works well for removing stock without leaving a lot of finish sanding work.

Keep the sander moving continuously so you don't sand one area too much. And don't bear down on the sander. Let the weight of the tool do the work.

**CHECK.** Finally, check your work with a straightedge (the longer the better) and stop as soon as the top is reasonably flat *(Step 3)*. You don't want to remove too much material from the top.

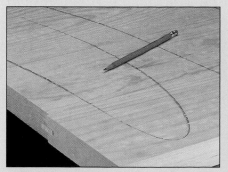

**1** Scribble a line across the entire surface of the top to serve as a reference. You'll sand until the line is gone.

**2** Work the sander across the grain at first to even up trouble spots on the joint line, but finish sanding with the grain.

**3** When the pencil line is gone, use a straightedge to check the progress. Stop when the top is flat.

Once you've reached this stage, all that remains is to add the breadboard end caps and attach the top to the base.

To make the breadboard ends, I started by cutting the end caps (Q) to width and length *(Fig. 21)*. The thickness of these pieces should match the thickness of the top panel (O).

Next, a long mortise is made in each end cap to fit over a tenon that will be cut on each end of the top panel *(Figs. 21 and 21b)*. This mortise is ³⁄₈" thick and stopped at both ends *(Fig. 21a)*.

An easy way to make a mortise this long is to use a router table and a ³⁄₈"-dia. spiral end mill bit. The workpiece is just dropped down over the rotating bit and pushed forward until you reach the end of the mortise.

The trick to routing the mortise is knowing where to stop and start. So I drew a couple of index lines on the top of my router table to serve as reference points *(Fig. 22)*. Since the mortise is fairly deep (1¹⁄₄"), I cut it in several passes, raising the bit ¹⁄₄" between each pass.

**TENON.** After completing the mortises in the end caps, you can cut the tenons on the ends of the top panel. These are also made with a router. But since the top panel is too large and heavy to maneuver safely on the router table, I found it easier to use a hand-held router with an edge guide *(Figs. 23 and 23a)*.

To allow the top to expand and contract with humidity changes, the ends of the tenon are trimmed off with a hand saw *(Fig. 21c)*. What you want here is for each tenon to end up about ¹⁄₂" shorter than the mortise at each end.

**HARDWARE.** Normally, a mortise and tenon joint is glued together. But if the end caps are glued to the top panel of the table, they won't allow for any wood movement. So instead, I used threaded rods and barrel nuts to hold the end caps

in place. The threaded rods act as draw bolts, allowing you to pull the end cap snug against the top panel again if the end cap should shrink over time.

Each end cap is held in place by four threaded rods. One end of each rod is threaded into a barrel nut that is inserted in the cap. On the other end, a nut and washer serve to hold the cap tight against the top panel. Drilling oversize holes for the threaded rods allows for expansion and contraction across the top.

All the hardware is installed from the bottom of the end caps and the top panel so that it won't be visible once the table is assembled. To start with, place the end cap on the top panel and lay out the locations for the hardware *(Fig. 24)*.

Now all you need to do is drill a series of holes for all the hardware. First, four ⁷⁄₁₆"-dia. holes are drilled in each end cap for the barrel nuts *(Fig. 24)*.

Next, 1"-dia. counterbores for the washers and nuts are drilled in the underside of the top panel with a Forstner bit. Then one side of the hole is squared off with a chisel to create a flat bearing surface for the washer and nut *(Fig. 24a)*.

Finally, you'll need to drill ³⁄₈"-dia. cross holes for the threaded rods in the ends of the panel and also in the end caps *(Figs. 25 and 25a)*. Drilling the cross holes in each end cap is pretty straightforward using a drill press.

But the top panel is too large to place on a drill press. To overcome this, I used a portable drill. And in order to be able to drill the holes deep enough, I created clearance notches in the tenons for the chuck of my drill *(Fig. 25b)*.

**ATTACHING END CAPS.** Once you've got all the holes drilled, all that's left is to attach the end caps. Start by inserting the barrel nuts into the holes in the end caps.

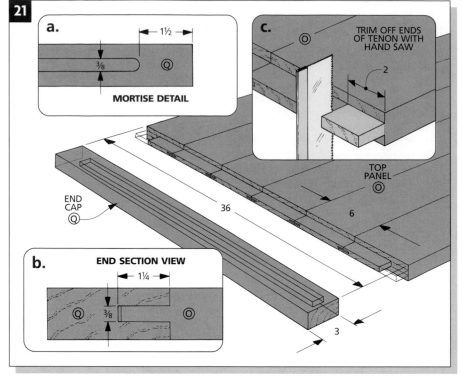

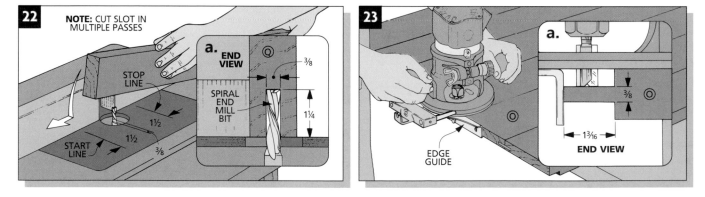

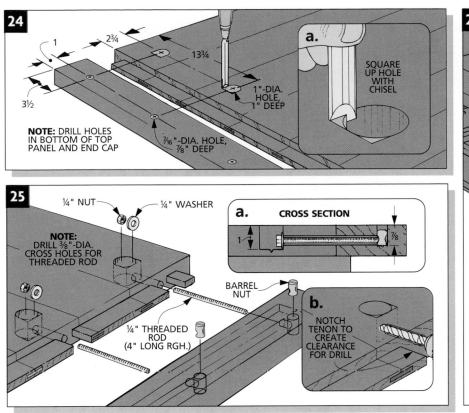

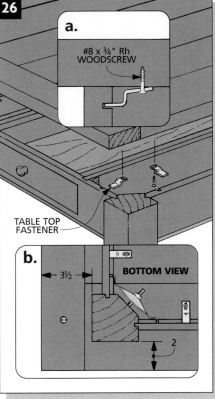

(Make sure the holes are facing into the cross holes.)

Next, insert the lengths of threaded rods into the cross holes in the end caps and thread them into the barrel nuts.

Now slip the end cap onto the end of the top panel, making sure that the threaded rods enter the shank holes in

the end of the panel. Finally, secure the end caps by placing a washer and nut on the end of each threaded rod.

**ROUNDOVER AND FINISH.** Now, before attaching the table top, I routed an $\frac{1}{8}$" roundover on all the edges. Then I finished the top and the base of the table separately (see the Finishing box below).

**ATTACHING THE TOP.** When the finish is dry, you can attach the top to the base. To do this, I used Z-shaped table top fasteners *(Figs. 26 and 26b)*. These simply fit into the kerfs cut near the top edge of the aprons. Then small woodscrews are used to secure the fasteners to the underside of the top *(Fig. 26a)*.  ∎

---

# FINISHING .................................................. *Colored Stain*

**N**ormally, I don't like to paint the projects I make because I feel that it hides the natural beauty of the wood. However, the country design of this table seems to lend itself to a more colorful finish. So I added color — but I didn't use paint.

Instead, I decided to use a colored stain on the base of the table. Unlike paint, stain allows the grain of the wood to show through a bit. And by leaving the top of the table natural, you still get the warm feeling of wood, and an interesting contrast with the colored stain.

**WASH COAT.** Before doing any staining, however, I applied a thin wash coat of orange shellac to the entire table (including the top). This serves two purposes. On the base of the table, the

shellac serves as a stain controller, preventing the stain from penetrating deeper in some places than in others.

And on the top of the table, the shellac gives the wood a warm, amber color similar to the patina that you might expect to find on an old piece of furniture.

To make the wash coat, I mixed about 2 to 3 ounces of orange shellac flakes with a quart of denatured alcohol. Then, after the shellac dried, I sanded very lightly with 400-grit sandpaper to knock off the "whiskers."

**STAIN.** Next, I stained the base of the table, using a commercially prepared water-based stain. I applied two coats of stain, sanding the surface lightly after each coat had dried.

**TOP COAT.** After the stain had dried, I finished the entire table with a wipe-on oil finish. I used two coats on the base of the table, again sanding lightly between coats. (You don't want to sand through the dye.) I applied a couple of extra coats to the table top, because it's subject to more wear and abuse.

# DESIGNER'S NOTEBOOK

*If you don't need (or have room) to feed a large crew, this table has all the charm of the full-size version in about half the space. Cut-out aprons and straight tapers on the legs give it a distinctive look.*

## CONSTRUCTION NOTES:

■ Besides being smaller, there are a few other design changes to this table. The aprons are wider, but have a notched profile to allow for knee space. The legs have also changed. I tapered just two faces of the legs and left off the bead at the top and the arcs toward the bottom. And since this table isn't as long, there is only one drawer. (It's the same size as before.)

■ The leg blanks (A) start out the same size as for the larger table. The first thing to do is to cut the mortises on the router table. Since the aprons on this table are wider, the mortises are longer *(Fig. 1)*.

■ Next, you can cut the notches for the corner brackets on the top inside corner of each leg. These notches are the same size as for the larger table.

■ Once the notches are cut, the legs can be tapered. These legs are tapered on just the two inside faces (the faces with the mortises). Start by laying out the end of the taper on the bottom of each leg *(Fig. 1)*. The top of the tapers start 6" from the top of the leg.

■ After sanding the tapers smooth, all that remains to complete the legs is to rout ³⁄₈" roundovers on the edges *(Fig. 2)*. I also rounded over the bottom end of

SQUARE TABLE

each leg so it wouldn't chip out if the table were dragged along the floor.

■ Now you can move on to the aprons (C). All four aprons are the same length and width, but one (the front apron) has an opening for the drawer *(Fig. 3)*. Start by gluing up the front apron and cutting the other three aprons to size.

■ Now you can make a series of cuts in the aprons as before. First, cut a ¹⁄₄"-deep kerf toward the top edge of each apron to hold the tabletop fasteners *(Fig. 3)*.

■ Next, I cut dadoes to hold the corner brackets on all four aprons *(Fig. 3)*.

## MATERIALS LIST

### CHANGED PARTS
| | | |
|---|---|---|
| A | Legs (4) | 3¹⁄₄ x 3¹⁄₄ - 29 |
| C | Aprons (4) | ³⁄₄ x 5¹⁄₂ - 26 |
| F | Drawer Supports (2) | ³⁄₄ x 3³⁄₄ - 29³⁄₄ |
| G | Glue Blocks (4) | 1¹⁄₂ x 1¹⁄₂ - 3¹⁄₂ |
| H | Drawer Front (1) | ³⁄₄ x 2⁵⁄₈ - 15⁷⁄₈ |
| I | Drawer Sides (2) | ¹⁄₂ x 2⁵⁄₈ - 26³⁄₄ |
| J | Drawer Back (1) | ¹⁄₂ x 2¹⁄₈ - 15³⁄₈ |
| K | Drawer Bottom (1) | ¹⁄₄ ply - 15³⁄₈ - 26¹⁄₂ |
| L | Upper Guides (2) | ³⁄₄ x ¹⁄₂ - 29¹⁄₄ |
| M | Lower Guides (2) | ³⁄₄ x ⁹⁄₁₆ - 29¹⁄₄ |
| N | Drawer Stop (1) | ¹⁄₂ x 2⁷⁄₈ - 16 |
| O | Top Panel (1) | 1¹⁄₄ x 36 - 36 |
| P | Splines | ¹⁄₄ hdbd. - ⁷⁄₈ x 180 (rough) |

### HARDWARE SUPPLIES
(8) No. 8 x ³⁄₄" Rh woodscrews
(8) Table top fasteners
(1) 1"-dia. wood knob w/ screw
**Note:** Do not need parts B, D, E, and 4d finish nails.

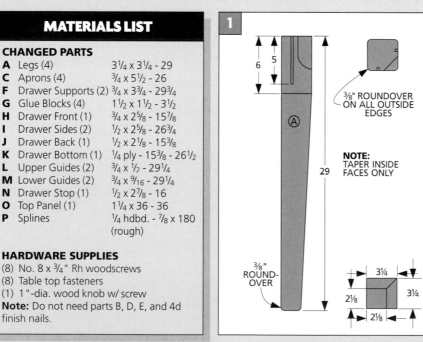

**1**

6  5

Ⓐ

³⁄₈" ROUNDOVER ON ALL OUTSIDE EDGES

**NOTE:** TAPER INSIDE FACES ONLY

29

³⁄₈" ROUND-OVER

3¹⁄₄
2¹⁄₈   3¹⁄₄
2¹⁄₈

**2**

³⁄₈" ROUNDOVER BIT

LEG Ⓐ

**NOTE:** ROUND OVER BOTTOMS AND LONG EDGES OF LEGS

The front and back aprons also need ³/₄"-wide dadoes to accept the drawer supports, which are added later *(Fig. 3)*.

Now go ahead and cut the tenons on each apron to fit the mortises in the legs.

Each apron has a profile cut along its lower edge to create leg room *(Figs. 3 and 3a)*. After laying out the profile, I rough-cut the shape on the band saw. Then I sanded up to the layout line with a drum sander and sanding block.

To complete the aprons, rout ³/₈" roundovers along their bottom edges.

Once the aprons are done, you can assemble the base of the table with the hanger bolts and corner brackets.

The next step is to add the drawer supports (F). These are cut to length to fit between the dadoes in the front and back aprons *(Fig. 4)*. They are glued in place flush with the top of the aprons. Then a glue block (G) is added in each outside corner to reinforce the joint.

Now you can build the drawer (nothing changes here), and add the upper and lower guides (L, M) to the drawer supports (these pieces are longer) *(Fig. 4)*.

To keep the drawer front flush with the apron, add a drawer stop (N) behind the drawer. It sits on top of the two lower guides, but it is wider than on the full-size table (2⁷/₈") *(Fig. 4a)*.

All that remains is to build the table top. Construction of the top panel (O) is the same as before, except that it's shorter (32³/₈") *(Fig. 5)*. The breadboard end caps (Q) and hardware for attaching them are also the same.

After attaching the end caps, rout a ¹/₂" roundover with a ¹/₈" shoulder around the top edge of the table top *(Fig. 5a)*.

Finally, turn the table top upside down and center the base on it. Then secure the base to the table top with Z-shaped fasteners in the kerfs *(Fig. 6)*.

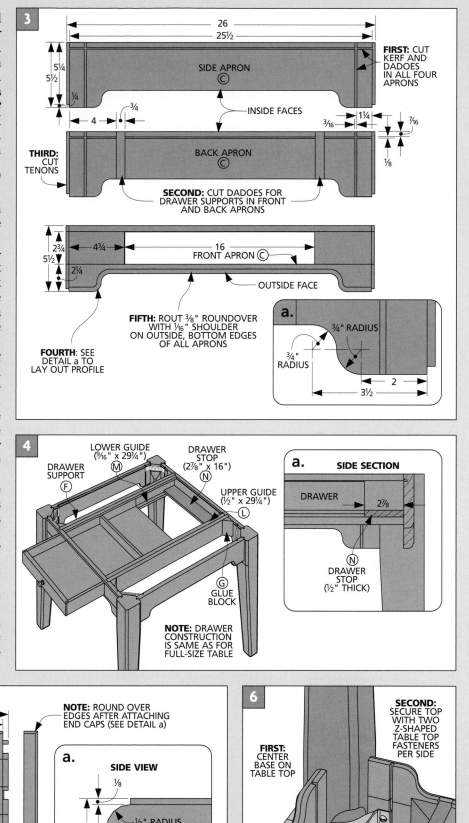

**3**

FIRST: CUT KERF AND DADOES IN ALL FOUR APRONS

26
25½
5¼
5½
¼

SIDE APRON ⓒ

INSIDE FACES

THIRD: CUT TENONS

BACK APRON ⓒ

¾
4
³/₁₆
1¼
⁷/₁₆
¹/₈

SECOND: CUT DADOES FOR DRAWER SUPPORTS IN FRONT AND BACK APRONS

2¾
5½
2¼
4¾
16
FRONT APRON ⓒ

OUTSIDE FACE

FIFTH: ROUT ³/₈" ROUNDOVER WITH ¹/₁₆" SHOULDER ON OUTSIDE, BOTTOM EDGES OF ALL APRONS

FOURTH: SEE DETAIL a TO LAY OUT PROFILE

**a.**
¾" RADIUS
¾" RADIUS
2
3½

**4**

LOWER GUIDE (⁹/₁₆" x 29¼") Ⓜ

DRAWER STOP (2⁷/₈" x 16") Ⓝ

DRAWER SUPPORT Ⓕ

UPPER GUIDE (½" x 29¼") Ⓛ

GLUE BLOCK Ⓖ

**a.** SIDE SECTION

DRAWER
2⁷/₈

Ⓝ DRAWER STOP (½" THICK)

NOTE: DRAWER CONSTRUCTION IS SAME AS FOR FULL-SIZE TABLE

**5**

32³/₈
30
3
36

TOP PANEL Ⓞ

END CAP Ⓠ

NOTE: ROUND OVER EDGES AFTER ATTACHING END CAPS (SEE DETAIL a)

**a.** SIDE VIEW
¹/₈
1¼
½" RADIUS

**6**

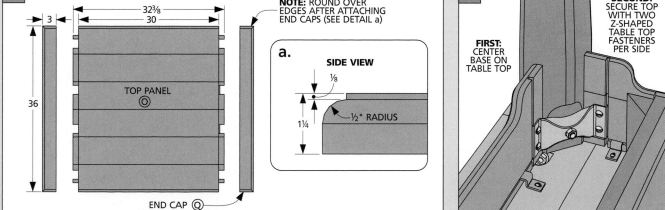

SECOND: SECURE TOP WITH TWO Z-SHAPED TABLE TOP FASTENERS PER SIDE

FIRST: CENTER BASE ON TABLE TOP

# CLASSIC CABINETS

There's something intriguing about the classics of the past revived. That's definitely the case with all three projects in this section. Although their present day function may be different from that of the past, each project offers more than nostalgia and is easily adapted to fit the needs of today's home.

Our Hoosier-style cabinet is a scaled-down version of the original. Reeded glass doors and authentic hardware highlight this reproduction of an American classic. A number of options make this cabinet easy to customize.

Punched tin panels and subtle "distressed" details make the pie safe look like an antique as soon as it's completed. And there is plenty of storage inside — two drawers and moveable shelves hold more than pies.

Finally, the old-fashioned icebox is now more versatile than ever. We offer a number of ways to build this classic cabinet to suit your tastes and needs.

# Hoosier-Style Cabinet

*A blending of old and new, like frame and panel construction, old-fashioned reeded glass, and specialty hardware, give this cabinet a "period" look while making it functional for homes of today.*

**B**efore built-in cabinets, many kitchens in America had a "Hoosier" cabinet. This was simply a free-standing workstation that was used for everything from kneading dough to storing flour and other food staples. (Most of these cabinets were built in Indiana — the Hoosier state.)

For quite some time, I've wanted to build a Hoosier cabinet. But I've been a little bit hesitant because of their sheer size. Most of the older Hoosier cabinets I've seen take up a whole wall, and that's just not very practical in today's kitchens.

The obvious solution was to build a scaled-down version. One that could be used not only in the kitchen, but in the rest of the house as well. The trick was to maintain the "look" of the older cabinets.

**OLD AND NEW.** One way I did this was to use some of the same elements found on older Hoosier cabinets, like frame and panel construction.

But what really gives this cabinet an old-time look is the hardware. I used a lot of specialty hardware. The brass bin pulls, door latches, and casters with ant traps are all typical of the hardware you'll find on originals. You can order a complete hardware kit from *Woodsmith Project Supplies* (see page 126).

Most Hoosier cabinets were mass-produced in furniture factories, where speed was the highest priority. So one of the things I did was to strengthen some of the joinery. For example, I used dovetails to join the drawer fronts to the sides. Mortises and tenons and stub tenons and grooves join the frame pieces.

**OPTIONS.** There are also a few options you might like to try. First, the cabinet has two sections so you can build just the bottom if you wish. Or build it with a maple butcher block top. Lastly, you could build just the top half and hang it on a wall. You can find out more about these changes in the Designer's Notebooks on pages 98 and 102.

# EXPLODED VIEW

**OVERALL DIMENSIONS:**
37½W x 24D x 73H

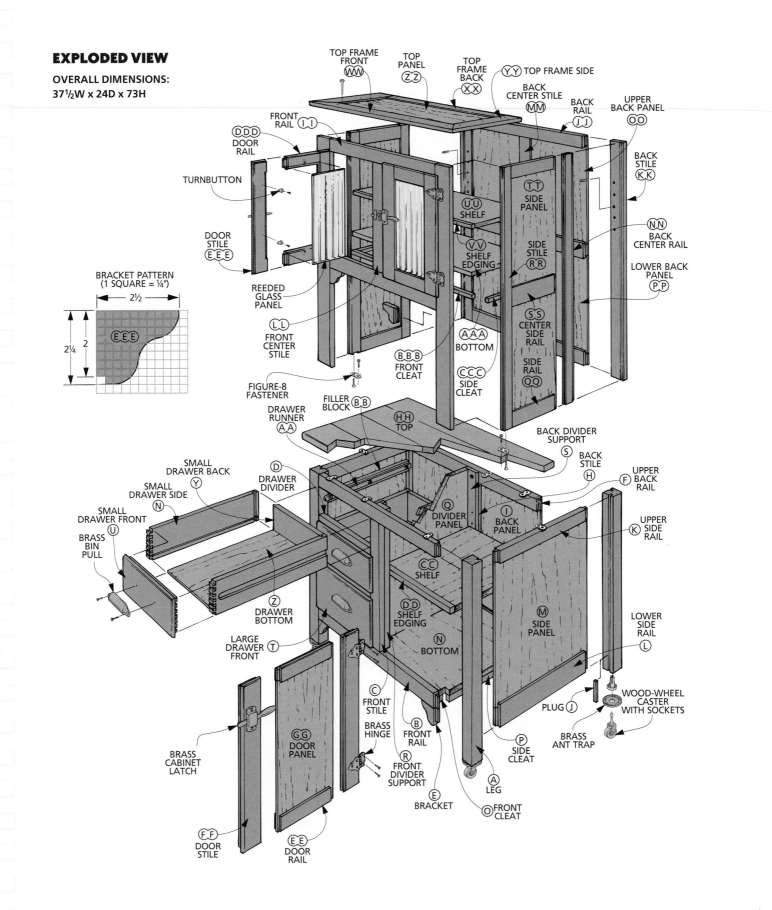

BRACKET PATTERN
(1 SQUARE = ¼")

# CUTTING DIAGRAM

**1³⁄₄ x 3¹⁄₄ - 72 RED OAK (3.25 Bd. Ft.)**

A · A

**³⁄₄ x 6¹⁄₂ - 96 RED OAK (4.3 Bd. Ft.)**

B · C · H · F · G · AA

**³⁄₄ x 6¹⁄₂ - 96 RED OAK (4.3 Bd. Ft.)**

K · K · BB · R · D · E E E E · L · L

**³⁄₄ x 6¹⁄₂ - 96 RED OAK (4.3 Bd. Ft.)**

U · U · T · T · FF · EE · EE · DD

**1 x 6¹⁄₂ - 84 RED OAK (Two Boards @ 4.7 Bd. Ft. Each)**

HH · HH

**¹⁄₂ x 2³⁄₄ - 84 RED OAK (1.6 Sq. Ft.)**

S · O · P · J

**³⁄₄ x 5¹⁄₄ - 96 RED OAK (3.5 Bd. Ft.)**

KK · II · LL · MM

**³⁄₄ x 5¹⁄₄ - 96 RED OAK (3.5 Bd. Ft.)**

KK · JJ · QQ · QQ · BBB · CCC

**³⁄₄ x 6 - 96 RED OAK (4 Bd. Ft.)**

RR · WW · RR · SS · SS · YY · YY

**³⁄₄ x 6 - 96 RED OAK (4 Bd. Ft.)**

EEE · EEE · DDD · DDD · VV · XX · NN · BBB

**¹⁄₂ x 5¹⁄₂ - 72 MAPLE (Two Boards @ 3.7 Sq. Ft. Each)**

W · W · Y

**¹⁄₂ x 8¹⁄₄ - 72 MAPLE (4.1 Sq. Ft.)**

V · V · X

**¹⁄₄" OAK PLYWOOD - 48 x 96**

PP · OO · I · TT · TT · OO · I · TT · TT · ZZ · Z · Z · Z · GG

**³⁄₄" OAK PLYWOOD - 48 x 48**

N · Q · CC

**³⁄₄" OAK PLYWOOD - 24 x 48**

UU · AAA

**¹⁄₄" OAK PLYWOOD - 48 x 48**

M · M

# MATERIALS LIST

## LOWER CABINET

| | | |
|---|---|---|
| **A** | Legs (4) | 1¹⁄₂ x 1¹⁄₂ - 30 |
| **B** | Front Rails (2) | ³⁄₄ x 2 - 34 |
| **C** | Front Stile (1) | ³⁄₄ x 2¹⁄₂ - 23¹⁄₈ |
| **D** | Drawer Dividers (2) | ³⁄₄ x 1¹⁄₂ - 16¹⁄₄ |
| **E** | Brackets (4) | ³⁄₄ x 2¹⁄₄ - 2¹⁄₂ |
| **F** | Upper Back Rail (1) | ³⁄₄ x 2 - 33¹⁄₂ |
| **G** | Lower Back Rail (1) | ³⁄₄ x 4 - 33¹⁄₂ |
| **H** | Back Stile (1) | ³⁄₄ x 2¹⁄₂ - 22¹⁄₈ |
| **I** | Back Panels (2) | ¹⁄₄ ply - 15³⁄₄ x 22¹⁄₈ |
| **J** | Plugs (6) | ¹⁄₄ x ¹⁄₄ - 2³⁄₈ |
| **K** | Upper Side Rails (2) | ³⁄₄ x 2 - 19¹⁄₄ |
| **L** | Lower Side Rails (2) | ³⁄₄ x 4 - 19¹⁄₄ |
| **M** | Side Panels (2) | ¹⁄₄ ply - 19¹⁄₄ x 22¹⁄₈ |
| **N** | Bottom (1) | ³⁄₄ ply - 20 x 34 |
| **O** | Front/Back Cleats (2) | ¹⁄₂ x 1 - 33 |
| **P** | Side Cleats (2) | ¹⁄₂ x 1 - 18³⁄₄ |
| **Q** | Divider Panel (1) | ³⁄₄ ply - 18³⁄₄ x 24¹⁄₈ |
| **R** | Fr. Dvdr. Support (1) | ³⁄₄ x 2¹⁄₂ - 24¹⁄₈ |
| **S** | Bk. Dvdr. Support (1) | ¹⁄₂ x 2¹⁄₂ - 24¹⁄₈ |
| **T** | Large Drwr. Front (1) | ³⁄₄ x 8⁵⁄₈ - 15³⁄₄ |
| **U** | Small Drwr. Fts. (2) | ³⁄₄ x 6 - 15³⁄₄ |
| **V** | Large Drwr. Sides (2) | ¹⁄₂ x 7⁷⁄₈ - 20 |
| **W** | Small Drwr. Sides (4) | ¹⁄₂ x 5¹⁄₄ - 20 |
| **X** | Large Drwr. Back (1) | ¹⁄₂ x 7⁷⁄₈ - 14¹⁄₂ |
| **Y** | Small Dwr. Backs (2) | ¹⁄₂ x 5¹⁄₄ - 14¹⁄₂ |
| **Z** | Drawer Bottoms (3) | ¹⁄₄ ply - 14¹⁄₂ x 19⁵⁄₈ |
| **AA** | Drawer Runners (6) | ⁵⁄₁₆ x ³⁄₄ - 19¹⁄₄ |

| | | |
|---|---|---|
| **BB** | Filler Blocks (3) | ³⁄₄ x 1¹⁄₂ - 18³⁄₄ |
| **CC** | Shelf (1) | ³⁄₄ ply - 17¹⁄₂ x 17⁵⁄₈ |
| **DD** | Shelf Edging (1) | ³⁄₄ x 1 - 17¹⁄₂ |
| **EE** | Door Rails (2) | ³⁄₄ x 2 - 12¹⁄₄ |
| **FF** | Door Stiles (2) | ³⁄₄ x 2 - 22⁵⁄₈ |
| **GG** | Door Panel (1) | ¹⁄₄ ply - 12¹⁄₄ x 19¹⁄₈ |
| **HH** | Top (1) | 1 x 24 - 37¹⁄₂ |

## UPPER CABINET

| | | |
|---|---|---|
| **II** | Front Rails (2) | ³⁄₄ x 2 - 32 |
| **JJ** | Back Rails (2) | ³⁄₄ x 2 - 31¹⁄₂ |
| **KK** | Fr./Bk. Stiles (4) | ³⁄₄ x 2¹⁄₂ - 39³⁄₄ |
| **LL** | Front Ctr. Stile (1) | ³⁄₄ x 2¹⁄₂ - 18¹⁄₂ |
| **MM** | Back Ctr. Stile (1) | ³⁄₄ x 2¹⁄₂ - 17¹⁄₂ |
| **NN** | Back Ctr. Rail (1) | ³⁄₄ x 2¹⁄₂ - 31¹⁄₂ |
| **OO** | Upr. Bk. Panels (2) | ¹⁄₄ ply - 14³⁄₄ x 17¹⁄₈ |
| **PP** | Lwr. Back Panel (1) | ¹⁄₄ ply - 31¹⁄₂ x 17¹⁄₈ |
| **QQ** | Side Rails (4) | ³⁄₄ x 2 - 9¹⁄₂ |
| **RR** | Side Stiles (4) | ³⁄₄ x 1¹⁄₂ - 39³⁄₄ |
| **SS** | Ctr. Side Rails (2) | ³⁄₄ x 2¹⁄₂ - 9¹⁄₂ |
| **TT** | Side Panels (4) | ¹⁄₄ ply - 9¹⁄₂ x 17¹⁄₈ |
| **UU** | Shelf (1) | ³⁄₄ ply - 10¹⁄₄ x 34¹⁄₄ |
| **VV** | Shelf Edging (1) | ³⁄₄ x 1 - 34¹⁄₄ |
| **WW** | Top Frame Fr. (1) | ³⁄₄ x 2¹⁄₂ - 37¹⁄₂ |
| **XX** | Top Frame Bk. (1) | ³⁄₄ x 2 - 33 |
| **YY** | Top Frame Sds. (2) | ³⁄₄ x 2¹⁄₂ - 13³⁄₄ |
| **ZZ** | Top Panel (1) | ¹⁄₄ ply - 9³⁄₄ x 33 |
| **AAA** | Bottom (1) | ³⁄₄ ply - 11¹⁄₂ x 34¹⁄₂ |
| **BBB** | Fr./Bk. Cleats (2) | ³⁄₄ x ³⁄₄ - 34¹⁄₂ |

| | | |
|---|---|---|
| **CCC** | Side Cleats (2) | ³⁄₄ x ³⁄₄ - 10 |
| **DDD** | Door Rails (4) | ³⁄₄ x 2 - 11³⁄₄ |
| **EEE** | Door Stiles (4) | ³⁄₄ x 2 - 18 |

## HARDWARE SUPPLIES

(18) No. 8 x ³⁄₄" Fh woodscrews
(38) No. 8 x 1" Fh woodscrews
(26) No. 8 x 1¹⁄₄" Fh woodscrews
(8) No. 8 x ⁵⁄₈" Ph woodscrews
(12) No. 6 x ¹⁄₂" brass woodscrews
(6) Brass cabinet hinges w/ screws
(3) Brass cabinet latches w/ screws
(3) Brass bin pulls w/ screws
(13) Figure-8 fasteners
(4) Wood-wheel casters w/ sockets
(4) Brass ant traps
(8) Brass spoon-type shelf supports
(2) 11³⁄₈" x 14⁵⁄₈" reeded glass panels
(12) Plastic turnbuttons

## LOWER CABINET

The lower cabinet is essentially four legs joined with a frame and panel back and sides. A face frame on the front provides openings for the drawers and a door. A divider panel slips down inside the cabinet to separate the interior into two compartments — one for the drawers and one for the door and shelf. A solid wood top completes the lower cabinet.

**LEGS.** The first step in building the lower cabinet is to make the legs (A). These start out as four identical square blanks *(Fig. 1)*. But they quickly become different as you begin to lay out and cut all the joints that will connect them to the other parts of the cabinet.

Grooves on all four legs hold the side and back panels that are added later. (These are sized to match the thickness of the 1/4" plywood panels.) Mortises on the front legs are drilled and chiseled out to support the face frame pieces. And a row of shelf pin holes are drilled on the inside faces of the two right legs.

**FACE FRAME.** The two front legs are connected with a lower and upper front rail (B) *(Fig. 2)*. In addition, a front stile (C) and a couple of drawer dividers (D) create the openings in the front of the cabinet for the drawers and cupboard door. These pieces are all joined with 1/4"-wide (thick) mortises and tenons.

When you assemble the face frame, you'll discover that the mortises in the legs for the lower rail are extra long. I did this intentionally. This way, each mortise is large enough to hold the rail and a bracket (E) that is glued in place after the face frame is assembled *(Figs. 2 and 3)*.

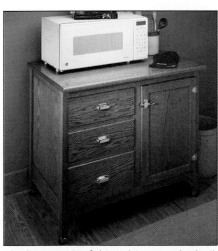

*The lower unit of this cabinet can be built and used separately as a microwave cart or a handy side serving table.*

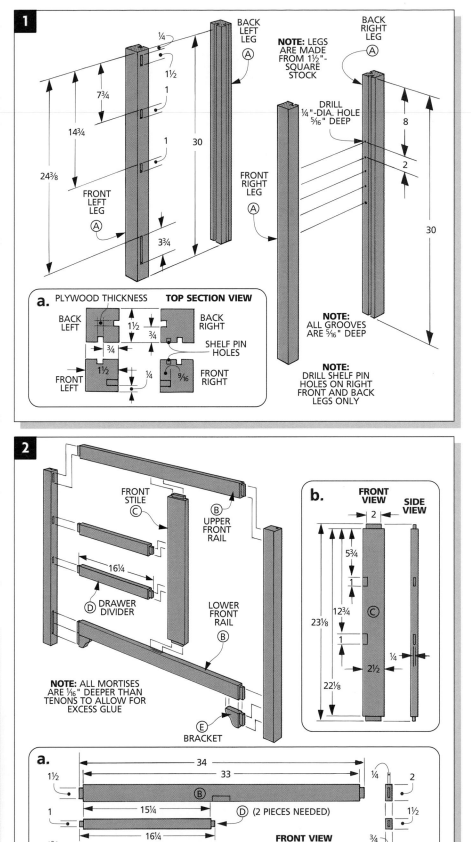

**3**

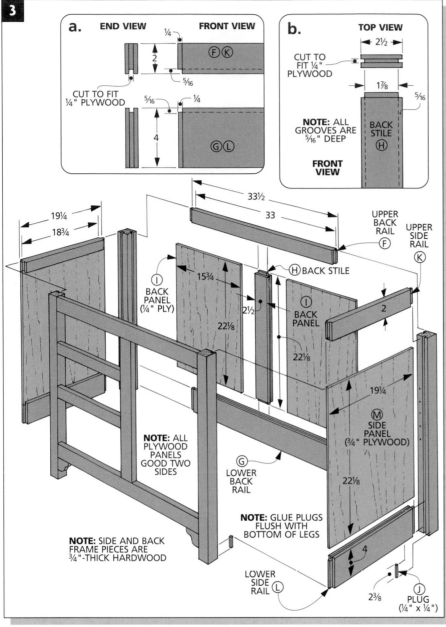

**a.** END VIEW    FRONT VIEW

CUT TO FIT ¼" PLYWOOD

¼
2
5⁄16

F  K

5⁄16
¼
4

G  L

CUT TO FIT ¼" PLYWOOD

**b.** TOP VIEW

CUT TO FIT ¼" PLYWOOD

2½
1⅞
5⁄16

BACK STILE
H

NOTE: ALL GROOVES ARE 5⁄16" DEEP

FRONT VIEW

33½
33

19¼
18¾

UPPER BACK RAIL
F

UPPER SIDE RAIL
K

H BACK STILE

15¾

I BACK PANEL (¼" PLY)

2½
22⅛

I BACK PANEL

2

22⅛

19¼

M SIDE PANEL (¾" PLYWOOD)

22⅛

NOTE: ALL PLYWOOD PANELS GOOD TWO SIDES

G LOWER BACK RAIL

NOTE: GLUE PLUGS FLUSH WITH BOTTOM OF LEGS

NOTE: SIDE AND BACK FRAME PIECES ARE ¾"-THICK HARDWOOD

LOWER SIDE RAIL  L

4

2⅜

J PLUG (¼" x ¼")

---

**4**

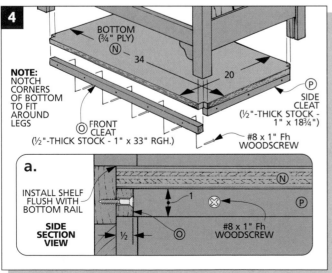

BOTTOM (¾" PLY)  N

34
20

NOTE: NOTCH CORNERS OF BOTTOM TO FIT AROUND LEGS

O FRONT CLEAT (½"-THICK STOCK - 1" x 33" RGH.)

SIDE CLEAT (½"-THICK STOCK - 1" x 18¾")  P

#8 x 1" Fh WOODSCREW

**a.**

INSTALL SHELF FLUSH WITH BOTTOM RAIL

N

P

1

½

O

#8 x 1" Fh WOODSCREW

SIDE SECTION VIEW

---

**5**

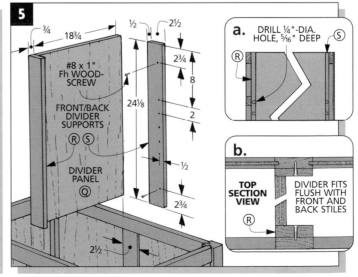

¾
18¾

½
2½

#8 x 1" Fh WOOD-SCREW

2¾

8

24⅛

FRONT/BACK DIVIDER SUPPORTS
R  S

2

DIVIDER PANEL
Q

½

2¾

2½

**a.** DRILL ¼"-DIA. HOLE, 5⁄16" DEEP

S
R

**b.**

TOP SECTION VIEW
R

DIVIDER FITS FLUSH WITH FRONT AND BACK STILES

---

**BACK FRAME AND PANEL.** After gluing up the face frame, you can make the back frame and panel *(Fig. 3)*. This consists of an upper and lower back rail (F, G) and a back stile (H). Centered grooves cut on the inside edges of these pieces hold ¼" plywood back panels (I).

**Note:** Since the inside of this Hoosier-Style Cabinet will be visible, I decided to use plywood with two "good" faces.

Unlike the face frame, the back is held together with stub tenon and groove joints. They're simple to make and the tenons are sized to fit in the same grooves that hold the plywood, so they're a bit thinner than ¼" *(Fig. 3a)*.

To help position the lower back rail during assembly (and hide the gap created in the leg by the groove), I glued wood plugs (J) into the grooves on all of the legs, flush with the bottom *(Fig. 3)*. Then the back assembly can be glued together. Later, the same plugs will be used to support the lower side rails.

**SIDE PANELS.** Now that the front and back of the cabinet is assembled, you just need to add the sides. Each side is made up of an upper and lower side rail (K, L) that sandwich a ¼" plywood side panel (M) *(Fig. 3)*.

**BOTTOM.** At this point, the four "walls" of the cabinet are up. The next step is to add a bottom *(Fig. 4)*. The bottom (N) is just a piece of ¾" plywood supported by front, back, and side cleats (O, P) that are attached to the inside faces of the lower rails *(Fig. 4a)*. (The bottom is glued down to the cleats.) I used a hand saw to notch the corners of the bottom to fit around the legs of the cabinet *(Fig. 4)*.

**CENTER DIVIDER.** Before you start working on the parts that fit inside the cabinet (the drawers and shelf), you need to add a center divider. The divider not only separates the cabinet into two compartments, but it also provides a place to mount the drawer runners.

The divider panel (Q) is sandwiched between a couple of narrow boards, the front and back divider supports (R, S) *(Fig. 5)*. Notice that the front divider support is slightly thicker than the back divider support *(Fig. 5b)*.

These support pieces each have a row of shelf pin holes drilled on one face (to match the holes on the legs) *(Figs. 5 and 5a)*. After they're glued to the divider panel, the entire assembly is screwed to the inside of the cabinet.

## DRAWERS & SHELF

With the basic carcase of the lower cabinet completed, you can now turn your attention to making the parts that fit inside it — the drawers and shelf.

The left side of the cabinet contains a set of three drawers — a large drawer on the bottom and two smaller drawers above it *(Fig. 7)*. The large and small drawer fronts (T, U) are joined to the large and small drawer sides (V, W) with rabbeted half-blind dovetails. (I used a router and a dovetail jig to make the dovetails.) Then the large and small drawer backs (X, Y) are joined to the sides with a rabbeted joint.

**RABBETED FRONT.** The only thing a little bit different about these drawers is the drawer fronts. A lip around the front edge of each drawer overlaps the drawer opening. Once all the drawer pieces are cut to size, creating this lip will be the first step in making the drawers.

To make this lip, start by routing a $3/8$" roundover on the outer edges of the drawer front. Then to finish the lip, rout a $3/8$" x $3/8$" rabbet around the inside edge of each drawer front with a rabbeting bit *(Fig. 6a)*. Once this is done, you can set up your router and dovetail jig to start cutting the $1/2$" half-blind dovetails on the drawer fronts and sides.

**LOCKING RABBET.** To join the drawer back to the sides, I used a simple, yet strong joint, called a locking rabbet joint. To do this, simply cut a dado near the end of each drawer side *(Fig. 6b)*. Then cut a tongue on each end of the drawer back to fit in the dadoes. A $1/4$"-deep groove cut on the lower inside face of each drawer piece holds a plywood drawer bottom (Z) *(Fig. 6a)*.

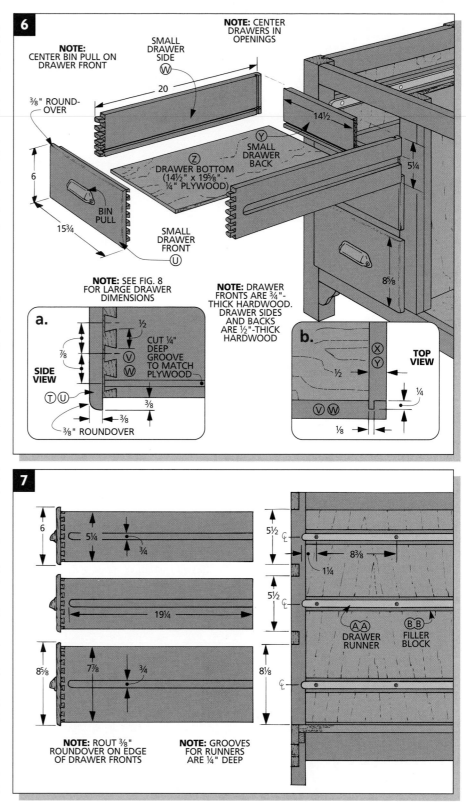

**STOPPED GROOVES.** Before assembling the drawers, there is one more detail you'll want to take care of. A stopped groove needs to be routed on the drawer sides to accept the drawer runners that will be made later. I cut this groove on the router table with a $3/4$"-dia. straight bit, using a stop block to position the end of the groove. If you don't have a bit this large, see the Technique article on page 97 for another option that will only require a $3/4$" Forstner bit and a $1/2$" straight bit. Now all that's left is to mount the runners and install the shelf.

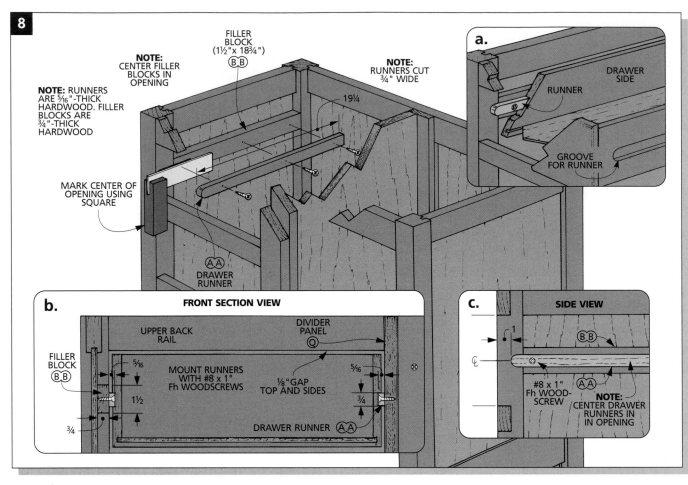

**NOTE:** RUNNERS ARE 5/16"-THICK HARDWOOD. FILLER BLOCKS ARE 3/4"-THICK HARDWOOD

**NOTE:** CENTER FILLER BLOCKS IN OPENING

FILLER BLOCK (1 1/2" x 18 3/4") BB

**NOTE:** RUNNERS CUT 3/4" WIDE

19 1/4

MARK CENTER OF OPENING USING SQUARE

AA DRAWER RUNNER

**a.**
DRAWER SIDE
RUNNER
GROOVE FOR RUNNER

**b.** FRONT SECTION VIEW

UPPER BACK RAIL
DIVIDER PANEL Q
FILLER BLOCK BB
5/16
MOUNT RUNNERS WITH #8 x 1" Fh WOODSCREWS
1/8 "GAP TOP AND SIDES
5/16
3/4
1 1/2
3/4
DRAWER RUNNER AA

**c.** SIDE VIEW
1
BB
#8 x 1" Fh WOOD-SCREW
AA
**NOTE:** CENTER DRAWER RUNNERS IN IN OPENING

**DRAWER RUNNERS.** Each drawer rides on a pair of hardwood runners that are mounted to the sides of the drawer openings. These runners not only support the drawers, but they also serve as guides, keeping each drawer centered in its opening. The drawer runners (AA) should be sized so they slide freely in the stopped grooves you routed in the sides of the drawers.

Mounting the runners to the right-hand side of the drawer opening is just a matter of installing a few screws. But in order to mount the left-hand runners, you'll need to glue some filler blocks (BB) to the side of the cabinet first. These fillers "flush out" the runners with the legs of the cabinet *(Fig. 8a)*. After they're cut to size, they can be glued to the side of the cabinet. But clamping the runners to the side of the cabinet poses a bit of a

## SHOP TIP .................................... *Spring Clamps*

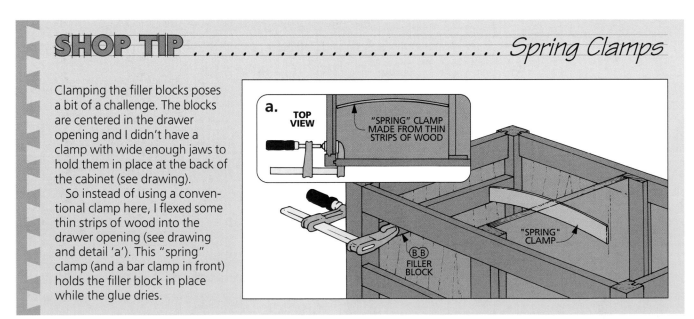

Clamping the filler blocks poses a bit of a challenge. The blocks are centered in the drawer opening and I didn't have a clamp with wide enough jaws to hold them in place at the back of the cabinet (see drawing).

So instead of using a conventional clamp here, I flexed some thin strips of wood into the drawer opening (see drawing and detail 'a'). This "spring" clamp (and a bar clamp in front) holds the filler block in place while the glue dries.

**a.** TOP VIEW
"SPRING" CLAMP MADE FROM THIN STRIPS OF WOOD
BB FILLER BLOCK
"SPRING" CLAMP

problem. That's because they're located inside the cabinet where a conventional clamp won't reach. As it turns out, there's an easy way to solve the problem (see the Shop Tip box on the previous page).

**MOUNTING THE RUNNERS.** There are a couple of things to watch for when installing the runners. First, each runner should be centered on the height of the drawer opening. And second, the front edge of each one should be set back 1" from the front of the cabinet *(Fig. 8c)*.

The easiest way I found to mount the runners was to mark the centerpoint of each drawer opening and then draw a layout line on the inside of the cabinet with a try-square *(Fig. 8)*. Next, I marked the centerpoint at the ends of each drawer runner. Then I simply lined up the marks on the runner with the centerline on the case while drilling the pilot holes for each of the mounting screws.

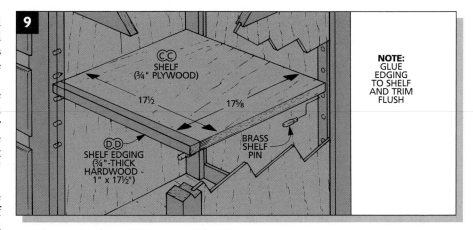

Test the fit of each drawer after you mount the runners. A little paste wax applied to the runners will make the drawers slide easier.

Now you can mount the brass bin pulls. These are centered on the drawer fronts (refer to *Fig. 6* on page 95).

**SHELF.** In comparison to the drawers, making the shelf (CC) is a piece of cake. It's just ¾"-thick plywood *(Fig. 9)*. And to hide the edge, I covered it with a strip of 1"-wide hardwood edging (DD) glued to the front. Brass shelf pins support the shelf inside the cabinet.

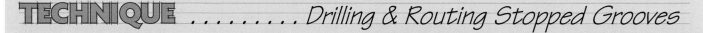

# TECHNIQUE . . . . . . . . . . *Drilling & Routing Stopped Grooves*

The wood drawer guides on the Hoosier-Style Cabinet required a stopped groove on each drawer side (see photo at right). The easiest way to do this is with a ¾"-dia. straight bit in the router table. This is a big bit, and if you don't have one this size, don't worry. You'll still be able to create the groove using a more common ¾"-dia. Forstner drill bit and a ½"-dia. straight bit.

**DRILL HOLE.** The first step is to lay out and drill a hole near the front of each drawer side *(Fig. 1)*. This will become the round end of the groove.

Since this part of the groove will be clearly visible every time the drawer is

opened, I wanted my hole to be flat-bottomed, so I used a ¾"-dia. Forstner bit.

**ROUT GROOVE.** With the hole drilled, the remainder of the groove can be routed with a ½"-dia. straight bit *(Fig. 2)*. This will require two separate steps — and two fence settings *(Figs. 2a and 2b)*.

The groove will be routed from the back end of the drawer side to the hole you just drilled. (Just rout till you reach the hole — you'll know you've reached the hole when you hear the bit stop cutting.) Then simply turn off the router and nudge the router table fence out a little for the next pass *(Fig. 2b)*.

**Note:** It's important to rout the grooves in the right order, or you'll end up back routing. (Back routing occurs when you move the router in the

same direction as the bit's rotation.) Rout the groove nearest the fence first *(Fig. 2a)*. Then slide the fence away from the bit to complete the groove.

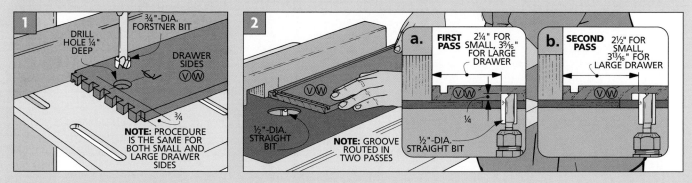

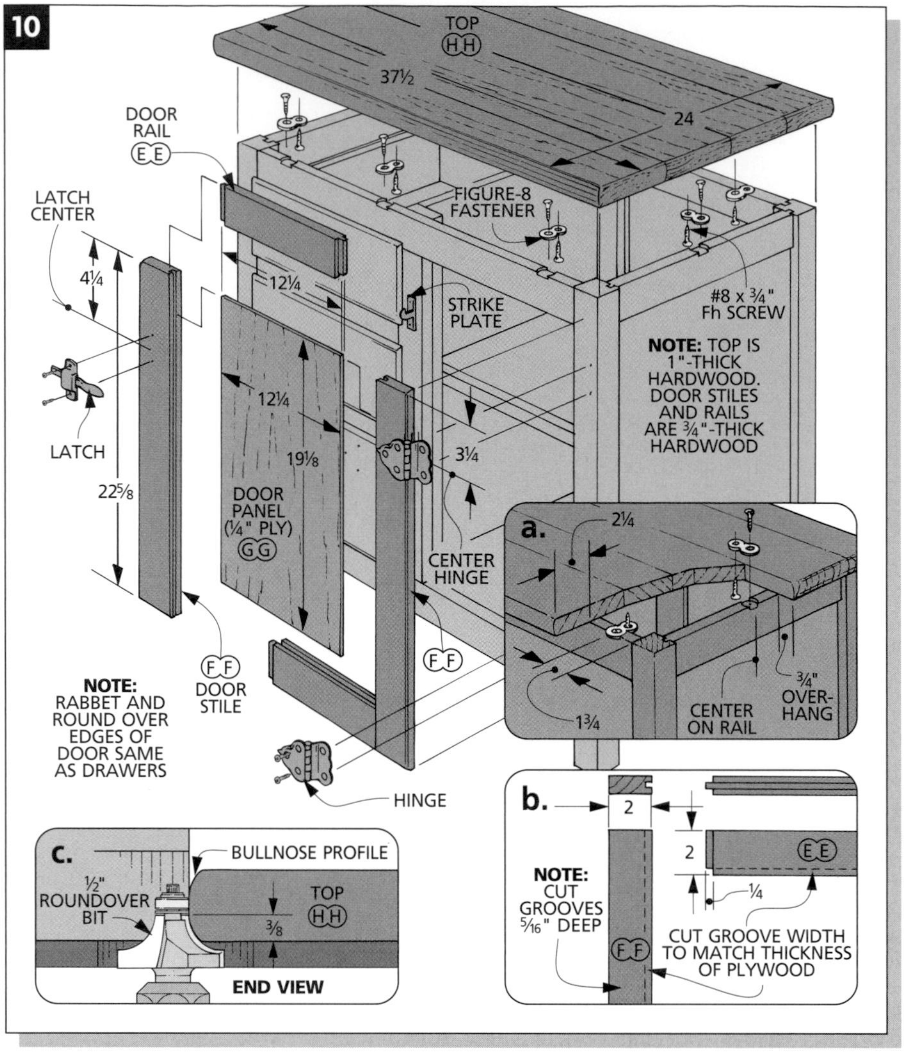
10
TOP
HH
37½
24
DOOR RAIL
EE
LATCH CENTER
4¼
12¼
FIGURE-8 FASTENER
STRIKE PLATE
#8 x ¾" Fh SCREW
NOTE: TOP IS 1"-THICK HARDWOOD. DOOR STILES AND RAILS ARE ¾"-THICK HARDWOOD
12¼
LATCH
22⅝
19⅛
3¼
DOOR PANEL (¼" PLY)
GG
CENTER HINGE
a.
2¼
1¾
CENTER ON RAIL
¾" OVER-HANG
FF
FF
DOOR STILE
NOTE: RABBET AND ROUND OVER EDGES OF DOOR SAME AS DRAWERS
HINGE
b.
2
2
EE
¼
NOTE: CUT GROOVES 5⁄16" DEEP
FF
CUT GROOVE WIDTH TO MATCH THICKNESS OF PLYWOOD
c.
BULLNOSE PROFILE
½" ROUNDOVER BIT
TOP
HH
⅜
END VIEW

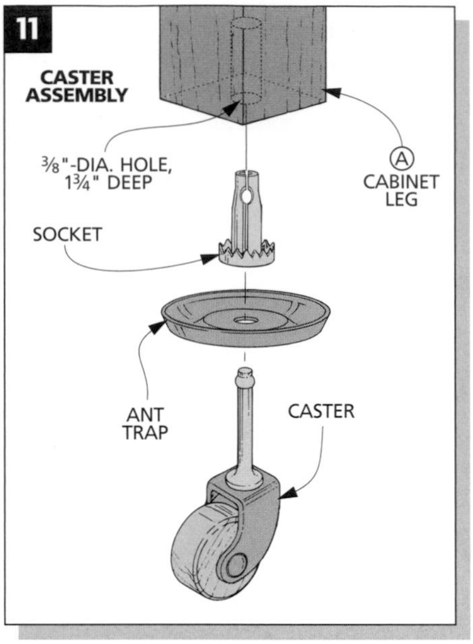
11
CASTER ASSEMBLY
⅜"-DIA. HOLE, 1¾" DEEP
A
CABINET LEG
SOCKET
ANT TRAP
CASTER

## DESIGNER'S NOTEBOOK

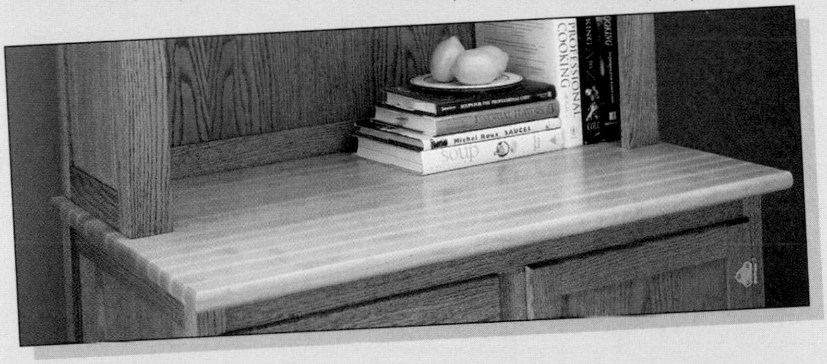

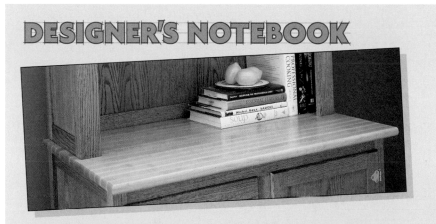

### BUTCHER BLOCK TOP

■ If you plan to do a lot of cutting or meal preparation on the surface of this cabinet (or if you just want a different look), you may want to build a butcher block top. I made this top out of glued-up strips of flat-sawn hard maple.

■ To do this, I ripped several narrow strips out of 1¾"-thick maple. (I made my strips just a hair over 1" in width.)

■ Now just turn each strip 90° before gluing them all together. Finally, sand the top and sides flat and smooth.

## DOOR & TOP

Like the drawers, the door has a lip around its edge. This allows it to overlap the opening in the cabinet. And like the lip on the drawers, it is also rounded over. But I'm getting ahead of myself.

**DOOR.** The door starts off as a plywood panel mounted in a hardwood frame. Grooves cut on the inside edges of the door rails (EE) and door stiles (FF) hold the door panel (GG). And stub tenons on the ends of the door rails join the frame pieces together *(Fig. 10b)*.

After the door is assembled, the edges are rounded over, and a rabbet is cut all around the door to create the lip to overlay the opening (like the drawers).

Mounting the door couldn't be simpler. I used surface-mount, offset hinges *(Fig. 10)*. To mount the hinges, start by centering the door in the opening and clamping it in place. Then just place the hinge where you want it and use it as a template to drill the screw holes.

**LATCH.** To match the period hinges, I used a brass cupboard latch on the door. The latch is mounted near the top of the door, while the strike plate is mounted to the front stile of the cabinet *(Fig. 10)*.

**TOP.** With the door in place, you can make the top. I made mine out of oak (like the rest of the cabinet). But if you're going to do a lot of cutting on the surface of the top, you might want to consider making a butcher block top out of maple (see the Designer's Notebook at left).

The top (HH) is just a flat panel made up of 1"-thick boards. After it's glued up, cut the panel to finished size. Then to

create a bullnose profile on the edges of the top, rout a partial roundover on both the top and the bottom edges *(Fig. 10c)*.

Finally, to allow the solid wood top to expand and contract, attach it to the case with figure-8 fasteners *(Figs. 10 and 10a)*.

Now that the lower cabinet is completed, you can lay it down on its back and drill holes in the bottom of the legs for the casters *(Fig. 11)*. There are three pieces to each caster. First, a socket is pounded into the hole in the leg. Then the caster is slipped through the hole in the ant trap and into the socket.

## UPPER CABINET

By itself, the lower cabinet is a pretty functional piece of furniture. But it's not until you add the upper cabinet that you really get the look of an authentic Hoosier cabinet (see the photo at right).

Like the lower cabinet, the upper cabinet consists of a face frame with a frame and panel back and a pair of frame and panel sides. But instead of being joined together by legs, the side panels are simply sandwiched between the face frame and the back frame.

**FACE FRAME**. I started building the upper cabinet by cutting out the various pieces for the front face frame — the front rails (II), stiles (KK), and the front center stile (LL) *(Fig. 12)*.

Once all these pieces were cut to size, I began cutting all the grooves and making the mortise and tenon joints, just like I did on the face frame of the lower cabinet *(Figs. 12a and 12b)*. But there's something a little different here. On the back face of the front stiles, there are grooves that run the length of each piece *(Fig. 12a)*. These grooves will hold the sides of the cabinet that are added later.

**Note:** The grooves on the faces of the front and back stiles are a full ¼" wide. They're sized to fit the tongues that will be cut on the edges of the panels later.

After making a couple more of the small brackets (E), the face frame can be glued up and clamped.

**BACK FRAME**. While the face frame was drying, I started making the back frame. It consists of three rails (JJ, NN), a pair of stiles (KK), and a short center stile (MM) *(Fig. 13)*. And again, the pieces are all joined together with stub tenons and grooves *(Figs. 13a, 13b, and 13c)*.

Just like the stiles on the face frame, the stiles on the back also have grooves to hold the sides of the cabinet, and holes for shelf pins *(Figs. 13, 13b, and 13c)*.

The back frame holds three ¼" plywood panels (OO, PP) — a wide panel on the bottom and two smaller panels above. These are cut to size, and then the back can be glued up.

*An upper cabinet completes the Hoosier cabinet. (This upper unit can be modified to hang on a wall. See the Designer's Notebook on page 102 for more on this.)*

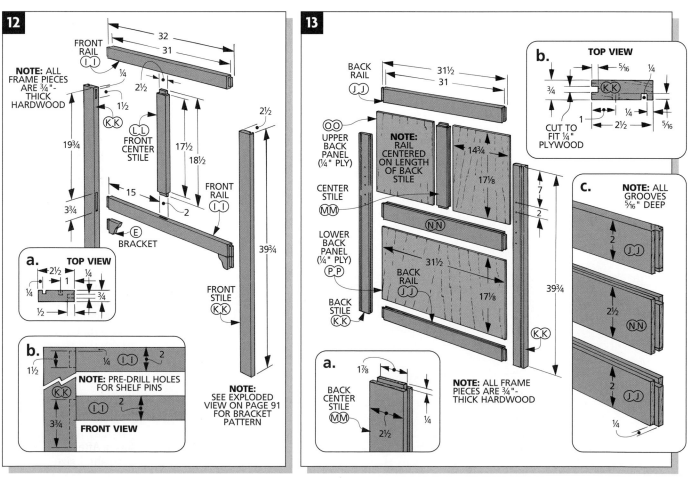

**SIDES.** The sides of the upper cabinet are sandwiched between the front and back *(Fig. 14)*. Each side is made up of a pair of rails (QQ), a pair of stiles (RR) and a center rail (SS). These pieces form a side frame that holds a pair of equally-sized plywood side panels (TT).

After these pieces have all been cut to size, grooves are cut on the edges for the panels, and tenons are cut on the ends of the rails *(Fig. 14b)*. Finally, a tongue is cut on one edge of each side stile to match the grooves you cut earlier in the front and back frames *(Fig. 14a)*.

With the joinery complete, the plywood side panels (TT) can be cut to size, and the sides can be glued together. Then the side assemblies can be glued up with the front and back assemblies.

When all the assemblies are glued together, the upper cabinet looks like an open box. To enclose this space, you'll need to add a top and bottom.

There's also a shelf that fits inside the upper cabinet. And since this shelf is actually captured inside the cabinet when the top and bottom are added later, I started by making it first.

**SHELF.** The shelf (UU) is nothing more than a piece of ³/₄" plywood with a strip of hardwood edging (VV) glued to the front *(Figs. 15 and 15b)*. The shelf is supported by shelf pins.

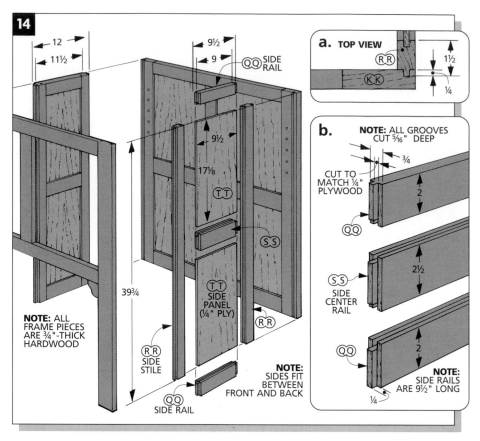

**TOP.** The top consists of a ¹/₄" plywood panel surrounded by a hardwood frame *(Fig. 15)*. The top frame front, back, and sides (WW, XX, YY) are grooved to hold the top panel (ZZ). I mitered the front corners of the frame, but left the back corners square. This makes construction easier and won't affect the looks.

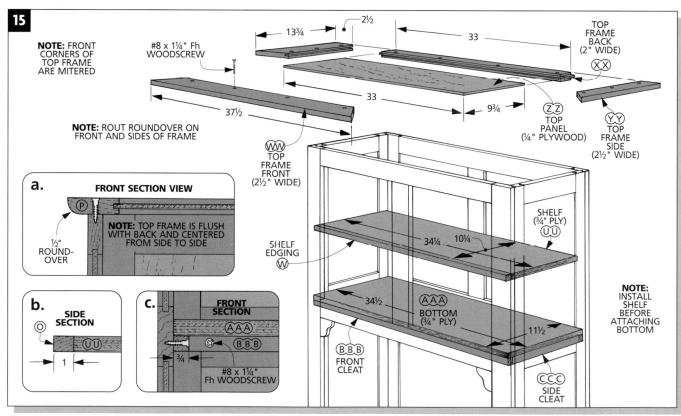

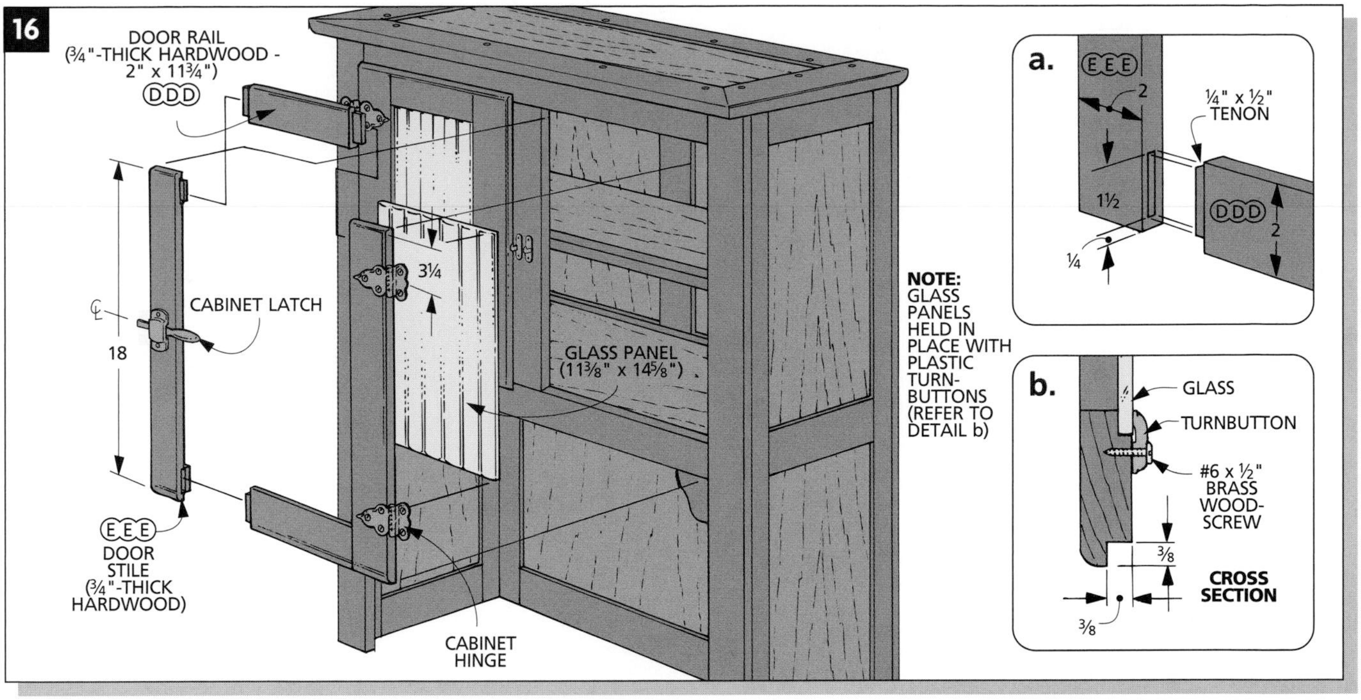
16
DOOR RAIL (¾"-THICK HARDWOOD - 2" x 11¾")
DDD
CABINET LATCH
18
3¼
GLASS PANEL (11⅜" x 14⅝")
EEE
DOOR STILE (¾"-THICK HARDWOOD)
CABINET HINGE
NOTE: GLASS PANELS HELD IN PLACE WITH PLASTIC TURN-BUTTONS (REFER TO DETAIL b)
a.
EEE
2
¼" x ½" TENON
1½
DDD
2
¼
b.
GLASS
TURNBUTTON
#6 x ½" BRASS WOOD-SCREW
⅜
CROSS SECTION
⅜

Once the top is glued up, a roundover is routed on the lower edges of the front and side pieces only *(Fig. 15a)*. Then the top can be screwed to the case.

**BOTTOM.** Like the shelf, the bottom (AAA) is also made out of ¾" plywood. But it doesn't need any edging. Instead, it's cut to fit in the case opening and then supported by front and side cleats (BBB, CCC), just like the bottom on the lower case *(Figs. 15 and 15c)*.

**DOORS.** Now all that remains to finish the upper cabinet is to add the two doors. These doors are similar to the door on the lower case, except that they have reeded glass panels instead of a plywood panel *(Fig. 16)*. This calls for a slightly different method of construction.

Go ahead and cut the door rails (DDD) and stiles (EEE) to size and make the mortise and tenon joints on the ends of the pieces *(Fig. 16a)*. But this time, don't worry about cutting any grooves for plywood panels. Instead, simply glue up the door frames nice and square.

Then after creating the rabbeted lip on the doors with a router and rabbetting bit, use the same bit to cut a rabbet on the inside opening of each door frame for the glass panel *(Figs. 17a and 17b)*.

**Note:** The rabbet bit will leave a round corner on the rabbets, so you'll have to square them up with a chisel *(Fig. 17)*.

**GLASS.** In keeping with the style of this cabinet, I chose a decorative reeded glass that seemed more appropriate than ordinary flat glass. (See Sources on page 126.) Several plastic turnbuttons hold the glass in place *(Fig. 16b)*.

Once the decorative hinges and latches are added and the doors are mounted to the case, you can attach the upper cabinet to the lower cabinet with figure-8 fasteners *(Figs. 18 and 18a)*. ■

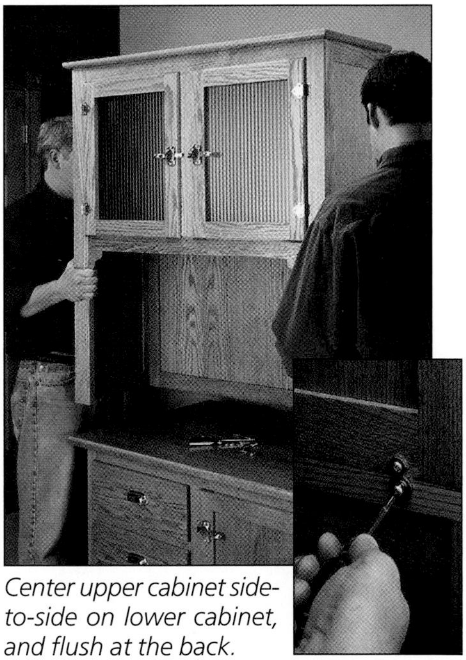

*Center upper cabinet side-to-side on lower cabinet, and flush at the back.*

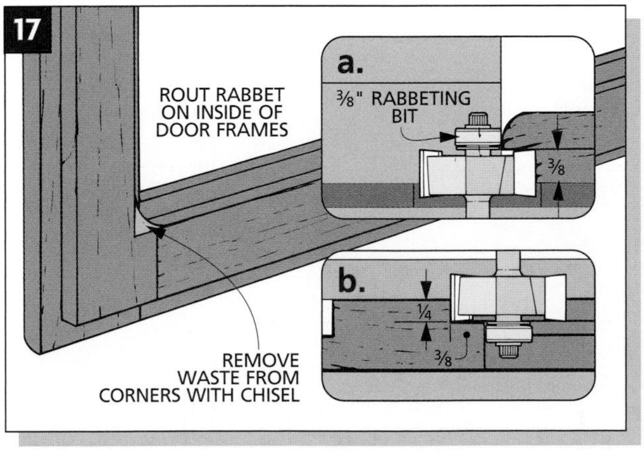
17
ROUT RABBET ON INSIDE OF DOOR FRAMES
a.
⅜" RABBETING BIT
⅜
b.
¼
⅜
REMOVE WASTE FROM CORNERS WITH CHISEL

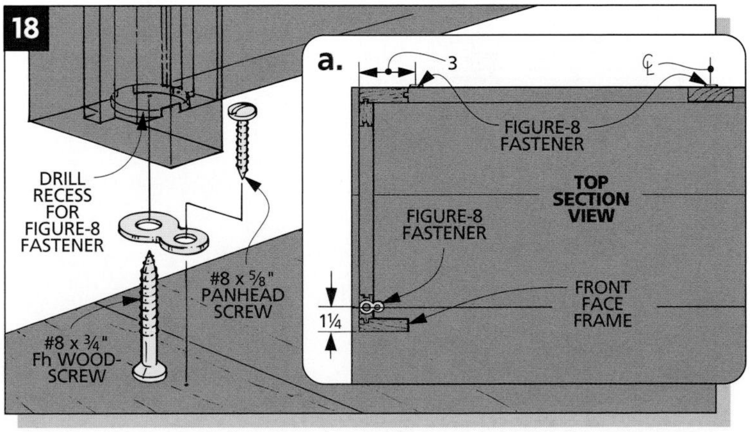
18
DRILL RECESS FOR FIGURE-8 FASTENER
#8 x ⅝" PANHEAD SCREW
#8 x ¾" Fh WOOD-SCREW
a.
3
FIGURE-8 FASTENER
TOP SECTION VIEW
FIGURE-8 FASTENER
FRONT FACE FRAME
1¼

# DESIGNER'S NOTEBOOK

*The great thing about the Hoosier cabinet is its versatility. With this wall-hung version all you do is shorten the top cabinet, then add a shelf and some support brackets for a fully-functional wall unit.*

## CONSTRUCTION NOTES:

■ Start by ripping the front (KK), back (KK), and side (RR) stiles for the Wall-Hung Cabinet to the same width as before. This time, though, the length of each stile is 33¾" *(Fig. 1)*.

■ The lower back panel and the bottom pair of side panels will also need to be shortened. I cut the new lower side panel (FFF) and a lower back panel (PP) to size from ¼" plywood *(Fig. 1)*. (Both of my panels ended up 11⅛" long.)

**Note:** Remaining workpieces for the upper cabinet remain the same size.

■ Once the new stiles and panels are complete, build all the remaining pieces, assemble them into a completed cabinet, and set it aside for now.

■ Because you're not building the lower cabinet, there is no longer the shelf that the top of the lower cabinet provided. Rather than waste this space by leaving it open, I decided to build a lower shelf that's supported by a pair of brackets.

The bottom shelf frame is built the same way as the top frame with a ¼" groove cut in all the pieces to accept the panel. But the bottom panel is made from ¾" plywood.

To build it, cut the bottom frame front, back, and sides (WW, XX, YY) to size. Then miter the pieces at the front and leave them square at the back just as before.

■ Now dry-assemble the frame and measure for the bottom panel (GGG), allowing for the ¼" wide, ¼" long tongue on all four sides. Now cut it to size and cut the tongue *(Fig. 2)*.

■ Next, glue up the frame. When the glue is dry, rout a ½" roundover on the top edge of the front and sides.

■ Now cut two brackets (HHH) from ¾"-thick stock and cut out the curved profile using a band saw *(Fig. 2)*.

■ Finally, drill countersunk shank holes through the top edge of the bottom frame and attach the brackets to the frame with screws *(Figs. 2 and 2a)*. Then attach the bottom frame and the brackets to the cabinet, this time screwing *up* through the bottom shelf and into the back frame and the front stiles *(Fig. 2a)*.

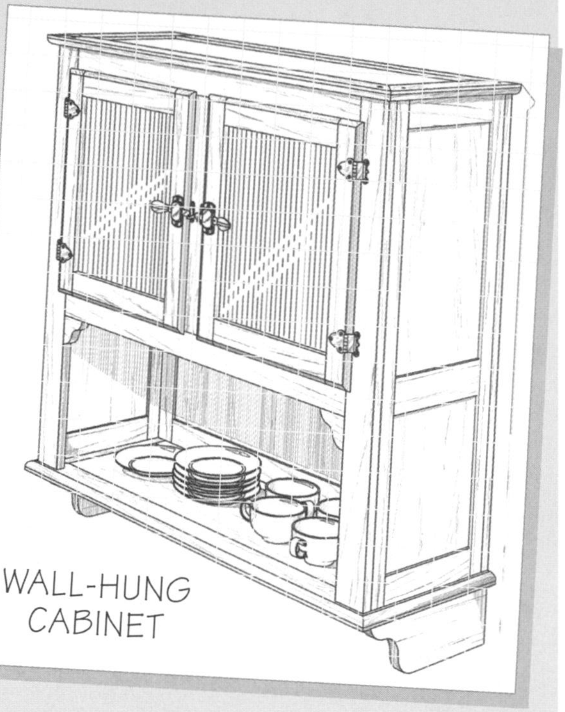

WALL-HUNG
CABINET


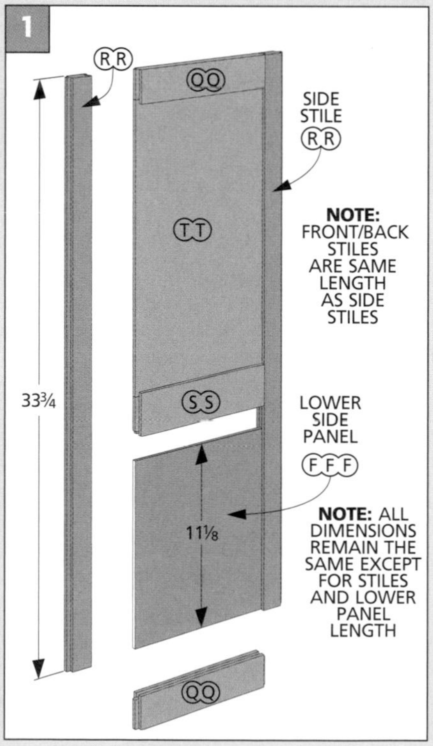

1
RR
QQ
SIDE STILE
RR
NOTE: FRONT/BACK STILES ARE SAME LENGTH AS SIDE STILES
TT
33¾
SS
LOWER SIDE PANEL
FFF
11⅛
NOTE: ALL DIMENSIONS REMAIN THE SAME EXCEPT FOR STILES AND LOWER PANEL LENGTH
QQ


### MATERIALS LIST

**CHANGED PARTS**

| | | |
|---|---|---|
| **KK** | Front/Back Stiles (4) | ¾ x 2½ - 33¾ |
| **PP** | Lower Back Panel (1) | ¾ x 31½ - 11⅛ |
| **RR** | Side Stiles (4) | ¾ x 1½ - 33¾ |
| **TT** | Side Panels (2) | ¼ ply x 9½ - 17⅛ |
| **WW** | Top/Btm. Frm. Fr. (2) | ¾ x 2½ - 37½ |
| **XX** | Top/Btm. Frm. Bk. (2) | ¾ x 2 - 33 |
| **YY** | Top/Btm. Frm. Sd. (4) | ¾ x 2½ - 13¾ |

**NEW PARTS**

| | | |
|---|---|---|
| **FFF** | Lwr. Side Panels (2) | ¼ ply - 9½ x 11⅛ |
| **GGG** | Bottom Panel (1) | ¾ ply - 9¾ x 33 |
| **HHH** | Brackets (2) | ¾ x 4½ - 12¼ |

**Note:** Do not need parts A through HH.

**HARDWARE SUPPLIES**

(10) No. 8 x 1¼" Fh woodscrews

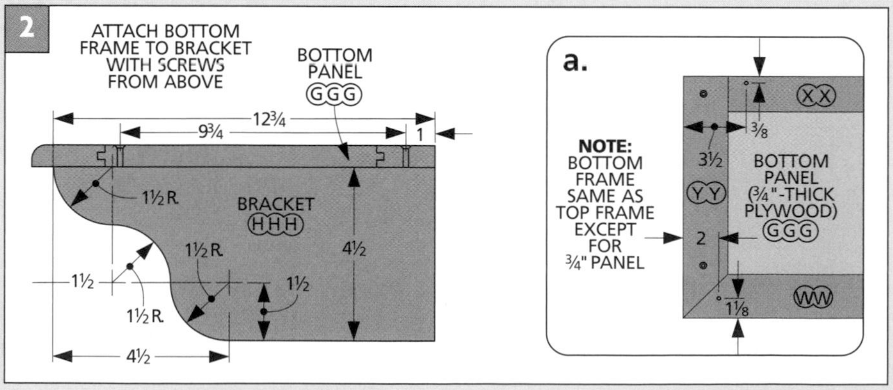

2
ATTACH BOTTOM FRAME TO BRACKET WITH SCREWS FROM ABOVE
BOTTOM PANEL
GGG
12¾
9¾
1
1½R
BRACKET
HHH
1½R
4½
1½
1½
1½R
4½
a.
XX
⅜
NOTE: BOTTOM FRAME SAME AS TOP FRAME EXCEPT FOR ¾" PANEL
3½
YY
BOTTOM PANEL (¾"-THICK PLYWOOD)
GGG
2
1⅛
WW

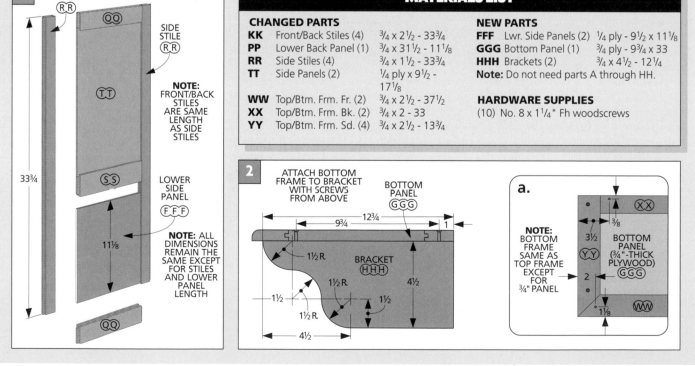

# Country Pie Safe

*The fun in building this project is that it's brand new, but it looks old. The challenge in building this "new" antique is to use time-tested materials like square nails and an easy technique for punching tin.*

There were a lot of questions to consider as I started building this pie safe. And all of them centered around making it look authentic.

The main attraction is the punched tin panels. I found a scratch awl with a short, tapered point to punch the holes, but you can buy pre-punched tin if you prefer. (For more on punched tin panels,

see the Technique article on page 112 and Sources on page 126.)

**MATERIALS.** Another important question was, what wood should be used? I decided on No. 2 common pine. It has just enough knots and defects to give the project a little "character."

**OLD BEFORE ITS TIME.** Finally, I wanted my safe to look like it might have been

built a hundred years ago. But how could it be distressed and finished to look old?

I used square nails and created a few joints that look loose (but aren't). Then to distress it I sanded down some edges to show wear and added fake wormholes (see the Technique on page 111).

**SPACE-SAVER.** For a smaller safe, see the Designer's Notebook on page 110.

# EXPLODED VIEW

OVERALL DIMENSIONS:
39½"W x 13¾"D x 54¾"H

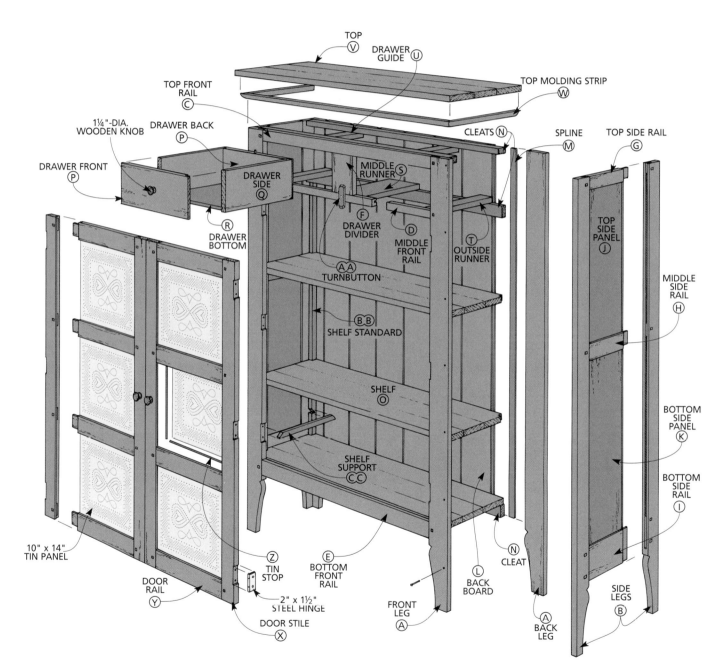

TOP
(V)

DRAWER GUIDE (U)

TOP FRONT RAIL (C)

TOP MOLDING STRIP (W)

1¼"-DIA. WOODEN KNOB

DRAWER BACK (P)

CLEATS (N)

SPLINE (M)

TOP SIDE RAIL (G)

DRAWER FRONT (P)

DRAWER SIDE (Q)

MIDDLE RUNNER (S)

TOP SIDE PANEL (J)

DRAWER BOTTOM (R)

DRAWER DIVIDER (F)

MIDDLE FRONT RAIL (D)

OUTSIDE RUNNER (T)

MIDDLE SIDE RAIL (H)

TURNBUTTON (AA)

SHELF STANDARD (BB)

SHELF (O)

BOTTOM SIDE PANEL (K)

10" x 14" TIN PANEL

SHELF SUPPORT (CC)

BOTTOM SIDE RAIL (I)

DOOR RAIL (Y)

TIN STOP (Z)

BOTTOM FRONT RAIL (E)

BACK BOARD (L)

CLEAT (N)

2" x 1½" STEEL HINGE

DOOR STILE (X)

FRONT LEG (A)

BACK LEG (A)

SIDE LEGS (B)

**104** CLASSIC CABINETS

## CUTTING DIAGRAM

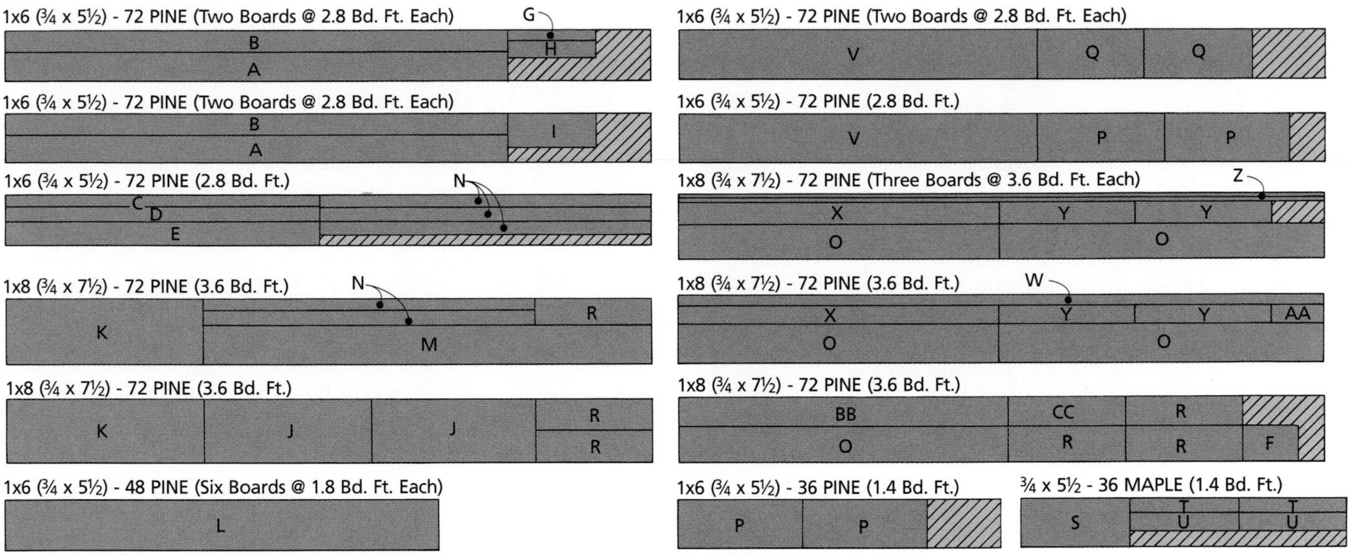
1x6 (3/4 x 5 1/2) - 72 PINE (Two Boards @ 2.8 Bd. Ft. Each)
G
B
H
A
1x6 (3/4 x 5 1/2) - 72 PINE (Two Boards @ 2.8 Bd. Ft. Each)
B
I
A
1x6 (3/4 x 5 1/2) - 72 PINE (2.8 Bd. Ft.)
N
C
D
E
1x8 (3/4 x 7 1/2) - 72 PINE (3.6 Bd. Ft.)
N
K
R
M
1x8 (3/4 x 7 1/2) - 72 PINE (3.6 Bd. Ft.)
K
J
J
R
R
1x6 (3/4 x 5 1/2) - 48 PINE (Six Boards @ 1.8 Bd. Ft. Each)
L
1x6 (3/4 x 5 1/2) - 72 PINE (Two Boards @ 2.8 Bd. Ft. Each)
V
Q
Q
1x6 (3/4 x 5 1/2) - 72 PINE (2.8 Bd. Ft.)
V
P
P
1x8 (3/4 x 7 1/2) - 72 PINE (Three Boards @ 3.6 Bd. Ft. Each)
Z
X
Y
Y
O
O
1x8 (3/4 x 7 1/2) - 72 PINE (3.6 Bd. Ft.)
W
X
Y
Y
AA
O
O
1x8 (3/4 x 7 1/2) - 72 PINE (3.6 Bd. Ft.)
BB
CC
R
O
R
R
F
1x6 (3/4 x 5 1/2) - 36 PINE (1.4 Bd. Ft.)
P
P
3/4 x 5 1/2 - 36 MAPLE (1.4 Bd. Ft.)
S
T
U
T
U

## MATERIALS LIST

**WOOD**

**A** Front/Back Legs (4) 3/4 x 3 - 56 rough
**B** Side Legs (4) 3/4 x 2 1/4 - 56 rough
**C** Top Front Rail (1) 3/4 x 1 3/4 - 34
**D** Middle Front Rail (1) 3/4 x 1 - 34
**E** Bottom Fr. Rail (1) 3/4 x 2 - 34
**F** Drawer Divider (1) 3/4 x 4 - 5
**G** Top Side Rails (2) 3/4 x 1 1/2 - 9 1/2
**H** Mdl. Side Rails (2) 3/4 x 2 - 9 1/2
**I** Btm. Side Rails (2) 3/4 x 4 - 9 1/2
**J** Top Side Panels (2) 1/2 x 6 7/8 - 17 7/8
**K** Btm. Side Panels (2) 1/2 x 6 7/8 - 21 3/8
**L** Back Boards (6) 3/4 x 5 1/4 - 46
**M** Splines (7) 1/4 x 3/4 - 46
**N** Cleats (5) 3/4 x 1 1/2 - 35 1/2
**O** Shelves (3) 3/4 x 10 7/8 - 35 1/2
**P** Drawer Fr./Bks. (4) 3/4 x 5 - 13 1/2
**Q** Drawer Sides (4) 3/4 x 5 - 11
**R** Drawer Bottoms (2) 1/2 x 10 1/2 - 12 1/2
**S** Middle Runner (1) 3/4 x 5 1/2 - 11 1/8
**T** Outside Runners (2) 3/4 x 2 - 11 1/8
**U** Drawer Guides (2) 3/4 x 2 - 11
**V** Top (1) 3/4 x 13 3/4 - 39 1/2
**W** Top Molding Strip (1) 3/4 x 3/4 - 72
**X** Door Stiles (4) 3/4 x 2 - 36 1/2
**Y** Door Rails (8) 3/4 x 2 - 14 1/2
**Z** Tin Stops 1/4 x 3/8 - 30 ln. ft.
**AA** Turnbutton (1) 1/2 x 7/8 - 3
**BB** Shelf Standards (4) 3/4 x 1/2 - 36 rough
**CC** Shelf Supports (4) 3/4 x 1/2 - 11 rough

**HARDWARE SUPPLIES**

(12) No. 8 x 2" Fh woodscrews
(2) No. 8 x 1 1/2" Fh woodscrews
(61) No. 8 x 1 1/4" Fh woodscrews
(2) No. 8 x 3/4" Rh woodscrews
(1 lb.) 1 1/2"-long square nails
(14) 1" brads
(72) 1/2" brads
(3 pr.) 2" x 1 1/2" steel hinges w/ screws
(6) 10" x 14" tin panels
(4) 1 1/4"-dia. wooden knobs w/ screws

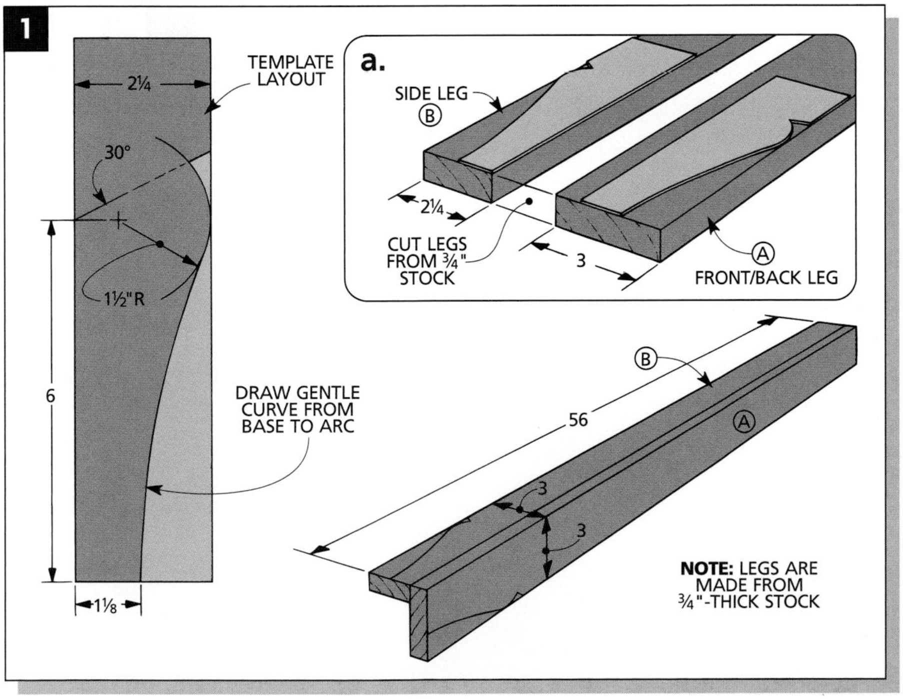
1
2 1/4
TEMPLATE LAYOUT
30°
1 1/2"R
6
1 1/8
DRAW GENTLE CURVE FROM BASE TO ARC
a.
SIDE LEG B
2 1/4
CUT LEGS FROM 3/4" STOCK
3
A
FRONT/BACK LEG
B
56
A
3
3
NOTE: LEGS ARE MADE FROM 3/4"-THICK STOCK

## LEGS

I started building the Country Pie Safe by making the legs. They run the full height of the cabinet and also serve as the stiles (uprights) for the front, side, and back frames. Begin by cutting the four front and back legs (A) from 3/4"-thick stock to size (3" x 56") *(Fig. 1)*. I used No. 2 common pine for all the frame pieces.

Each corner of the pie safe is actually two legs (a front or back leg and a side leg) nailed together *(Fig. 1)*. Since I wanted the width of the legs to appear the same from the front and the sides, I cut the side legs (B) 3/4" narrower than the front and back legs (A).

**BOTTOM PROFILE.** Next, I added a curved profile on the bottom of all eight leg pieces. To make doing this easier, I made a cardboard template *(Fig. 1)* and then used it to lay out and cut identical profiles on all eight legs *(Fig. 1a)*.

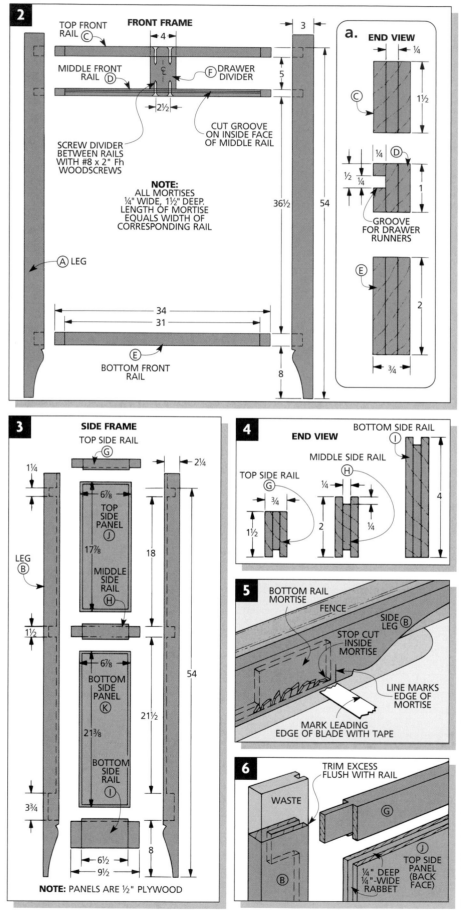

## FRONT FRAME

To build the front frame of the pie safe start by ripping three rails to width: a top front (C), middle front (D), and a bottom front (E) *(Figs. 2 and 2a)*. All three front rails are 34" long.

**MORTISE AND TENONS.** These rails are joined to the front legs by cutting mortises along the legs' *inside* edges *(Fig. 2)*. Then centered tenons are cut on the ends of all the rails to fit the mortises.

**GROOVE MIDDLE RAIL.** Now cut a $1/4$"-deep groove, $1/4$" wide on the inside face of the middle rail *(Fig. 2a)*. This groove will hold the tongue on the front of the drawer runners you'll be adding later.

**DRAWER DIVIDER.** Next, dry-assemble the frame and measure the distance between the top and middle rails. Then cut a 4"-wide drawer divider (F) to this length (5") *(Fig. 2)*. Center the divider on the rails and screw it in place.

**ASSEMBLY.** Now the rails can be glued to the front legs. I also added square wooden pegs through the joints (see the Shop Tip on the next page).

## SIDE FRAMES

After the front frame is clamped up, you can begin work on the side frames.

**RAILS.** First, rip the top side (G), middle side (H), and the bottom side (I) rails to width *(Fig. 4)*. Then cut all six rails to the same length *(Fig. 3)*.

**JOINERY.** After the rails are cut to size, cut mortises on the inside edges of the side legs (B) *(Fig. 3)*.

These mortises accept matching centered tenons cut on the rails. Then cut $1/4$" grooves on the edges of the rails *(Fig. 4)*.

**Note:** The top and bottom faces of the side rail tenons are trimmed away when grooves for the panels are cut in the rails.

**GROOVES IN LEGS.** There's one more set of grooves to cut for the panels. These are on the inside edge of the side legs. The trick is to stop the groove before it cuts through the profile at the bottom of the legs. I used a pencil mark on the leg and a piece of tape on the table saw to mark where to stop the cut *(Fig. 5)*.

**PANELS.** Now the panels can be made. Start by gluing up enough $1/2$"-thick stock to make two top side panels (J) and two bottom side panels (K) *(Fig. 3)*. To allow for expansion, trim the panels $1/8$" less than the distance between the grooves.

**TONGUE.** Next, to fit the panels into the grooves, I cut a rabbet on the back face

## SHOP TIP . . . . . . . . . . . . . . . . . . . . . . . . Square Pegs

On the pie safe, I added a peg through each of the mortise and tenon joints. With today's glues, this isn't necessary, but it makes the project more authentic. At one time, glue quality was so poor that joints needed more support — a peg or two to hold it together.

Not only are square pegs more authentic, but when a square peg is driven into a round hole, the corners wedge in tight and hold.

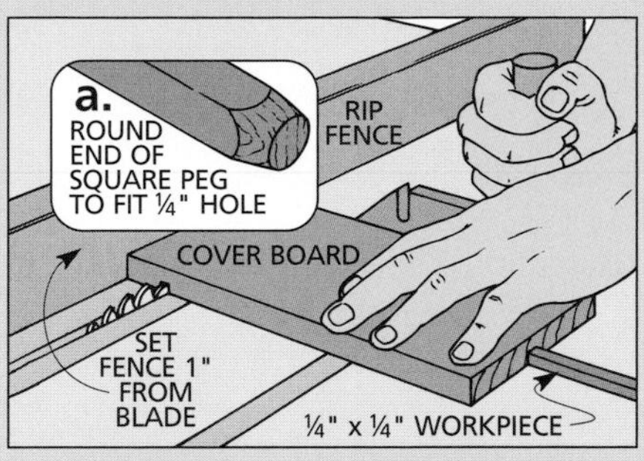

a.
ROUND END OF SQUARE PEG TO FIT 1/4" HOLE
RIP FENCE
COVER BOARD
SET FENCE 1" FROM BLADE
1/4" x 1/4" WORKPIECE


**1** *Round the end of a 1/4" x 1/4" stick with a pencil sharpener. With the rip fence as a stop, place the stick in a groove in a scrap cover board and safely cut it to length.*

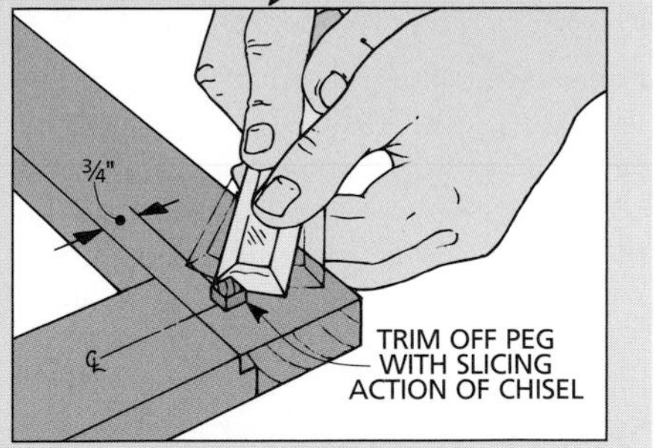

3/4"
TRIM OFF PEG WITH SLICING ACTION OF CHISEL


**2** *Drill a stopped 1/4" hole centered on the mortise. Glue in a peg with its edges parallel to the joint line. Saw the peg off 1/8" proud and then chisel it flush.*

of each panel to form a tongue along the front face *(Fig. 6)*.

**ASSEMBLY.** After the rabbets are cut, the side frames can be glued and clamped square. Don't glue the panels into the grooves. Just a dot of glue at the center of the top and bottom will keep the panel centered in the frame.

Once the side frames were assembled, I cut the excess off the top ends of the side legs and front legs *(Fig. 6)*.

### BACK FRAME

After the side frames were complete, I began work on the back. It's made from six boards aligned vertically between the two back legs. To connect the boards and still allow for expansion and contraction, I used a pair of cleats.

**BACK BOARDS.** The total width of all six back boards (L) must equal the shoulder-to-shoulder distance of the front frame rails (31"). After I ripped the boards so they added up to a total of 31", I trimmed an extra 1/16" off each board to allow for seasonal expansion. Then cut all the boards 46" long *(Fig. 7)*.

**SPLINES.** To align the boards for the back, I used 1/4" splines set into grooves cut in the edges of the boards *(Fig. 8)*.

After you cut the grooves, cut the splines (M) to fit the grooves. Then glue the splines into one side of each board *(Fig. 8)*. (Don't glue the splines into adjoining edges or the boards won't be able to expand and contract.)

**ASSEMBLE THE BACK.** Now to assemble the back, space the pieces out evenly until the overall width of the back (including the legs) equals the width of the front frame (37"). Also, make sure that the bottom ends of the boards are up 8" from the bottom of the legs *(Fig. 7)*.

Next, cut two cleats (N) to hold the back together. Cut them to length so they stop 3/4" from each side *(Fig. 9)*.

Screw (don't glue) the two cleats down across the assembly (two screws in each board) to prevent racking *(Figs. 7 and 9)*.

When the back is assembled, cut the excess "ears" off the top *(Fig. 7)*.

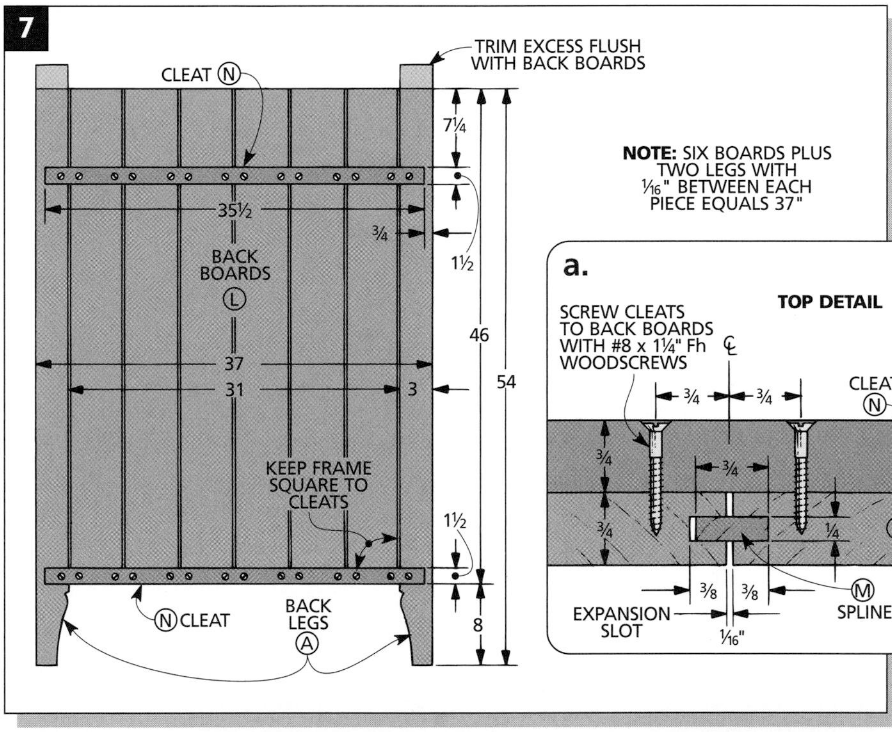

7
TRIM EXCESS FLUSH WITH BACK BOARDS
CLEAT (N)
7 1/4
NOTE: SIX BOARDS PLUS TWO LEGS WITH 1/16" BETWEEN EACH PIECE EQUALS 37"
35 1/2
3/4
1 1/2
BACK BOARDS (L)
46
54
37
31
3
KEEP FRAME SQUARE TO CLEATS
1 1/2
(N) CLEAT
BACK LEGS (A)
8
a.
TOP DETAIL
SCREW CLEATS TO BACK BOARDS WITH #8 x 1 1/4" Fh WOODSCREWS
3/4
3/4
CLEAT (N)
3/4
3/4
3/4
1/4
(L)
3/8
3/8
EXPANSION SLOT
1/16"
(M) SPLINE


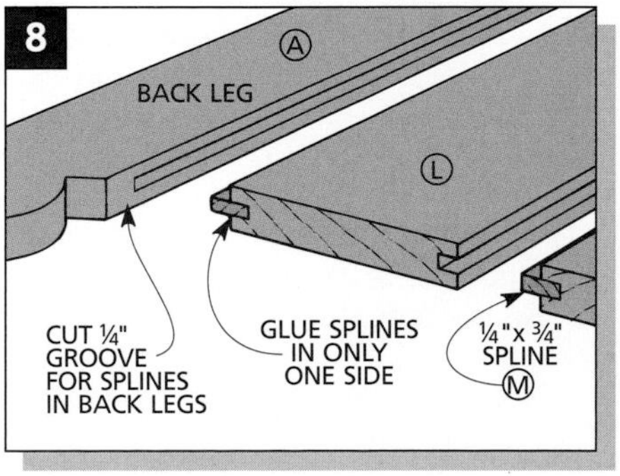

8
(A)
BACK LEG
(L)
CUT 1/4" GROOVE FOR SPLINES IN BACK LEGS
GLUE SPLINES IN ONLY ONE SIDE
1/4" x 3/4" SPLINE (M)


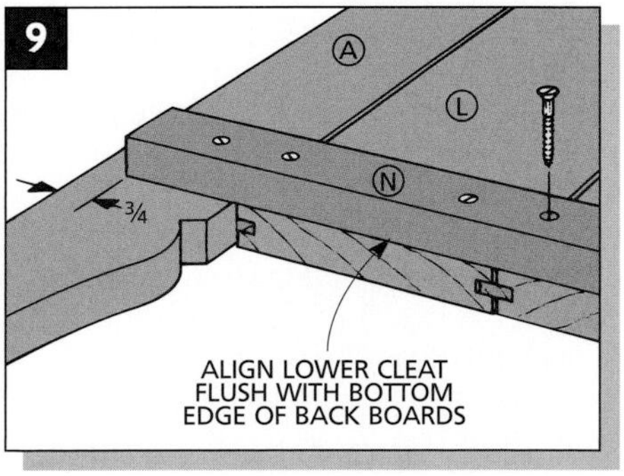

9
(A)
(L)
(N)
3/4
ALIGN LOWER CLEAT FLUSH WITH BOTTOM EDGE OF BACK BOARDS

Before assembling the cabinet frame, cut two more cleats (N), and screw them on edge to the inside of the front frame and the back assembly flush with the top (*Figs. 10 and 11*). To support the bottom shelf, screw one more cleat to the inside of the front frame (*Fig. 12*).

**ASSEMBLY.** Now the cabinet can be nailed together (*Fig. 11*). You could use standard 4d finishing nails, but I used square nails. (See Sources on page 126.) To prevent splitting when driving square nails, drill $1/8$" holes (every 8").

**SHELVES.** Once the cabinet is assembled, edge-glue enough $3/4$" stock to make three shelves (O) (one fixed and two adjustable). To allow for expansion, cut the shelves $1/8$" narrower than the inside depth of the cabinet (*Fig. 12*). Install the bottom shelf and nail it to the front cleat.

## DRAWERS

With the cabinet assembled, you can build the two drawers. Start by cutting four drawer fronts and backs (P) to fit the openings (*Fig. 13*). Next, cut four drawer sides (Q) to length (11").

**JOINERY.** To join these pieces, I cut rabbets in the fronts and backs (*Fig. 13*). I also cut grooves (for the bottom panel) in the front and side pieces.

**BOTTOM.** To make the drawer bottoms (R), I glued up $3/4$"-thick blanks and planed them down to $1/2$" thick. Then I cut a $1/4$" tongue on the front and sides.

**ASSEMBLY.** Once all the pieces are cut, glue and nail the front (P) to the sides (Q). Then slide the bottom (R) into the grooves from the back. (Don't glue it in.)

The drawer back sits on the bottom after the back is ripped to width. Then glue and nail it to the sides (*Fig. 13b*). To hold the bottom in the grooves, tack a nail up into the back (*Fig. 13a*).

After the drawers are assembled, plane them slightly for clearance in the cabinet. Then a roundhead screw is placed into each drawer back to act as a depth stop (*Fig. 13a*). Adjust the screws in or out until the drawers are flush with the front of the cabinet.

**DRAWER RUNNERS.** The drawers ride on maple runners. Cut one wide middle runner (S) ($5\frac{1}{2}$") and two narrow outside runners (T) (2"). Their length equals the inside depth of the cabinet plus $1/8$". 

To mount the runners, cut rabbets on the front end to produce a $1/4$" tongue

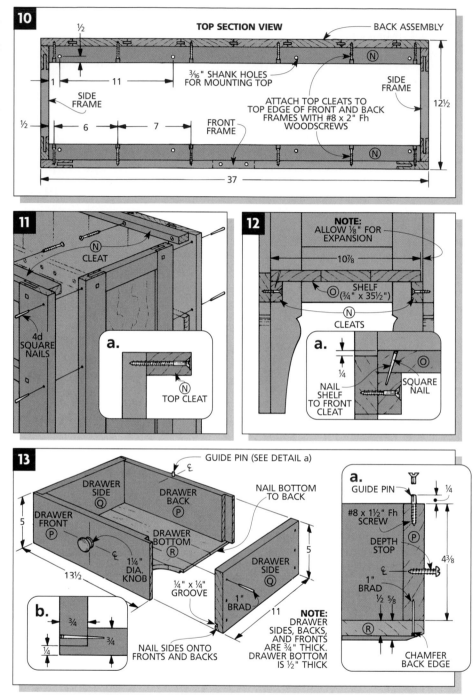

(*Fig. 14c*). Then slip the tongues in the groove in the middle front rail and screw the back end to the cleat (*Fig. 14*).

**DRAWER GUIDES.** My drawer guide system has a single maple guide (U) mounted above each drawer. The guide has a groove (*Fig. 14b*) to accept a guide pin made from a woodscrew. This pin is screwed into the top of the drawer back and the head is removed (*Fig. 13a*).

Before mounting the guides, plane a chamfer on the bottom back edge of the drawer sides so the drawers can be tipped into the opening (*Fig. 13a*).

Then to mount a drawer guide, hold the guide up under the top cleats and slide the drawer in. Then screw the back end of the guide in place.

Next pull the drawer until it's almost out of the cabinet and centered in the opening. Then screw the front of the guide in place from above.

## CABINET TOP

Now the cabinet is ready for the top. Edge-glue the top (V) from three pieces of $3/4$"-thick stock and cut the blank $1\frac{1}{4}$"

wider and 2½" longer than the cabinet *(Fig. 14)*. (Mine was 13¾" x 39½".)

To attach the top, first drill shank holes through the top cleats *(Fig. 10)*. Then center the top across the width of the cabinet and flush with the back, and screw it down from the inside (no glue).

**MOLDING.** I also routed a ¾" quarter-round profile on the top molding strip (W) and nailed it under the top *(Figs. 14 and 14a)*. The strips are mitered at the front corners and cut flush at the back.

## DOORS

The focal point of this whole cabinet is the doors with the punched tin panels.

**STILES.** To make the door frames, begin by cutting four door stiles (X) to a width of 2" and to length to match the exact height of the cabinet opening (36½" in my case) *(Fig. 15)*.

**Note:** I usually find it easiest to cut the door parts to fit tight and then plane them down after assembly.

After the stiles are cut to size, cut four mortises on the inside edge of each stile to accept the rails *(Fig. 15)*.

**RAILS.** To determine the length of the door rails (Y), measure one half the cabinet opening (15½"), subtract the width of two stiles (4") and add in the length of two 1½"-long tenons (3"). My total came to 14½". Then cut eight rails to this length and 2" wide *(Fig. 16)*.

**RABBETS.** Before cutting the tenons on the rails, I cut a ¼"-wide, ½"-deep rabbet to hold the tin panels. These rabbets are cut on the back edge of the rails and on the stiles *(Figs. 15 and 16)*.

**TENONS.** Next, cut tenons on all the rails. There's just one problem — when the rabbets were cut on the backs of the stiles, it created staggered shoulders *(Fig. 15a)*. So, you need to cut the tenon's shoulder on the *front* face 1½" from the end. But the shoulder on the *back* face is cut only 1¼" from the end to allow the tenon to "fill in" the rabbet *(Fig. 15b)*.

**ASSEMBLY.** After the tenons fit the mortises, dry-assemble the doors and test fit them in the openings. If they fit, glue all the parts together.

**Note:** After assembly, I clamped the parts for about two minutes until the glue "grabbed" and then fit the doors into the opening to hold them until they dried.

After the glue dries, remove each door and plane the edges to create a ¹⁄₁₆" gap between the door and the frame and a ⅛" gap between the doors.

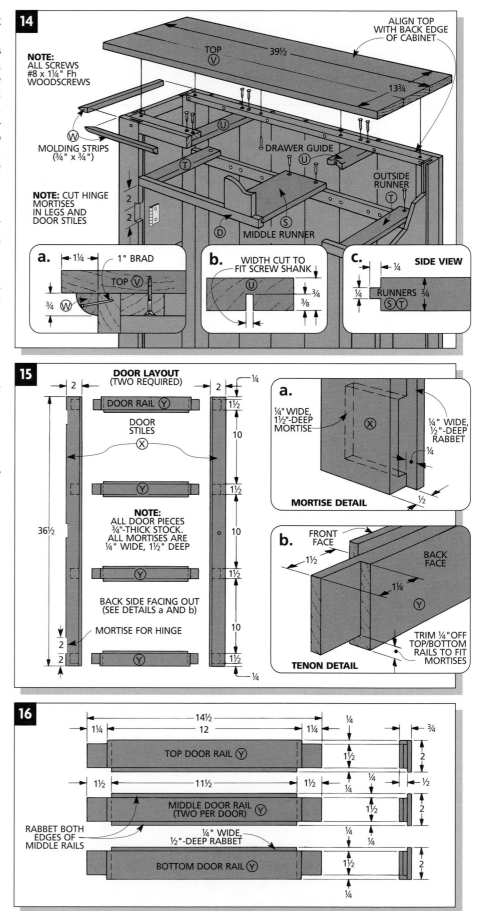

# DESIGNER'S NOTEBOOK

*For a different look, you can remove the two drawers and shorten the doors so there are just two tin panels on each side. What you'll end up with is a great space-saving version of the Country Pie Safe.*

## CONSTRUCTION NOTES:

■ The biggest change from the original is to shorten the front, back, and side legs. To make the width of the legs appear to be the same from the front and sides, cut the side legs (B) $^3/_4$" narrower than the front and back legs (A) *(Fig. 1)*.

■ Go ahead and cut the bottom profile on each of the legs exactly as before.

■ By shortening the legs, you'll now need only one hardwood panel on each side. So I glued up enough stock for a couple of bottom side panels (K) and made them slightly longer than before (23$^1/_2$").

■ Now cut the back boards (L), splines (M), and cleats (N) to size. Note that the back boards and splines have been shortened (28$^1/_2$") and that you'll only need four cleats instead of five. (Since I've left out the drawers, there's no need for a cleat for the drawer guides.)

■ After you've cut *all* of the pieces to size and cut the joinery on each, you can glue up the front, side, and back frames. Once again, use square pegs to pin the mortise

and tenon joints, then glue and nail (or screw) each joint the same as before.

■ With the cabinet assembled, I made the only new workpiece for this pie safe.

Since there's not enough room here for a turnbutton, I added a door stop to the case instead. The door stop (DD) is just a $^3/_4$"-thick piece of stock that I cut to size *(Fig. 2)*. Then it's glued in place to the back edge of the top front rail at the top of the case *(Fig. 2a)*. And to keep the doors closed, I installed a pair of rare-earth magnets in the stop and steel screws in the doors.

■ Now make the top and two shelves (O) and install them in the pie safe cabinet.

■ Next I made the doors using the same construction methods as I did with the larger version of the pie safe. This time though, the door stiles (X) are only 25" long and only six rails and four tin panels are needed. Add the door knobs, again centering them on the inside stiles.

■ Once the doors were complete, I cut hinge mortises for just two sets of hinges and installed them to the cabinet.

■ To complete the Space-Saving Pie Safe, all that's left is to cut four shelf standards (BB) to length (24$^3/_4$") and cutting the

notches before installing them inside the cabinet. Then I cut the two shelf supports (CC) and notched the corners.

SPACE-SAVING PIE SAFE

## MATERIALS LIST

**CHANGED PARTS**

| | | |
|---|---|---|
| A | Front/Back Legs (4) | $^3/_4$ x 3 - 36$^1/_2$ |
| B | Side Legs (4) | $^3/_4$ x 2$^1/_4$ - 36$^1/_2$ |
| K | Btm. Side Panels (2) | $^1/_2$ x 6$^7/_8$ - 23$^1/_2$ |
| L | Back Boards (6) | $^3/_4$ x 5$^1/_4$ - 28$^1/_2$ |
| M | Splines (7) | $^1/_4$ x $^3/_4$ - 28$^1/_2$ |
| N | Cleats (4) | $^3/_4$ x 1$^1/_2$ - 35$^1/_2$ |
| O | Shelves (2) | $^3/_4$ x 10$^7/_8$ - 35$^1/_2$ |
| X | Door Stiles (4) | $^3/_4$ x 2 - 25 |
| Y | Door Rails (6) | $^3/_4$ x 2 - 14$^1/_2$ |
| Z | Tin Stops | $^1/_4$ x $^3/_8$ - 20 ln. ft. |
| BB | Shelf Standards (4) | $^3/_4$ x $^1/_2$ - 24$^3/_4$ |
| CC | Shelf Supports (2) | $^3/_4$ x $^1/_2$ - 11 rough |

**NEW PART**

| | | |
|---|---|---|
| DD | Door Stop (1) | $^3/_4$ x 1$^1/_2$ - 35$^1/_2$ |

**HARDWARE SUPPLIES**

(37) No. 8 x 1$^1/_4$" Fh woodscrews
(12) 1" brads
(48) $^1/_2$" brads
(2 pr.) 2" x 1$^1/_2$" steel hinges w/ screws
(4) 10" x 14" tin panels
(2) 1$^1/_4$"-dia. wooden knobs w/ screws
(2) $^3/_8$" x $^1/_4$" rare-earth magnets w/ screws

**Note:** Do not need parts D, F, H, J, P, Q, R, S, T, U, AA, No. 8 x 1$^1/_2$" Fh woodscrews, and No. 8 x $^3/_4$" Fh woodscrews.

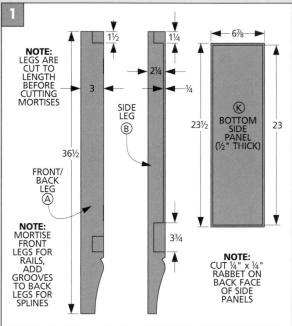

**1**

NOTE: LEGS ARE CUT TO LENGTH BEFORE CUTTING MORTISES

FRONT/BACK LEG (A)

NOTE: MORTISE FRONT LEGS FOR RAILS, ADD GROOVES TO BACK LEGS FOR SPLINES

SIDE LEG (B)

(K) BOTTOM SIDE PANEL ($^1/_2$" THICK)

NOTE: CUT $^1/_4$" x $^1/_4$" RABBET ON BACK FACE OF SIDE PANELS

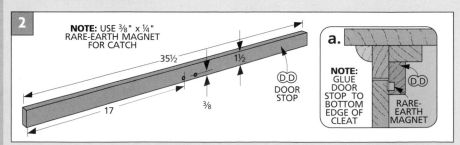

**2**

NOTE: USE $^3/_8$" x $^1/_4$" RARE-EARTH MAGNET FOR CATCH

DD DOOR STOP

**a.**

NOTE: GLUE DOOR STOP TO BOTTOM EDGE OF CLEAT

DD

RARE-EARTH MAGNET

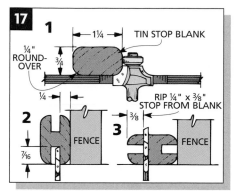

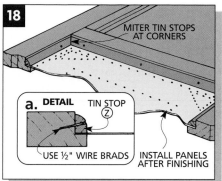

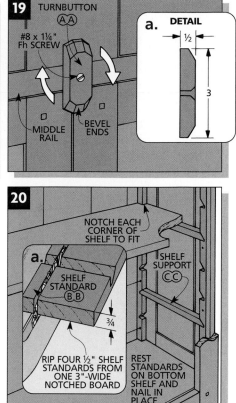

## TIN PANELS & HARDWARE

After the doors are planed to fit in the openings, the stops that hold the tin panels in place can be made.

**STOPS.** To make the tin stops (Z), round over all four edges of a piece of $3/4$" stock *(Step 1 in Fig. 17)*. Then make four cuts to form an "H-shaped" block *(Step 2)*. Finally, rotate the block on its side and trim off the tin stops *(Step 3)*.

After the tin stop molding is made, it can be mitered to fit *(Fig. 18)*.

**Note:** I used $1/2$" wire brads to hold the stops in place, but I didn't install the tins until later, after the finish was applied.

**HINGES AND KNOBS.** Now the doors are mounted to the front frame with three butt hinges on each door. Cut the mortises for the hinges in the door frame and front frame (refer to *Figs. 14 and 15* on page 109). Also, drill holes centered on the stiles for the door knobs.

**TURNBUTTON.** The doors are held closed with a turnbutton (AA) *(Fig. 19)*. Pare bevels on the ends of the turnbutton with a chisel, then position it on the middle rail and screw it in place so when it's turned it holds both doors closed.

## SHELVES

The last step is to install the adjustable shelves. I decided to use an old-fashioned notched system to hold them *(Fig. 20)*.

**STANDARDS.** I cut all four standards (BB) from one 3" x 36" (rough length) board *(Fig. 20a)*. (This keeps the notches in all four shelf standards aligned.) Lay out the notches on the edge of the board and make the 45° angled cuts.

Then make 90° cuts so they meet the ends of the angled cuts. (If the two cuts don't meet perfectly, clean out the bottom of the notch with a chisel.)

To cut the workpiece to length, measure the distance from the bottom shelf to the bottom of the cleat below the drawers. Then cut it this length, and rip it into four standards *(Fig. 20a)*.

Now you can nail each shelf standard into a corner of the cabinet. Just make sure the bottom edge rests firmly on the bottom shelf *(Fig. 20)*.

**SUPPORTS.** Next, cut four shelf supports (CC) with chamfered ends to fit the notches in the standards *(Fig. 20)*.

**NOTCH SHELVES.** Finally, notches are cut in the corners of the shelves to allow them to fit around the standards.

The only steps left are to distress the pie safe (see the Technique box below), finish it, and install the tin panels. (For more information on punching and aging tin, see the Technique on page 112.) ■

## TECHNIQUE ....................................... *Distressing*

When building this piece I decided I wanted it to look 100 years old. To do that, I needed to ask myself how much wear the Country Pie Safe might show after 100 years of use in the home.

**JOINTS.** After that much time, the joints would probably be a little loose. So to create the appearance of a gap in a mortise and tenon (but keep a strong joint), I sanded a slight round on the edges of the two matching pieces. This creates a shadow line that looks like a gap (see photo).

To create a gap on miters, I wasn't quite as careful when setting up the miter gauge to exactly 45° or clamping the joint perfectly tight.

**SANDING.** When sanding, round corners and edges by hand so it looks like there has been some natural wear. Concentrate on the bottom third of the project. That's where years of a broom bumping against it shows up.

**WORMHOLES.** To make "wormholes," bend some fine wire into a wavy pattern and tap it into the wood until an impression is left. Then use the wire to poke some holes.

**DIRT.** To make the project look "dirty," set the nails just below the surface of the wood. The stain soaks in and looks like a natural build-up of dirt.

Or try rubbing a little rottenstone or even fine dirt into the gouges, nail holes, around the knobs and turnbutton, and

along some of the edges of the doors and drawers.

Be careful not to overdo the distressing. It's a fine line, and too much looks phony.

# TECHNIQUE ............ *Punching Tin*

**W**hen I first started designing the pie safe I thought punching the tin would be the easiest and quickest part of the project. I found out it's not too difficult, but it sure isn't quick.

There are 1343 holes in each panel of the "Hearts on a Blanket" design I used (see below). It took an hour to punch the first panel, but after developing a technique I was able to punch the remaining panels in about 45 minutes each.

Punching a panel is fun, but tedious work. I found it easier to spread the task of punching the tin over a couple of days.

**PATTERNS.** The ideas for the patterns shown below came from some quilt design books. It can also be fun to create and punch your own design. (For sources of tin, pre-punched panels, and full-size patterns of the three designs below and other designs, see page 126.)

The two easier designs ("Fruit Basket" and "Daisy Swirl") only have one size hole and should only take about 20 minutes per panel to punch.

Since you punch right through the paper pattern and destroy it, you'll need a new copy of the pattern each time you punch a new panel (six copies for the Country Pie Safe). If you design your own pattern, photocopies can be made from your original for each panel.

| HEARTS ON A BLANKET | FRUIT BASKET | DAISY SWIRL |
| --- | --- | --- |

## SETTING UP

After selecting the pattern you want to use on your pie safe, the next step is fastening the pattern to the tin.

**PATTERN TO TIN.** To do this, start by aligning the pattern with the top edge of the tin and center it on the length. Then tape it down with masking tape *(Fig. 1)*. Because the 10" x 12" pattern is smaller than the 10" x 14" tin, there will be 1" of waste on the sides. Don't worry about it. The waste is trimmed off and it gives you some room to practice punching.

**BACKING BOARD.** The next step is to fasten the tin to a 12" x 16" backing board *(Fig. 2)*. To keep from punching into existing holes, I used a new ¼" hard-board backing board for each panel that I punched. Since hardboard is very consistent, it's easy to control the depth of the punches from board to board.

**KEEPER STRIPS.** Finally, to keep the tin from curling or moving while I was punching, I screwed a ¼" x 1" keeper strip along each side *(Fig. 2)*.

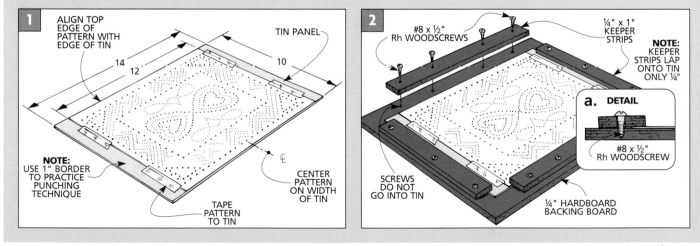

## PUNCHING THE TIN

Once the tin is fastened to the backing board, you're almost ready to start punching. Before you start, you'll want to select a punching tool and take a little practice to get the hang of it.

**PUNCHING TOOL.** What's the best tool for punching? I tried some metal center punches, but the point angle was too flat to pierce the tin *(Fig. 3)*. A scratch awl punched the small holes just fine, but it couldn't make the large holes.

To punch the tin for the pie safe, I found a scratch awl with a thick shaft that

tapers quickly down to a point starting about $3/16''$ from the end *(Fig. 3)*. That's the best shape for punching various size holes. An old nail set could also be ground down to this shape on a grinder.

To make punching the tin as easy as possible, sharpen your punching tool by spinning it against a grinder or honing it sharp on a stone. It should be sharp enough to easily pierce the tin.

**PRACTICE MAKES PERFECT.** After the tool is sharp, practice punching in the border areas to develop a technique that

will consistently give you the correct size holes. The more complicated pattern has two different size holes *(Fig. 4)*.

The larger holes should be about $3/32''$ in diameter. The smaller holes should be $1/32''$ in diameter. If the pattern has only one size hole, $1/16''$ is about right.

**SMALL HOLES.** To punch the small holes, grip the shaft of the awl with one hand and hold the point on the dot in the pattern. Then choke half way up the hammer handle with the other hand.

**Note:** I used a 16 oz. claw hammer. Experiment to find what works best.

Now raise the hammer about six inches above the awl and drop it onto the awl. There shouldn't be any muscle behind it. If the awl is sharp enough, the point will pierce the tin and leave a hole about $1/32''$ in diameter *(Fig. 4a)*.

**LARGE HOLES.** To produce the larger $3/32''$-dia. holes *(Fig. 4b)*, you have to give the awl a firm blow. It's about like setting a nail with a nail set.

Practice in the waste area until you can punch holes of a fairly consistent size (large or small). Don't worry if your holes vary a bit — it adds character to the piece.

**FLATTEN THE TIN.** After all the holes are punched, remove the tin from the backing board and carefully flatten out any large, rolling bumps with your fingers. But don't cut off the borders yet. The borders serve as "handles" when you age the tin next.

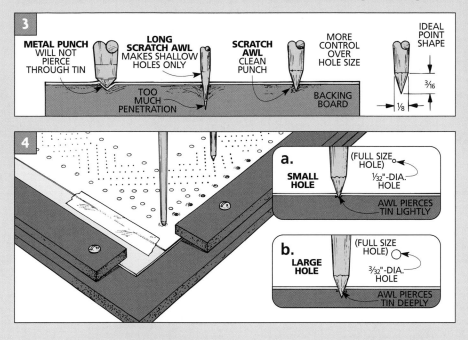

## AGING THE TIN

At this point, the tin looks too new and shiny to fit into an "antique" project. So to develop an "aged" appearance, the tin (and steel hinges) have to oxidize.

**WASH THE TIN.** The first step in this process is to wash off any fingerprints or dirt with dishwashing detergent.

**SOAKING TANK.** Next, make a soaking tank from 1x3s and a plastic garbage bag *(Fig. 5)*. Then soak the panels (two at a time) in a gallon of white vinegar.

To keep the tin panels from touching each other or the bottom, separate them with scraps of wood *(Fig. 5a)*. If the wood floats the panels, add some weight, but make sure the weight and spacers only touch the waste areas.

The face side of the tin should face up in the tank. As the tin oxidizes, bubbles develop and float up under the bottom side leaving a blotchy surface.

**RINSE.** After the tin has soaked overnight, lift it out of the tank by the waste borders. Immediately rinse off the entire panel under running water, wiping off any residue with a soft rag.

**DRY AND CUT TO SIZE.** Then, to prevent water spots, dry it off immediately with a hair dryer. Once it's dry, cut off the

waste with tin snips so the panel fits the opening and the design is centered.

**PREVENTING RUST.** Over time, the tin might rust from humidity. To keep it from rusting, I sealed the panels with a spray matte varnish. It's used by artists to seal acrylic and oil paintings and is available at art and hobby supply stores.

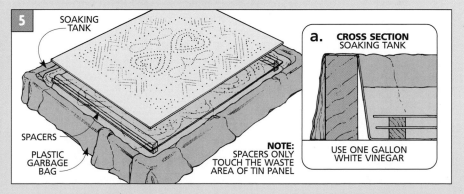

# Oak Icebox

*Although the ice wagon may be a thing of the past, the icebox lives on here as a beautiful storage cabinet. Our design can be modified in a number of ways to make this piece suit your needs.*

The memories of opening the door of the icebox and chipping off a piece of ice for a refreshing summertime treat have long since melted away. But these old iceboxes still have enough charm to encourage a whole new generation of woodworkers to take up the challenge of building one.

So what is an icebox used for these days? Well, inside this one, there's plenty of open space with movable shelves in each compartment. So you could use it as a home for table linens and dishes, or as a small pantry in the kitchen.

**HARDWARE.** The biggest stumbling block with building an icebox is finding authentic-looking brass hardware. But now beautiful reproductions of that hardware are available again. A hardware kit that includes the hinges, latches, and the name plate for the bottom of the cabinet is available from *Woodsmith Project Supplies*. Details and ordering information can be found on page 126.

The solid-brass hinges and latches I used on this project require a $3/8''$ offset on the doors. If you find your hardware from another source it may have a different offset. So it's best to have it in hand before construction begins.

**CONSTRUCTION.** The bulk of the icebox is frame and panel construction.

The sides, back, doors, and even the shelves are built this way. The panels are plywood, so any concerns about wood movement are reduced. But the top of the icebox is solid wood. So you have to allow it to expand and contract as the humidity changes. Some simple Z-shaped fasteners do the trick here.

**OPTIONS.** You have several options to customize this project. The first option, shown on page 124, is to use a panel of reeded refrigerator glass instead of wood in the large door. Or by building the icebox with drawers where the small doors are, it can serve as a dresser. Details about this option are on page 125.

## EXPLODED VIEW

**OVERALL DIMENSIONS:**
43½W x 21½D x 47¾H

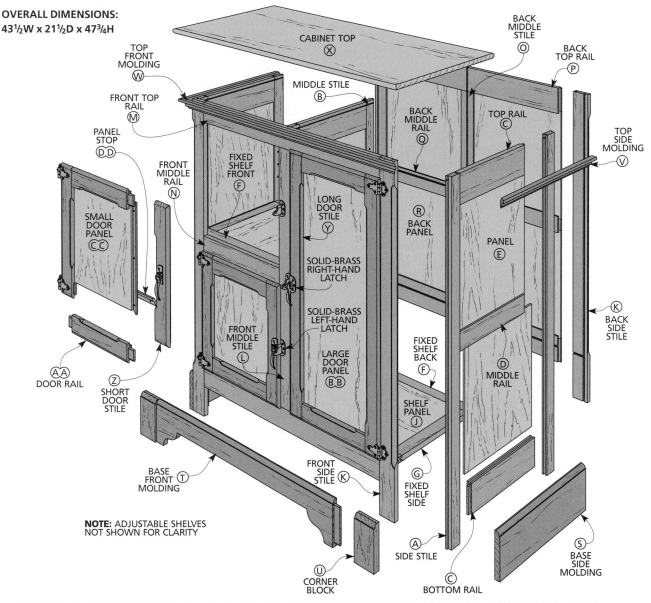

TOP FRONT MOLDING — W

FRONT TOP RAIL — M

PANEL STOP — DD

SMALL DOOR PANEL — CC

FRONT MIDDLE RAIL — N

FIXED SHELF FRONT — F

MIDDLE STILE — B

CABINET TOP — X

BACK MIDDLE STILE — O

BACK TOP RAIL — P

BACK MIDDLE RAIL — Q

TOP RAIL — C

TOP SIDE MOLDING — V

LONG DOOR STILE — Y

SOLID-BRASS RIGHT-HAND LATCH

SOLID-BRASS LEFT-HAND LATCH

LARGE DOOR PANEL — BB

FRONT MIDDLE STILE — L

BACK PANEL — R

PANEL — E

BACK SIDE STILE — K

FIXED SHELF BACK — F

MIDDLE RAIL — D

AA — DOOR RAIL

Z — SHORT DOOR STILE

BASE FRONT MOLDING — T

FRONT SIDE STILE — K

SHELF PANEL — J

FIXED SHELF SIDE — G

A — SIDE STILE

BASE SIDE MOLDING — S

U — CORNER BLOCK

C — BOTTOM RAIL

**NOTE:** ADJUSTABLE SHELVES NOT SHOWN FOR CLARITY

---

## MATERIALS LIST

### SIDE/MIDDLE FRAMES

| | | |
|---|---|---|
| **A** | Side Stiles (4) | ¾ x 2 - 47 |
| **B** | Middle Stiles (2) | ¾ x 2 - 42½ |
| **C** | Top/Bottom Rails (6) | ¾ x 4 - 15¼ |
| **D** | Middle Rails (3) | ¾ x 2½ - 15¼ |
| **E** | Panels (6) | ¼ ply - 15¼ x 16¾ |

### SHELVES

| | | |
|---|---|---|
| **F** | Fixed Shelf Fr./Bk. (6) | ¾ x 2 - 19 . |
| **G** | Fixed Shelf Sides (6) | ¾ x 2 - 15¼ |
| **H** | Adj. Shelf Fr./Bk. (6) | ¾ x 1¾ - 18¼ |
| **I** | Adj. Shelf Sides (6) | ¾ x 1¾ - 15¼ |
| **J** | Shelf Panels (6) | ¾ ply - 15¼ x 15½ |

### FRONT/BACK FRAMES

| | | |
|---|---|---|
| **K** | Fr./Bk. Side Stiles (4) | ¾ x 2½ - 47 |
| **L** | Front Middle Stile (1) | ¾ x 2½ - 38½ |
| **M** | Fr. Top/Btm. Rails (2) | ¾ x 3 - 36½ |

### MOLDING/TOP

| | | |
|---|---|---|
| **N** | Front Middle Rail (1) | ¾ x 2½ - 18 |
| **O** | Back Middle Stile (1) | ¾ x 2½ - 35¼ |
| **P** | Bk. Top/Btm. Rails (2) | ¾ x 4 - 35¼ |
| **Q** | Back Middle Rails (2) | ¾ x 2½ - 16¾ |
| **R** | Back Panels (4) | ¼ ply - 16¾ x 16¾ |

### MOLDING/TOP

| | | |
|---|---|---|
| **S** | Base Side Mldg. (2) | ¾ x 6 - 19½ |
| **T** | Base Fr. Molding (1) | ¾ x 6 - 36½ |
| **U** | Corner Blocks (2) | 1¹/₁₆ x 3¼ - 6 |
| **V** | Top Side Moldings (2) | ¾ x 2¾ - 21 |
| **W** | Top Fr. Molding (1) | ¾ x 2¾ - 42 |
| **X** | Cabinet Top (1) | ¾ x 21½ - 43½ |

### DOORS

| | | |
|---|---|---|
| **Y** | Long Door Stiles (2) | ¾ x 2½ - 37 |
| **Z** | Short Door Stiles (4) | ¾ x 2½ - 17½ |
| **AA** | Door Rails (6) | ¾ x 2½ - 13½ |

| | | |
|---|---|---|
| **BB** | Large Door Panel (1) | ¼ ply - 12 x 32½ |
| **CC** | Small Door Panels (2) | ¼ ply - 12 x 13 |
| **DD** | Panel Stop | ⅜ x ¾ - 16 ln. ft. |

### HARDWARE SUPPLIES

(22) No. 8 x 1¼" Fh woodscrews
(42) No. 6 x ¾" Fh woodscrews
(8) No. 8 x ¾" Rh woodscrews
(2) No. 15 x ½" brass brads
(8) Table top fasteners
(12) Brass-plated pin-style shelf supports
(2) Solid brass left-hand latches w/ screws
(1) Solid brass right-hand latch w/ screws
(6) Solid brass hinges (⅜" offset) w/ screws
(1) "White Clad" nameplate

## CUTTING DIAGRAM

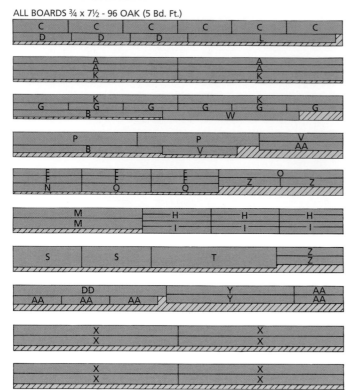

ALL BOARDS ¾ x 7½ - 96 OAK (5 Bd. Ft.)

¼" OAK PLYWOOD - 48 x 96

¾" OAK PLYWOOD - 48 x 48

1¹⁄₁₆ x 6½ - 24 OAK (1.6 Bd. Ft.)

---

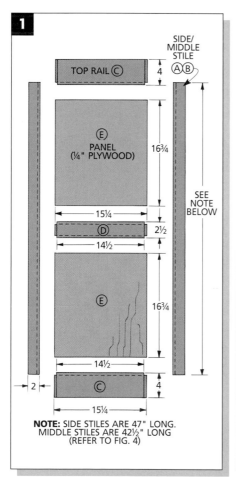

TOP RAIL Ⓒ

SIDE/MIDDLE STILE ⒶⒷ

4

Ⓔ
PANEL
(¼" PLYWOOD)

16¾

15¼

Ⓓ 2½

14½

Ⓔ

16¾

14½

Ⓒ 4

2

15¼

SEE NOTE BELOW

**NOTE:** SIDE STILES ARE 47" LONG. MIDDLE STILES ARE 42½" LONG (REFER TO FIG. 4)

## SIDE FRAMES

I started work on the icebox by building the two side frames and the middle divider frame. All three frames are built the same way: solid-wood frames with ¼" plywood panels.

**STILES.** Begin by ripping enough stock for all six stiles (A, B) to finished width and to rough length *(Fig. 1)*. Then cut the four side stiles (A) 47" long, and the two middle stiles (B) 42½" long *(Fig. 1)*. The extra length on the side stiles allows for 4½"-long legs to extend below the bottom edge of the frame (refer to *Fig. 4*).

**RAILS.** The next thing to work on is the top and bottom rails (C) and the middle rails (D) *(Figs. 1, 2, and 3)*.

**GROOVES.** After the stiles and rails have been cut to size, ⅜"-deep, centered grooves are cut on the inside edge of each piece to accept the plywood panels.

**TONGUES.** Then, cut ⅜"-long tongues on each end of the rails to fit the grooves *(Figs. 2 and 3)*. I cut these tongues by making multiple passes on the table saw.

**PLYWOOD PANELS.** After the joints are cut, dry-assemble the frames and take measurements for the plywood panels (E). For the best appearance, try to cut

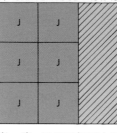

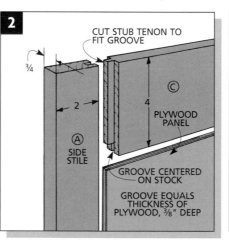

CUT STUB TENON TO FIT GROOVE

¾

2

4

Ⓒ

PLYWOOD PANEL

Ⓐ SIDE STILE

GROOVE CENTERED ON STOCK

GROOVE EQUALS THICKNESS OF PLYWOOD, ⅜" DEEP

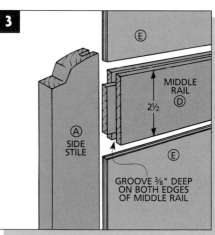

Ⓔ

MIDDLE RAIL Ⓓ

2½

Ⓐ SIDE STILE

Ⓔ

GROOVE ⅜" DEEP ON BOTH EDGES OF MIDDLE RAIL

the panels so the grain pattern of the plywood continues from the bottom panel up to the top panel (refer to the Cutting Diagram on the facing page).

Be sure to position the bottom rail on the side frames $4^{1}/_{2}$" from the bottom of the stiles to produce the "legs" *(Fig. 4)*. Also, make sure these rails line up with the bottom rails on the middle frame. If everything checks out, spread glue in all the grooves and clamp the frames and panels together.

**HOLES FOR SHELVES.** After the frames are assembled, holes are drilled to mount adjustable shelves inside the cabinet. (See the Shop Tip on the next page for an easy way to do this.)

**GROOVE FOR TOP.** The last step in constructing the frames is to cut a $^{1}/_{8}$"-wide groove for the hardware used to mount the top of the cabinet *(Fig. 4a)*.

## SHELVES

After the holes were drilled in the frames, I started work on the shelves. There are two kinds of shelves: fixed shelves that serve as the bottom of each of the three compartments, and adjustable shelves that sit inside each compartment.

All the shelves are $^{3}/_{4}$" plywood with a solid-wood frame. To make the frame pieces for the fixed shelves, start by ripping the front (F), back (F), and the sides (G) 2" wide *(Fig. 5)*. Then cut the front and back pieces (F) to a length of 19".

The shelf side pieces (G) are then cut to length so the shelf will end up exactly as wide as the cabinet's side frame. To do this, measure the width of the side frame, subtract the width of the shelf's front and back pieces, and add $^{3}/_{4}$" for the two $^{3}/_{8}$"-long tongues. (Mine were $15^{1}/_{4}$" long.)

Now you can cut the pieces for the adjustable shelf. First, rip the front (H), back (H), and sides (I) $1^{3}/_{4}$" wide *(Fig. 6)*. Then cut the front and back pieces $18^{1}/_{4}$" long, and cut the side pieces the same length as the fixed shelf side pieces.

**GROOVES.** After the frame pieces are cut to size, cut grooves on the inside edges of all the pieces *(Figs. 5a and 6a)*. Then cut tongues on the ends of the side pieces to fit the grooves.

**PLYWOOD INSERTS.** Now dry-assemble the frames and take measurements for the plywood shelf panels (J) *(Fig. 5)*. Then cut tongues on the panels to fit the grooves in the frame pieces.

**ASSEMBLY.** Finally, glue and clamp the frame pieces around the plywood panels.

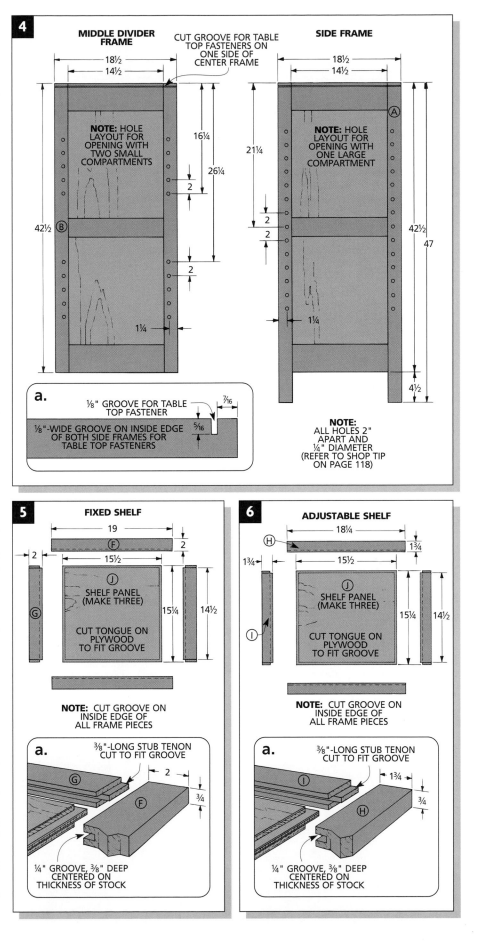

Each compartment of the icebox has an adjustable shelf that rests on four shelf pins. All told, there are 48 holes for the pins.

Laying out each hole would be time-consuming. And if I mismarked one hole, the shelf wouldn't sit properly. So instead, I made a couple of drilling templates. This way, I knew the holes would align between both sides of each compartment.

**Note:** The spacing for the holes is different on each side of the cabinet

(refer to *Fig. 4* on page 117). The large compartment has a continuous series of holes. The two small compartments have an "interrupted" pattern.

All that's needed to make each template is to mark and drill the positions of the holes on a piece of scrap, and then nail a cleat to the end of it (see drawing).

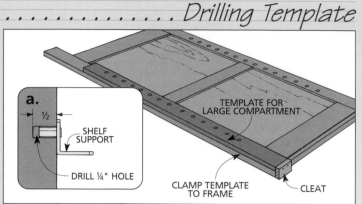

To use the templates, all you need to do is hook the cleat over the top edge of each frame and drill the holes (see drawing).

To prevent drilling through the frame, I used a depth stop on my drill bit so that all the holes ended up $\frac{1}{2}$" deep (detail 'a').

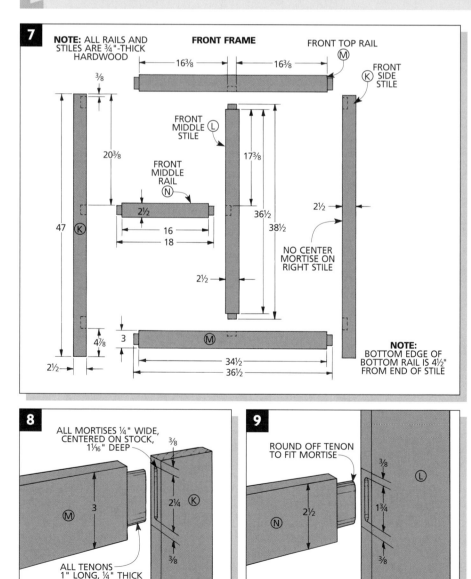

## FRONT FRAME

To complete the basic cabinet, the side frames and shelves are joined to a front face frame and a back frame (refer to *Fig. 14* on page 120). I started with the front face frame.

Begin by ripping all six pieces for the front frame (K, L, M, N) to final width and rough length *(Fig. 7)*. Next, the front side stiles (K) can be trimmed to length to match the side frame stiles.

**MORTISES AND TENONS.** Now you can start on the joinery. First, cut mortises at the top of the side stiles (K) *(Fig. 8)*.

The mortises at the bottom of the stiles are $4\frac{7}{8}$" up from the bottom edge to allow for the "leg" and the shoulder of the tenon. Then there's one more mortise in the middle of the left-hand stile only. To find its position, use the side frame as a guide. What you want is for the middle rail (N) of the face frame to align with the middle rail of the side frame.

**RAIL TENONS.** After the mortises are cut, trim the front top and bottom rails (M) to length and cut tenons to fit the mortises in the stiles *(Fig. 8)*. Finally, cut the mortises for the middle stile.

**MIDDLE STILE.** Now dry-assemble the stiles and rails and measure for the length of the middle stile (L). (Mine was $38\frac{1}{2}$" long.) Then cut the middle stile to length and cut tenons on each end *(Fig. 7)*. And finally, cut a mortise on the middle stile for the front middle rail (N) *(Fig. 9)*.

**MIDDLE RAIL.** For the middle rail (N) just repeat the same procedure: Add the middle stile to the dry assembly, measure for the length of the middle rail, cut the rail to length, and cut tenons on the ends.

**ASSEMBLY.** Finally, test the fit and then glue and clamp the front frame together.

## BACK FRAME

The construction of the back frame is similar to the side frames *(Fig. 10)*. Begin by cutting the seven frame pieces (K, O, P, Q) to size *(Fig. 10)*.

**JOINERY.** Now cut $3/8$"-deep grooves centered on the thickness of each piece to accept the plywood panels (refer to *Figs. 11 and 12 on page 120*).

The rest of the procedure is similar to building the front frame. Trim the back side stiles (K) and the back top and bottom rails (P) to final length and cut tenons on the rails *(Fig. 10)*.

**MIDDLE STILE AND RAILS.** Now dry-assemble the stiles and rails to find the length of the back middle stile (O).

**Note:** Be sure to position the bottom rail $4^{1}/2$" up from the bottom.

Add the middle stile to the assembly and measure and cut the middle rails (Q) to final length ($16^{3}/4$") *(Fig. 10)*.

**PANELS.** Finally, assemble the frame and measure for the back panels (R). Cut the panels to size and then glue and clamp the whole back frame together.

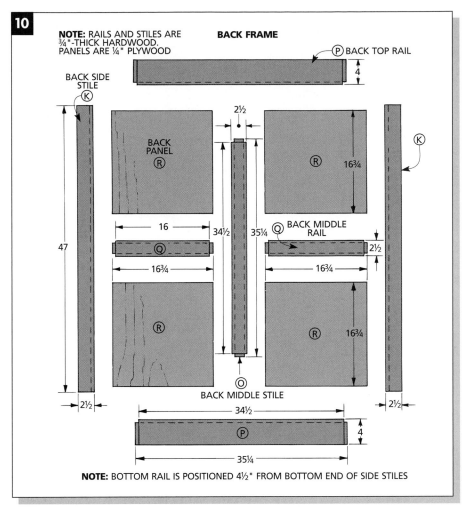

**10**

**NOTE:** RAILS AND STILES ARE $3/4$"-THICK HARDWOOD. PANELS ARE $1/4$" PLYWOOD

**BACK FRAME**

**NOTE:** BOTTOM RAIL IS POSITIONED $4^{1}/2$" FROM BOTTOM END OF SIDE STILES

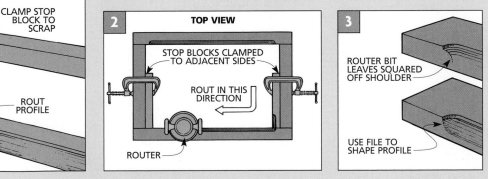

**SHOP TIP** . . . . . . . . . . . . . . . . . . *Stopped Roundovers*

When routing a stopped profile on an edge (refer to *Fig. 14* on page 120 and *Fig. 25* on page 123), it's easy to determine the end of the cut with a couple of simple stop blocks.

To make the stop blocks, clamp a block to a piece of scrap *(Fig. 1)*. Then rout the inside corner formed by the block and the scrap.

Now it's just a matter of marking the points on the finished workpiece where you want the profile to start and stop.

Then, by clamping a stop block next to each mark, I was able to stop the cuts at the correct position.

To make the stopped cuts on the inside edge of the icebox door frames, you may need to trim each stop block to width so the profile routed on it lines up with the mark *(Fig. 2)*.

After routing the edges, there is still some hand work to be done.

At both the start and stop points, the bit leaves a squared-off shoulder *(Fig. 3)*. Round this shoulder with a file and sandpaper to match the rest of the profile *(Fig. 3)*.

**1** CLAMP STOP BLOCK TO SCRAP | STOP BLOCK | ROUT PROFILE

**2** TOP VIEW | STOP BLOCKS CLAMPED TO ADJACENT SIDES | ROUT IN THIS DIRECTION | ROUTER

**3** ROUTER BIT LEAVES SQUARED OFF SHOULDER | USE FILE TO SHAPE PROFILE

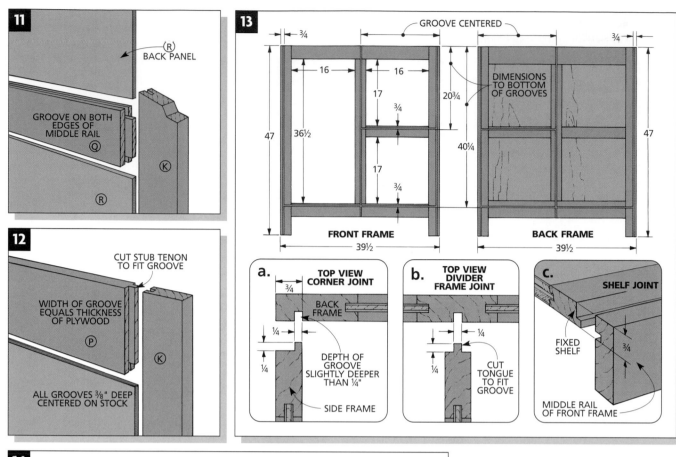

**11**

BACK PANEL ℞

GROOVE ON BOTH EDGES OF MIDDLE RAIL Ⓠ

Ⓚ

℞

**12**

CUT STUB TENON TO FIT GROOVE

WIDTH OF GROOVE EQUALS THICKNESS OF PLYWOOD Ⓟ

Ⓚ

ALL GROOVES ³⁄₈" DEEP CENTERED ON STOCK

**13**

GROOVE CENTERED

¾

16    16

17

¾

20¾

DIMENSIONS TO BOTTOM OF GROOVES

¾

47    36½

40¼

17

¾

47

**FRONT FRAME**

39½

**BACK FRAME**

39½

**a.**    **TOP VIEW CORNER JOINT**

¾

BACK FRAME

¼

¼

DEPTH OF GROOVE SLIGHTLY DEEPER THAN ¼"

SIDE FRAME

**b.**    **TOP VIEW DIVIDER FRAME JOINT**

¼

¼

CUT TONGUE TO FIT GROOVE

**c.**    **SHELF JOINT**

FIXED SHELF

¾

MIDDLE RAIL OF FRONT FRAME

**14**

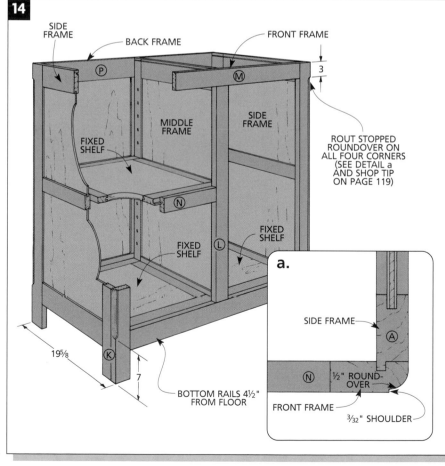

SIDE FRAME

BACK FRAME

FRONT FRAME

Ⓟ

Ⓜ

3

MIDDLE FRAME

SIDE FRAME

FIXED SHELF

Ⓝ

ROUT STOPPED ROUNDOVER ON ALL FOUR CORNERS (SEE DETAIL a AND SHOP TIP ON PAGE 119)

FIXED SHELF

Ⓛ

FIXED SHELF

19⅝

Ⓚ

7

BOTTOM RAILS 4½" FROM FLOOR

**a.**

SIDE FRAME

Ⓐ

Ⓝ    ½" ROUND-OVER

FRONT FRAME

³⁄₃₂" SHOULDER

## GROOVES FOR ASSEMBLY

After the front and back frames are assembled, grooves are routed on the inside faces to attach the side frames and the fixed shelves *(Fig. 13)*.

The grooves on the side stiles are set in a distance exactly equal to the thickness of the side frames (³⁄₄") *(Fig. 13a)*.

Likewise, the grooves on the middle rails are positioned so the shelf is flush with the top of the middle rail *(Fig. 13c)*.

Use the same procedure to locate the groove on the bottom rail of the front frame. However, this procedure cannot be used on the back frame because the bottom rail is wider. To position this groove, use the groove on the front frame as a reference. Measure down from the top edge of the front frame, and mark off this same distance on the back frame.

The last set of grooves (for the middle divider frame) is centered on the total width of the frame *(Figs. 13 and 13b)*.

**TONGUES**. After the grooves are routed, rout tongues on the front and back edges of the side frames, the middle frame, and the fixed shelves *(Figs. 13a, 13b, and 13c)*. I did this on a router table, sneaking up on the depth of cut until the tongues fit the grooves.

**ASSEMBLY.** After the joints are completed, dry-assemble the frames and trim the three fixed shelves to final width to fit between the frames *(Fig. 14)*.

When the shelves fit, they can be glued and clamped to the frames.

**ROUT EDGES.** After assembly, I routed a stopped roundover with a $^3/_{32}$" shoulder on each corner of the cabinet *(Fig. 14a)*.

## BASE MOLDING

At this point, the project is starting to look like an icebox. The next step is to add molding around the base of the cabinet. The base side molding (S) and the front molding (T) are cut to a width of 6" and to rough length *(Fig. 15)*. Also cut the corner blocks (U) from $1^1/_{16}$"-thick stock.

**SIDE PIECES.** Now the side molding can be cut to length to equal the depth of the cabinet from front to back *(Fig. 19)*.

**FRONT PIECES.** To assemble the three pieces for the front of the cabinet, first cut the corner blocks to size. They should overlap the ends of the base side pieces and extend to the inside edge of the front leg (stile) *(Fig. 19)*. Then cut the front molding to fit between the corner blocks, adding 2" for the tenon on each end.

Next cut mortises in the corner blocks, and cut tenons on the front molding *(Fig. 19)*. After the joints are done, mark out the scroll cuts at the ends of the front molding *(Fig. 17)* and cut them on a band saw.

Now rout a $^1/_2$" roundover on the top edges of all pieces *(Fig. 18a)*. Next, screw the side pieces to the cabinet from the back side. And finally, glue the front molding to the end blocks and glue and screw this assembly to the cabinet.

## TOP

The top of the icebox is a glued-up panel. When the glue is dry, plane the top smooth and trim it to final size *(Fig. 20)*.

**ROUND EDGES.** Next, round over the front and side edges of the top (leaving the back edge square). I chose a bullnose profile here, routing the top edge with a $^1/_4$" roundover bit, and the bottom edge with a $^1/_2$" roundover bit *(Fig. 21)*.

**ATTACH THE TOP.** Since the top is solid wood, it must be attached to allow for expansion and contraction. Mount the front edge of the top by counterboring the front frame for pocket screws *(Fig. 22)*. Then secure the rest of the top with Z-shaped table top fasteners *(Fig. 21)*.

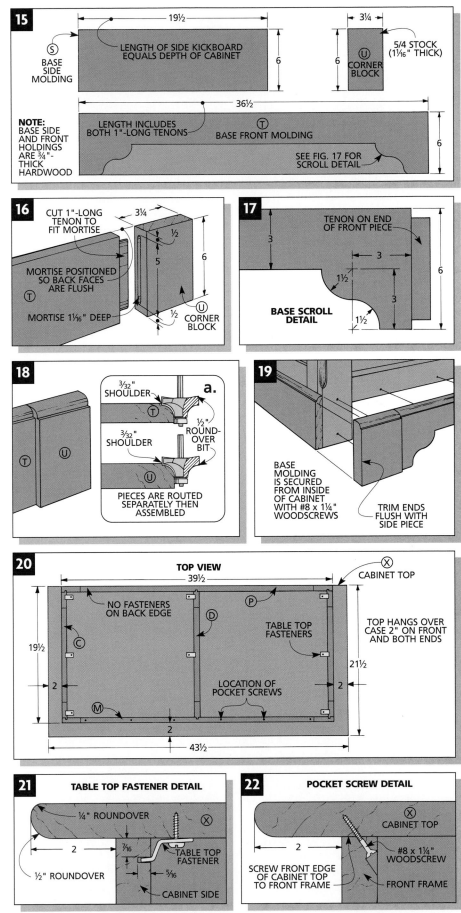

Next, I made the molding pieces that mount under the top of the cabinet. To make the molding, start with two pieces of $3/4$"-thick stock, $2^3/4$" wide and about 48" long *(Step 1 in Fig. 23)*. Then cut a $1/4$"-deep and 1"-wide cove *(Step 2)*.

After the cove is cut, trim the stock to a final width of $2^1/2$", making sure the cove is centered on the width *(Step 2)*.

Next, use a point-cutting ogee bit on the router table to rout a rounded groove on both shoulders of the cove *(Step 3)*. Also, round off one edge with the same bit *(Step 4)*. And finally, cut off the edges at 45° *(Steps 5 and 6)*.

**CUT MOLDING TO LENGTH.** To mount the molding it must be cut at a compound miter. But don't panic. There's an easy way to do this without a lot of head scratching or trial and error. (See the Technique box below.)

Start by mitering the front piece to length, sneaking up on the cuts so the inside corners of the molding strip mate with the outside corners of the cabinet *(Fig. 24)*. Then cut the side strips to length, mitering the front end and cutting the back end square.

**MOUNT THE MOLDING.** To mount the molding, glue and tack the bottom edge of the molding to the cabinet *(Fig. 24a)*.

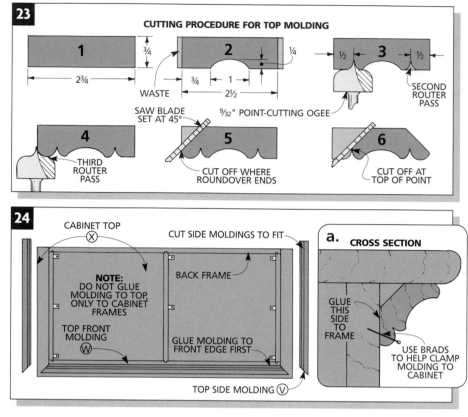

## DOORS

All that remains is to build three doors. The door frame pieces are all the same width. And all six rails are identical. So begin by cutting the door pieces $2^1/2$" wide and to rough length *(Fig. 25)*. Then trim the tall and short stiles (Y, Z) so they're $1/2$" longer than the height of each door opening.

---

# TECHNIQUE · · · · · · · · · · · · · · · · · · · · · · · · · · · *Compound Miters*

Compound miters are often made on the table saw with the miter gauge angled and the blade tilted. This procedure can be tricky and involves referring to a chart for the correct angles to set the miter gauge and the blade.

But if the workpiece can be held at the angle it will be installed on the project, the blade can stay at 90°, and only the miter gauge needs to be angled. I was able to use this simpler technique for the top moldings on the icebox.

**AUXILIARY FENCE.** To make the cut, begin by fastening an auxiliary fence to the miter gauge. The fence has to be tall enough to support the molding when it's held at the desired angle.

Since the bottom edge of the molding for the icebox is cut at 45°, there's a flat surface that can rest on the surface of the table saw. The top edge is then supported by the auxiliary fence *(Fig. 1)*.

To prevent the molding piece from sliding up during the cut, clamp a small stop block to the auxiliary fence so it rests on the top edge of the molding.

**MAKING THE CUT.** To cut the molding to length, begin by rotating the miter gauge to 45° and place it in the left slot of the table saw. Tip the workpiece to the correct incline and bring it up tight under the stop block and against the auxiliary fence. Then push the workpiece through the blade *(Fig. 2)*.

To miter the other end of the workpiece, move the miter gauge to the right slot and swing the head of the gauge to the opposite 45° setting.

If the molding can be cut by holding it against an auxiliary fence this way, the cut is likely to be much more accurate than the normal compound miter procedure.

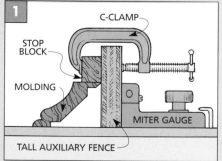

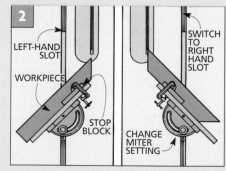

Cutting the rabbets on the inside of the icebox doors isn't complicated, even though it's done after the doors are assembled. I just use a hand-held router.

**SCORING PASS.** Whenever I rout a rabbet, I worry about chipout along the edge. There is a way around this — by taking a light backrouting pass first. This means a pass in the direction opposite in which the router usually runs (counter-clockwise inside the frame).

**BACKROUT.** The reason this works is that the bit is cutting *into* the workpiece. The material behind the cut supports the material being removed (see drawing). On a normal pass, the bit cuts *out* of the workpiece. The unsupported wood at the edge of the workpiece is what chips out.

So if backrouting is so great, why not do it all the time? The problem is that the router bit won't pull itself into the workpiece, as it normally would. Instead, the bit will bounce along the edge, trying to pull the router along. This can make it harder to control. So whenever back-routing, take a light pass, keep a firm grip on the router, and brace your arms against your body.

The idea is to remove just the material at the front edge of the cut so there won't be chipout when the cut is completed.

**ROUT RABBET.** After the edge has been scored, you can make deeper passes to cut the rabbet to full width. But this time rout in the normal direction (clockwise around the inside of the frame).

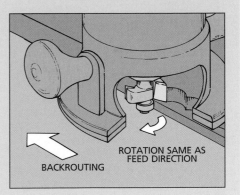

**SQUARE CORNERS.** When the rabbet is completed, you'll notice the corners where the bit couldn't reach are rounded. They are easily squared up by paring away the waste with a chisel.

Next, cut the door rails (AA) to length (allowing for the tenons) so the width of the assembled door overlaps the opening ½". Then the mortises and tenons can be cut on the stiles and rails *(Fig. 25)*. Once that's done, the doors can be glued up.

Now a series of profiles is routed on the edges of the doors. First, rout a 5/16"-deep rabbet on the inside edge of the frame for the plywood panel *(Step 1 in Fig. 26)*. (See the Technique box above for a tip about routing these rabbets.)

Then rout another rabbet to form a lip on the outside edge of the door. This rabbet is 3/8" wide, but the depth depends on the hardware you have. The hinges I used require a 3/8" lip, so I routed the rabbet deep enough to leave a 3/8"-thick lip on the front side of the door *(Step 2)*.

To complete the door frame, rout a 3/8" roundover along the front outside edge of the door frame *(Step 3)*. And finally, rout a stopped roundover with a shoulder on the inside edges of the frame *(Step 4)*. This roundover stops 4" from the outside corners of the door *(Fig. 25)*.

**PANELS.** After all the molding cuts are made, the panels can be cut to size. I used ¼" oak plywood on the two small doors. But on the large door you have an option: oak plywood (see the photo on page 114), or reeded glass (see the Designer's Notebook on page 124).

**STOPS.** The last step is to cut panel stops (DD) to hold the panels (or glass) in place. To make the stops, rout a ⅛" roundover on two edges of a piece of ¾"-thick stock. Then rip ⅜"-thick strips and cut shoulders to fit the rabbet *(Fig. 27a)*.

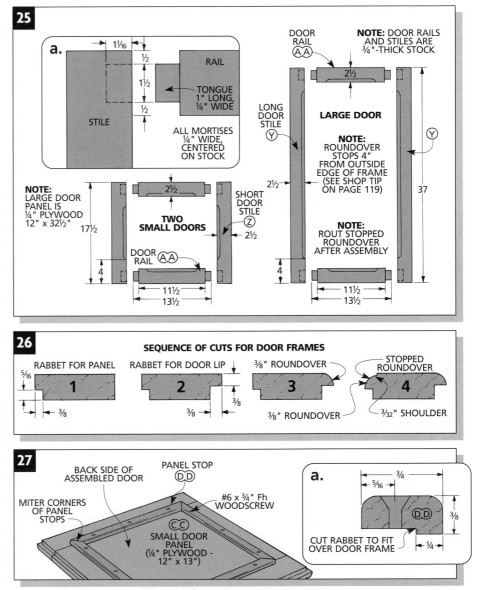

## HARDWARE & FINISH

The last step is to mount the brass reproduction hardware. The hardware I used is designed for doors with a lip that's $\frac{3}{8}$" thick *(Fig. 29)*. (A hardware kit is available from *Woodsmith Project Supplies*. See page 126 for details.)

Mount the hinges so they're centered on the width of the rails *(Fig. 28)*. The only tricky part is to position the knuckle of the hinge about $\frac{1}{8}$" from the edge of the door to allow clearance when the door is opened *(Fig. 29)*. You'll also need to allow some clearance between each catch and door *(Fig. 30)*.

**FINISHING**. Before applying the finish, remove the hardware. (Note that each piece is slightly different so it must be returned to the same place.) Then I applied two coats of stain and followed with two coats of tung oil varnish. ■

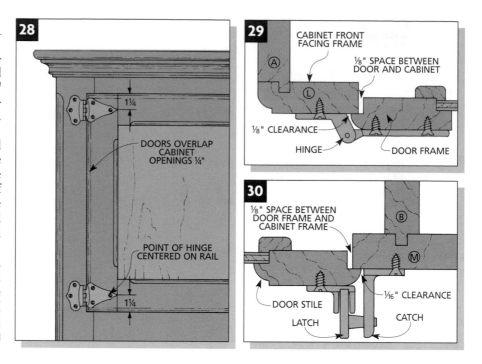

# DESIGNER'S NOTEBOOK

*Liven up the front of the icebox with a glass panel that gives you a hint of what's inside.*

## REEDED GLASS DOOR

■ When iceboxes were still a fixture in homes and grocery stores, some models came with insulated glass panels in the doors. The idea was that you could see what was inside before opening the door.

■ Installing a glass panel instead of plywood in one (or more) of the icebox doors is a simple modification. Instead of insulated glass, I used a reeded refrigerator glass (see photo). But if you intend to display collectibles in the cabinet, use a piece of tempered $\frac{1}{8}$"-thick glass so you can see into the cabinet clearly.

■ When measuring for the glass, I allowed $\frac{1}{16}$" of "breathing room" on all sides. In other words, the glass is sized $\frac{1}{8}$" less than the distance between the rabbets in the door frame.

■ Installing the glass is the same as installing a plywood panel. Just miter some panel stop (DD) to hold the glass in place (see drawing).

**Note:** To hold the glass securely, you may need to cut a deeper rabbet in the panel stop, depending on the thickness of your glass.

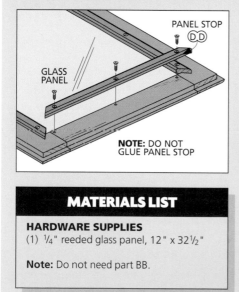

NOTE: DO NOT GLUE PANEL STOP

### MATERIALS LIST

**HARDWARE SUPPLIES**
(1) $\frac{1}{4}$" reeded glass panel, 12" x $32\frac{1}{2}$"

**Note:** Do not need part BB.

■ Finally, the stops are screwed in place (no glue). That way, they can be removed if the glass should need replacing.

# DESIGNER'S NOTEBOOK

*Organizing smaller items in the icebox is easier if you divide one (or both) of the compartments into drawer space. Dovetailed drawers and full-extension slides provide sturdy, easy-to-access storage.*

## CONSTRUCTION NOTES:

■ To add drawers to the icebox, you'll need to add a second front middle rail (N) to the front face frame *(Fig. 1)*. This separates the two drawers.

■ Once the case has been assembled, you can build the drawers. The drawer sides (EE), fronts (FF), and backs (FF) are built from ¹/₂"-thick stock and are joined with ¹/₂" half-blind dovetails at the front and back *(Fig. 2)*. I cut the dovetails with a dovetail jig and my router.

■ Once the dovetails have been routed, you can cut a groove on the inside face of all four pieces to hold a ¹/₄" plywood bottom. Align this groove with the bottom pin in the drawer sides *(Fig. 2)*.

■ Next, dry-assemble the drawers and measure for the drawer bottoms (GG). After they have been cut to size, glue up the drawers around the bottoms.

■ Before mounting the drawer slides, you'll need to cut spacers so the slides will clear the front frame. Note that the left slide spacers (HH) are wider than the right spacers (II) *(Fig. 1)*.

■ Once the spacers are cut to size, they can be glued and screwed to the stiles of the middle and side frames *(Fig. 1a)*.

■ Now screw the slides to the spacers so they rest on the middle and bottom rails and are set back ³/₈" from the front of the frame *(Figs. 1 and 1a)*.

■ After the slides are mounted to the cabinet, screw them to the drawers so there is ¹/₈" of clearance below each drawer.

■ Each drawer has a ³/₄"-thick false front (JJ) with a lip that overlays the face frame by ¹/₄" *(Fig. 2a)*. Start by cutting the false fronts to size *(Fig. 2)*.

■ Then rout a ³/₈" roundover around the outside face and a ³/₈" rabbet around the inside face of each false front *(Fig. 2a)*.

■ Now stick the false fronts to the drawers using carpet tape so you can drill pilot holes and screw them in place.

■ Finally, center and screw a bin pull to each false front.

TWO-DRAWER ICEBOX

## MATERIALS LIST

**CHANGED PARTS**

| | | |
|---|---|---|
| N | Front Middle Rails (2) | ³/₄ x 2¹/₂ - 18 |
| Z | Short Door Stiles (2) | ³/₄ x 2¹/₂ - 17¹/₂ |
| AA | Door Rails (4) | ³/₄ x 2¹/₂ - 13¹/₂ |
| CC | Small Door Panel (1) | ¹/₄ ply - 12 x 13 |
| DD | Panel Stop | ³/₈ x ³/₄ - 12 ln. ft. |

**NEW PARTS**

| | | |
|---|---|---|
| EE | Drawer Sides (4) | ¹/₂ x 7 - 17³/₄ |
| FF | Drawer Fr./Bk. (4) | ¹/₂ x 7 - 15 |
| GG | Drawer Bottoms (2) | ¹/₄ ply - 14¹/₂ x 17¹/₂ |
| HH | Left Slide Spacers (2) | 1 x 1³/₄ - 18 |
| II | Right Slide Spacers (2) | 1 x ⁷/₈ - 18 |
| JJ | Drawer False Fronts (2) | ³/₄ x 7³/₄ - 16¹/₂ |

**HARDWARE SUPPLIES**

(8) No. 8 x 1" Fh woodscrews
(4) No. 8 x 1¹/₂" Fh woodscrews
(4) No. 8 x 2¹/₄" Fh woodscrews
(4) 18" full-extension drawer slides w/ screws
(2) 3³/₄" x 1¹/₈" brass bin pulls w/ screws

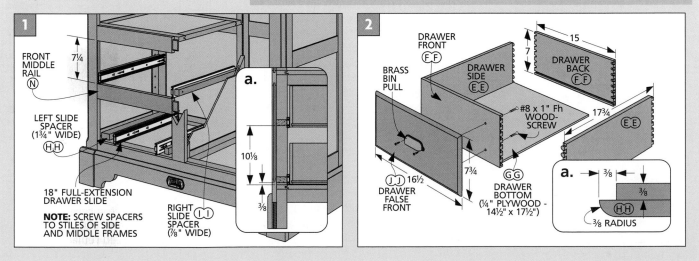

Something we take into consideration when designing projects at *Woodsmith* is the hardware. Does it complement the project and is the style appropriate? Is it affordable and readily available?

You should be able to find much of the hardware and supplies for the projects in this book at local hardware stores or home centers. For some of the less common items, you may have to order hardware through the mail. If that's the case, we've tried to find reputable sources with toll-free phone numbers and web sites (see the Mail Order Sources box at right).

## MAIL ORDER SOURCES

Some of the most important "tools" you can have in your shop are your mail order catalogs. The ones listed below are filled with special hardware, tools, finishes, lumber, and other supplies that can't be found at hardware stores or home centers. You should be able to find many of the supplies for the projects in this book in one or more of these catalogs. Many even offer online ordering.

**Note:** The information below was current when this book was printed. August Home Publishing does not guarantee these products will be available nor endorse any specific mail order company, catalog, or product.

### THE WOODSMITH STORE

**10320 Hickman Road**
**Clive, IA 50325**
**800-835-5084**
**www.woodsmithstore.com**
Our own retail store with hand tools, router bits, hardware, and finishing supplies. We don't have a catalog, but we do send out items mail order.

### LEE VALLEY TOOLS LTD.

**P.O. Box 1780**
**Ogdensburg, NY 13669-6780**
**800-871-8158**
**www.leevalley.com**
In their hardware catalog you'll find knobs, bumpers, square nails, spindles, and veneers. There's also an impressive line of brass hardware including cabinet latches, hinges, bin pulls, shelf supports, and hooks.

### ROCKLER WOODWORKING & HARDWARE

**4365 Willow Drive**
**Medina, MN 55340**
**800-279-4441**
**www.rockler.com**
A full line of hardware and finishing supplies including knobs, hinges, Z-shaped and figure-8 fasteners, screw hole buttons, file card frame pulls, plastic bumpers, and tin panels. Also find veneering supplies and Hoosier cabinet hardware.

### COUNTRY ACCENTS

**1723 Scaife Road**
**Williamsport, PA 17701**
**570-478-4127**
**www.piercedtin.com**
A huge selection of pre-punched tin panels in a variety of finishes. They also sell patterns and punching tools if you want to punch your own panels.

### WOODCRAFT

**560 Airport Industrial Park**
**P.O. Box 1686**
**Parkersburg, WV 26102-1686**
**800-225-1153**
**www.woodcraft.com**
From tools to project supplies, chances are you can find it here. They have all types of hinges and pulls, plus screw hole buttons, shelf supports, knobs, Z-shaped fasteners, barrel nuts, and plastic bumpers. You'll also find spindles, veneers, and veneering supplies.

### VAN DYKE'S RESTORERS

**39771 S.D. Hwy. 34 E.**
**P.O. Box 278**
**Woonsocket, SD 57385**
**800-558-1234**
**www.vandykes.com**
This is a great catalog full of hard-to-find period hardware and supplies. They have a good selection of hinges, knobs, and Hoosier cabinet hardware. In addition, they carry square nails, tin panels, veneers, veneering supplies, antiquing solution, and finishing supplies.

### WOODWORKER'S SUPPLY

**Attn.: Order Dept.**
**1108 North Glenn Rd.**
**Casper, WY 82601**
**800-645-9292**
**www.woodworker.com**
Another full-line catalog with a wide selection of hardware supplies including hinges, knobs, file card frame pulls, screw hole buttons, spindles, wood-wheel casters, brass hooks, veneers and veneering supplies, and toy wooden wheels.

# INDEX

## AUGUST HOME
PUBLISHING COMPANY

President & Publisher: Donald B. Peschke
Executive Editor: Douglas L. Hicks
Project Manager/Senior Editor: Craig L. Ruegsegger
Creative Director: Ted Kralicek
Art Director: Doug Flint
Senior Graphic Designers: Robin Friend, Chris Glowacki
Assistant Editor: Joel Hess
Editorial Intern: Cindy Thurmond
Graphic Designers: Jonathan Eike, Vu Nguyen

Designer's Notebook Illustrator: Chris Glowacki
Photographer: Crayola England
Electronic Production: Douglas M. Lidster
Production: Troy Clark, Minniette Johnson
Project Designers: Chris Fitch, Ryan Mimick, Ken Munkel, Kent Welsh
Project Builders: Steve Curtis, Steve Johnson
Magazine Editors: Tim Robertson, Terry Strohman
Contributing Editors: Vincent S. Ancona, Jon Garbison, Phil Huber,
Brian McCallum, Bryan Nelson, Ted Raife
Magazine Art Directors: Cary Christensen, Todd Lambirth
Contributing Illustrators: Harlan Clark, Mark Higdon, David Kreyling,
Erich Lage, Roger Reiland, Kurt Schultz, Cinda Shambaugh, Dirk Ver Steeg

Corporate V.P., Finance: Mary Scheve
Controller: Robin Hutchinson
Production Director: George Chmielarz
Project Supplies: Bob Baker
New Media Manager: Gordon Gaippe

For subscription information about
*Woodsmith* and *ShopNotes* magazines, please write:
August Home Publishing Co.
2200 Grand Ave.
Des Moines, IA 50312
800-333-5075
www.augusthome.com/customwoodworking

*Woodsmith*® and *ShopNotes*® are registered trademarks of August Home
Publishing Co.

## Oxmoor House®

Oxmoor House, Inc.
Book Division of Southern Progress Corporation
P.O. Box 2463, Birmingham, Alabama 35201

ISBN: 0-8487-2689-8
Printed in the United States of America

To order additional publications, call 1-800-765-6400.
For more books to enrich your life, visit **oxmoorhouse.com**